# Scheduling in Real-Time Systems

# Scheduling in Real-Time Systems

Francis Cottet
*LISI/ENSMA, Futuroscope, France*

Joëlle Delacroix
Claude Kaiser
*CNAM/CEDRIC, Paris, France*

Zoubir Mammeri
*IRIT–UPS, Toulouse, France*

JOHN WILEY & SONS, LTD

This publication is designed to provide accurate and authoritative information in regard to the
subject matter covered. It is sold on the understanding that the Publisher is not engaged in rendering
professional services. If professional advice or other expert assistance is required, the services of a
competent professional should be sought.

*Other Wiley Editorial Offices*

John Wiley & Sons Inc., 111 River Street, Hoboken, NJ 07030, USA

Jossey-Bass, 989 Market Street, San Francisco, CA 94103-1741, USA

Wiley-VCH Verlag GmbH, Boschstr. 12, D-69469 Weinheim, Germany

John Wiley & Sons Australia Ltd, 33 Park Road, Milton, Queensland 4064, Australia

John Wiley & Sons (Asia) Pte Ltd, 2 Clementi Loop #02-01, Jin Xing Distripark, Singapore 129809

John Wiley & Sons Canada Ltd, 22 Worcester Road, Etobicoke, Ontario, Canada M9W 1L1

*Library of Congress Cataloging-in-Publication Data*

Cottet, Francis.
  Scheduling in real-time systems / Francis Cottet, Joëlle Delacroix, Zoubir Mammeri.
    p. cm.
  Includes bibliographical references and index.
  ISBN 0-470-84766-2 (alk. paper)
  1. Real-time data processing.   2. Scheduling.   I. Delacroix, Joëlle. II. Mammeri, Zoubir.
  III. Title.

  QA76.54.C68 2002
  004'.33 — dc21

                                                                      2002027202

*British Library Cataloguing in Publication Data*

A catalogue record for this book is available from the British Library

ISBN 0-470-84766-2

Typeset in 10/12pt Times by Laserwords Private Limited, Chennai, India
Printed and bound by CPI Antony Rowe, Eastbourne
This book is printed on acid-free paper responsibly manufactured from sustainable forestry
in which at least two trees are planted for each one used for paper production.
Reprinted 2006

# Contents

# Notations and Symbols

| | |
|---|---|
| $AT_s^{c,p}$ | Arrival time, at switch $s$, of packet $p$ on connection $c$. |
| $auxVC_s^c$ | Auxiliary virtual clock of connection $c$ at switch $s$. |
| $B_i$ | Worst case blocking time of task $i$. |
| $b_L$ | Number of slots assigned, per round, by server $L$ to server $L + 1$. |
| BR | Bit-by-bit round-robin. |
| $C$ | Worst case computation time of task. |
| $C_i$ | Worst case computation time of task $i$. |
| | It also denotes the transmission delay of message $i$. |
| $C_i(t)$ | Pending computation time of task $i$ at time $t$. |
| $d$ | Absolute task deadline. |
| $d_i$ | Absolute deadline of task $i$. |
| $d_{i,j}$ | Absolute deadline of the $j + 1$th instance of task $i$ |
| | $\quad (d_{i,j} = r_{i,j} + D_i = r_{i,0} + D_i + j \times T_i)$. |
| $d_i^*$ | Modified deadline of task $i$. |
| $D$ | Relative deadline. |
| $D^c$ | End-to-end delay of connection $c$. |
| $D_s^c$ | Local delay fixed for connection $c$ at switch $s$. |
| $D_i$ | Relative deadline of task $i$ (or of message $i$). |
| $D_{i,j}(t)$ | Relative deadline of the $j + 1$th instance of task $i$ at time $t$ |
| | $\quad (D_{i,j}(t) = d_{i,j} - t)$. |
| DM | Deadline monotonic. |
| EDD | Earliest-due-date. |
| $e_i$ | Finishing time of task $i$. |
| $e_{i,j}$ | Finishing time of the $j + 1$th instance of task $i$. |
| EDF | Earliest deadline first. |
| $ET_s^{c,p}$ | Eligibility time assigned, by switch $s$, to packet $p$ from connection $c$. |
| $ExD_s^{c,p}$ | Expected deadline of packet $p$, on connection $c$, at switch $s$. |
| $F_s^{c,p}$ | Finish number, at switch $s$, of packet $p$ on connection $c$. |
| GPS | Generalized processor sharing. |
| $H$ | Major cycle (also called hyper period or scheduling period). |
| HRR | Hierarchical round-robin. |
| ID | Inverse deadline. |
| $I^c$ | Averaging interval for inter-arrival on connection $c$. |
| $Imp$ | Importance (or criticality) of a task. |
| $Imp_i$ | Importance (or criticality) of task $i$. |
| $J^c$ | End-to-end jitter of connection $c$. |
| $J_s^c$ | Local jitter fixed for connection $c$ at switch $s$. |
| $L^{c,p}$ | Length (in bits) of packet $p$ on connection $c$. |

| | |
|---|---|
| $L_i$ | Laxity of task $i$ ($L_i = D_i - C_i$). |
| $L_i(t)$ | Laxity of task $i$ at time $t$ ($L_i(t) = D_i(t) - C_i(t)$). |
| $L_{i,j}(t)$ | Laxity of the $j + 1$th instance of task $i$ at time $t$ ($L_{i,j}(t) = D_{i,j}(t) - C_i(t)$). |
| $LC_i(t)$ | Conditional laxity of task $i$ at time $t$. |
| LLF | Least laxity first. |
| $Lmax^c$ | Maximum length of packet on connection $c$. |
| $LP(t)$ | Laxity of the processor at time $t$. |
| $M_i$ | Message $i$. |
| $N_i$ | Node $i$ in distributed system. |
| $ns_L$ | Number of slots assigned, per round, to server $L$. |
| $OD_s^c$ | Local delay offered by switch $s$ for connection $c$. |
| $OJ_s^c$ | Local jitter offered by switch $s$ for connection $c$. |
| PGPS | Packet-by-packet generalized processor sharing. |
| $Prio_i$ | Priority of task $i$. |
| $Proc_i$ | Processor $i$. |
| $Q_i$ | Synchronous allocation time of node $i$. |
| $r_i^*$ | Modified release time of task $i$. |
| $r$ | Task release time (task offset). |
| $r_s^c$ | Bit rate assigned to connection $c$ at switch $s$. |
| $r_i$ | Release time of task $i$. |
| $r_{i,0}$ | First release time of task $i$. |
| $r_{i,j}$ | Release time of the $j + 1$th instance of task $i$ ($r_{i,j} = r_{i,0} + j \times T_i$). |
| $R_i$ | Resource $i$. |
| $r_s$ | Bit rate of the output link of switch $s$. |
| $R_s(t)$ | Round number of switch $s$. |
| RCSP | Rate-controlled static-priority. |
| RL | Round length. |
| $RL_L$ | Round length of server $L$. |
| RM | Rate monotonic. |
| $S_s^{c,p}$ | Start number, at switch $s$, of packet $p$ on connection $c$. |
| $s_i$ | Start time of task $i$. |
| $s_{i,j}$ | Start time of the $j + 1$th instance of task $i$. |
| S&G | Stop-and-go. |
| $T_i$ | Period of task $i$ (or of message $i$). |
| TR | Worst case response time of task. |
| $TR_i$ | Worst case response time of task $i$ ($TR_i = \max_j \{TR_{i,j}\}$). |
| $TR_{i,j}$ | Response time of the $j + 1$th instance of task $i$ ($TR_{i,j} = e_{i,j} - r_{i,j}$). |
| TTRT | Target token rotation time. |
| $u_i$ | Processor utilization factor of task $i$ ($= C_i / T_i$). |
| $U$ | Processor utilization factor ($= \Sigma u_i$). |
| $VC_s^c$ | Virtual clock of connection $c$ at switch $s$. |
| WBR | Weighted bit-by-bit round-robin. |
| WFQ | Weighted fair queuing. |
| $Xave^c$ | Average packet inter-arrival time on connection $c$. |
| $Xmin^c$ | Minimum packet inter-arrival time on connection $c$. |
| $\tau$ | Task set. |

| | |
|---|---|
| $\tau_i$ | Task $i$. |
| $\tau_{i,j}$ | $j + 1$th instance of task $i$. |
| $\tau_i \rightarrow \tau_j$ | Task $i$ precedes task $j$. |
| $\Delta_j^i$ | Communication delay between nodes $i$ and $j$. |
| $\rho$ | Rate of leaky bucket. |
| $\sigma$ | Depth of leaky bucket. |
| $\pi$ | End-to-end propagation delay. |
| $\pi_l$ | Delay of link $l$. |
| $\theta_{l',l}$ | Constant delay, introduced by S&G discipline, to synchronize frames. |
| $\phi_s^c$ | Weight assigned to connection $c$ at switch $s$. |
| $\omega^c$ | Number of slots assigned, per round, to connection $c$. |
| $\uparrow$ | Graphical symbol to indicate a task release. |
| $\downarrow$ | Graphical symbol to indicate a task deadline. |
| $\updownarrow$ | Graphical symbol to indicate a task with period equal to deadline. |

# Introduction

*Real-time computing systems* must react dynamically to the state changes of an environment, whose evolution depends on human behaviour, a natural or artificial phenomenon or an industrial plant. Real-time applications span a large spectrum of activities; examples include production automation, embedded systems, telecommunication systems, automotive applications, nuclear plant supervision, scientific experiments, robotics, multimedia audio and video transport and conditioning, surgical operation monitoring, and banking transactions. In all these applications, *time* is the basic constraint to deal with and the main concern for appraising the quality of service provided by computing systems.

Application requirements lead to differentiation between hard and soft real-time constraints. Applications have hard real-time constraints when a single failure to meet timing constraints may result in an economic, human or ecological disaster. A time fault may result in a deadline being missed, a message arriving too late, an irregular sampling period, a large timing dispersion in a set of 'simultaneous' measurements, and so on. Soft real-time constraints are involved in those cases when timing faults cause damage whose cost is considered tolerable under some conditions on fault frequency or service lag.

This book concerns applications where a computer system controls (or supervises) an environment in real-time. It is thus reasonable to split such applications into two parts: the *real-time computing system* and the *controlled environment*. The latter is the physical process to which the computing system is connected for controlling its behaviour. Real-time is a serious challenge for computing systems and its difficulties are often misunderstood. A real-time computing system must provide a time management facility; this is an important difference compared to conventional computing systems, since the value of data produced by a real-time application depends not only upon the correctness of the computation but also upon the time at which the data is available. An order which is computed right but sent late is a wrong command: it is a timing fault.

In a real-time application, the computing system and the environment are two partners that behave in different time domains. The environment is ruled by precise duration measurements of *chronometric time*. The computing system determines a sequence of machine instructions and defines a *chronological time*. The real-time application that is controlled by a computing system is not concerned by the high-fidelity or low-fidelity of the chronometric time or chronological time, but by the correct control of their synchrony. As the chronological time is fixed by the physical process and is an intangible datum, the computing system has to adapt the rate of its actions to the clock of the environment. In the context of real-time applications, the actions are *tasks* (also called processes) and the organization of their execution by the processors of the computing architecture (sequencing, interleaving, overlapping, parallel computing) is called *real-time scheduling* of tasks. The schedule must meet the timing constraints of the application; the procedure that rules the task execution ordering is called the *scheduling policy*.

If some properties of the scheduling policy are required, their guarantee must be formally derived; this has to be supported by a behavioural model of the tasks. Each class of model gives rise to the study of specific and various policies. However, all these policies rely on the 'truthfulness' of the model. In an industrial context, the timing parameters of tasks are not perfectly known and in addition some unusual events may occur: this may lead to unforeseen timing faults. A robust schedule must be able to cope with these situations, which means being able to limit the impact of a timing fault on the application and to divert its consequences to the least important tasks. Thus, it is easy to understand that the implementation of a real-time application requires scheduling expertise and also a thorough understanding of the target application.

This book is a basic treatise on real-time scheduling. The main objectives are to study the most significant real-time scheduling policies which are in use today in the industry for coping with hard real-time constraints. The bases of real-time scheduling and its major evolutions are described using unified terminology and notations. The first chapters concern centralized computing systems. We deal also with the case of distributed systems in the particular context where tasks are permanently assigned and managed by local schedulers that share a global system clock; the decisions remain local to each computer of the system. The use of local area networks to support real-time applications raises the problem of message scheduling and also of the joint scheduling of tasks and messages. Larger networks used in loosely coupled systems need to master packet scheduling.

We do not consider the case of asynchronous distributed systems, which do not share a global clock and where decisions may rely on a global consensus, with possibly the presence of faults; their study is a question that would require significant development and right now it remains a subject of research in the scientific community.

The primary objective of this book is to serve as a text book with exercises and answers, and also some useful case studies. The second objective of this book is to provide a reference book that can be used by practitioners and developers in the industry. It is reinforced by the choice of industrial realizations as case studies. The material is based on the pedagogical experience of the authors in their respective institutions for several years on this topic. This experience is dual. Some of our assistants are able to follow top-down and deductive reasoning; this is the case of master students in computer science with a good mathematical background. Other assistants prefer inductive reasoning based on their field experience and on case studies; this bottom-up approach concerns an audience already working in the industry and willing to improve its knowledge in evolving technologies.

Chapter 1 presents the real-time application domain and real-time scheduling, expresses their differences with conventional systems (non-real-time systems) and their scheduling, and introduces the basic terminology. The second chapter covers the simplest situation, consisting of scheduling independent tasks when their processing times and deadlines are known or estimated with enough accuracy. Chapter 3 considers the modifications to the former scheduling policies which are necessary to cope with precedence relationships and resource sharing. Chapter 4 presents some ways of reducing the timing fault consequences when unforeseen perturbations occur, such as processing overload or task parameter variations. Chapter 5 is devoted to symmetric multiprocessor systems sharing a common memory. Chapter 6 discusses how to evaluate the message transmission delays in several kinds of widely used real-time industrial networks and how to schedule messages exchanged between tasks of a distributed application supported by a local area network. Chapter 7 considers the case of packet-switching networks and the scheduling of packets in order to guarantee the packet transfer delay and to limit the delay jitter. Chapter 8 approaches different software environments for real-time applications, such as operating systems, asynchronous and synchronous languages, and distributed platforms. Chapter 9 deals with three relevant case studies: the first example describes the real-time acquisition and analysis of the signals providing from an aluminium rolling mill in the *Pechiney* plant, which manufactures aluminium reels for the packaging market; the second example presents the control system of the robot that the Pathfinder space vehicle landed on Mars, and it analyses the failure that was caused by a wrong sharing of the bus of the control computer. The last example describes the tasks and messages that are present in a distributed architecture supporting a car control system, and it analyses some temporal behaviours of these tasks.

Exercises appear at the end of some of the chapters. Other exercises can be deduced from the case studies (rolling mill, robot control and car control system) presented in Chapter 9. A glossary, given at the end of the book, provides definitions for many of the technical terms used in real-time scheduling.

# 1

# Basic Concepts

## 1.1 Real-Time Applications

### 1.1.1 Real-time applications issues

In real-time applications, the timing requirements are the main constraints and their mastering is the predominant factor for assessing the quality of service. Timing constraints span many application areas, such as industrial plant automation, embedded systems, vehicle control, nuclear plant monitoring, scientific experiment guidance, robotics, multimedia audio and video stream conditioning, surgical operation monitoring, and stock exchange orders follow-up.

Applications trigger periodic or random events and require that the associated computer system reacts before a given delay or a fixed time. The timing latitude to react is limited since transient data must be caught, actions have a constraint on both start and finish times, and responses or commands must be sent on time.

The time scale may vary largely, its magnitude being a microsecond in a radar, a second in a human–machine interface, a minute in an assembly line, or an hour in a chemical reaction.

The source of timing constraints leads to classifying them as hard or soft. A real-time system has *hard timing constraints* when a timing fault (missing a deadline, delivering a message too late, sampling data irregularly, too large a scatter in data supposed to be collected simultaneously) may cause some human, economic or ecological disaster. A real-time system has *soft timing constraints* when timing faults can be dealt with to a certain extent.

A real-time computer system is a computer system whose behaviour is fixed by the dynamics of the application. Therefore, a real-time application consists of two connected parts: the controlling real-time computer system and the controlled process (Figure 1.1).

Time mastery is a serious challenge for real-time computer systems, and it is often misunderstood. The correctness of system reactions depends not only on the logical results of the computations, but also on the time at which the results are produced. Correct data which are available too late are useless; this is a timing fault (Burns and Wellings, 1997; Lelann, 1990; Stankovic, 1988).

A controlling real-time computer system may be built as:

- a cyclic generator, which periodically samples the state of the controlled process, computes the measured data and sends orders to the actuators (this is also called synchronous control);

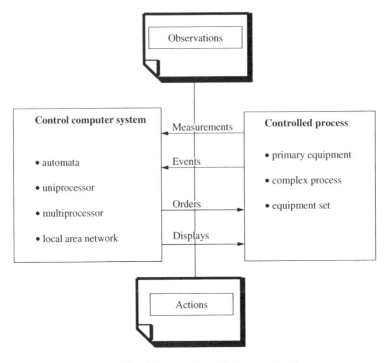

**Figure 1.1**   Scheme of a real-time application

- a reactive system, which responds instantaneously to the stimuli originating in the controlled process and thus is triggered by its dynamics;

- a union of both aspects, which schedules periodic and aperiodic tasks; this results in an asynchronous system.

## 1.1.2  Physical and logical architecture, operating systems

*Software design of a real-time application*

Several steps are usually identified to analyse and implement real-time applications. Some of them are:

- requirements analysis and functional and timing specifications, which result in a functional view (the question to answer is: what should the system do?).

- preliminary design, which performs an operational analysis (the question is: how to do it?) and leads to the choice of logical components of a logical architecture.

- specific hardware and software development. They are often developed concurrently with similar design processes. The hardware analysis (the question is: with which hardware units?) leads to a physical architecture, to the choice of commercial off-the-shelf components and to the detailed design and development of special hardware. The conceptual analysis (the question is: with which software modules?) leads to a software architecture, to the choice of standard software components and to the implementation of customized ones. These acquisition and realization steps end with unit testing.

- integration testing, which involves combining all the software and hardware components, standard ones as well as specific ones, and performing global testing.

- user validation, which is carried out by measurements, sometimes combined with formal methods, and which is done prior to acceptance of the system.

These steps are summarized in Figure 1.2, which gives an overview of the main design and implementation steps of real-time applications. Once the logical and hardware architecture is defined, an allocation policy assigns the software modules to the hardware units. In distributed fault-tolerant real-time systems, the allocation may be undertaken dynamically and tasks may migrate. The operational analysis must define the basic logical units to map the requirements and to express concurrency in the system, which is our concern. The operational behaviour of the application is produced by their concurrent execution.

The major computing units are often classified as:

- passive objects such as physical resources (devices, sensors, actuators) or logical resources (memory buffers, files, basic software modules);

- communication objects such as messages or shared variables, ports, channels, network connections;

- synchronization objects such as events, semaphores, conditions, monitors (as in Modula), rendezvous and protected objects (as in Ada);

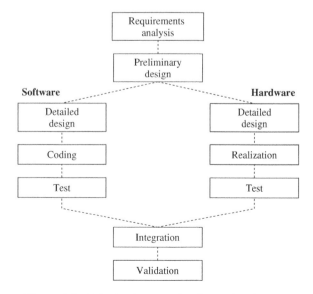

**Figure 1.2**   Joint hardware and software development

- active objects such as processes, threads, tasks;

- structuring, grouping and combining objects such as modules, packages (as in Ada), actors (as in Chorus), processes (as in Unix, Mach).

In real-time systems, the word *task* is most often used as the unit for representing concurrent activities of the logical architecture. The physical parallelism in the hardware architecture and the logical parallelism in the application requirements are usually the base for splitting an application into concurrent tasks. Thus a task may be assigned to each processor and to each input–output device (disk reader, printer, keyboard, display, actuator, sensor), but also to each distinct functional activity (computing, acquisition, presentation, client, server, object manager) or to each distinct behavioural activity (periodic, aperiodic, reactive, cyclic, according to deadline or importance).

## *Physical architecture*

Real-time systems hardware architectures are characterized by the importance of input–output streams (for example the VME bus in Figure 1.3). An example of physical architecture, the robot engine of the Pathfinder mission, will be presented in Chapter 9. The configuration of the embedded architecture is given in Figure 9.10. Figure 1.3 shows an example of a symmetric multiprocessor architecture with shared memory (Banino et al., 1993).

Distributed architectures over networks are being developed more and more. Chapter 6 is devoted to message scheduling, which is a major element in the mastery of timing constraints. We shall use the term *interconnected sites*. Figure 1.4 summarizes an architecture using local networks to interconnect several sites.

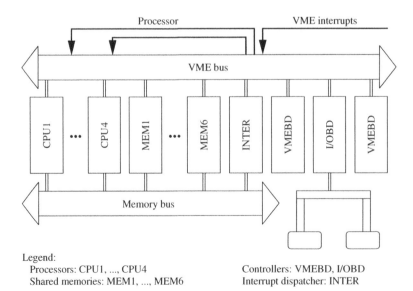

**Figure 1.3** Dune 3000 symmetric multiprocessor architecture with shared memory

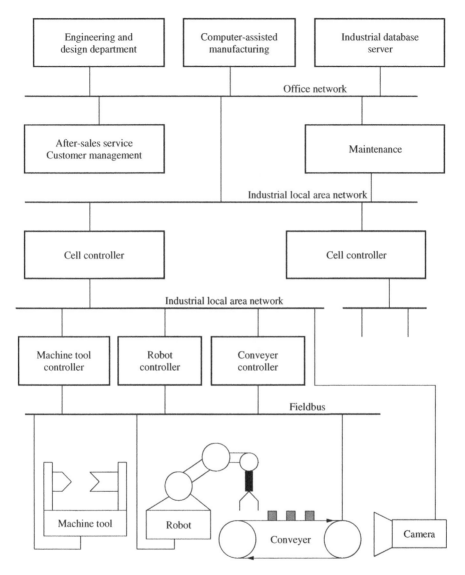

**Figure 1.4**   Example of a distributed architecture of real-time application

## Logical architecture and real-time computing systems

*Operating systems*   In order to locate real-time systems, let us briefly recall that computing systems may be classified, as shown by Figure 1.5, into transformational, interactive and reactive systems, which include asynchronous real-time systems.

The transformational aspect refers to systems where the results are computed with data available right from the program start and usable when required at any moment. The relational aspect between programming entities makes reference to systems where the environment-produced data are expected by programs already started; the results

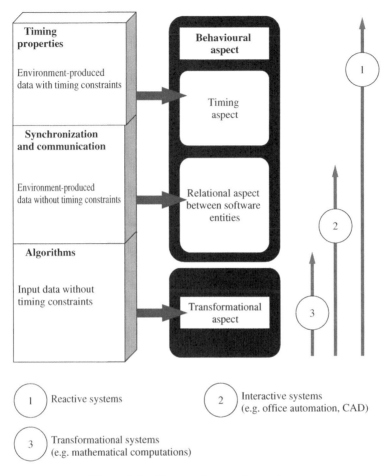

**Figure 1.5**   Classes of computing systems

of these programs are input to other programs. The timing aspect refers to systems where the results must be given at times fixed by the controlled process dynamics.

A system is centralized when information representing decisions, resource sharing, algorithms and data consistency is present in a shared memory and is directly accessible by all tasks of the system. This definition is independent of the hardware architecture. It refers to a uniprocessor or a shared memory multiprocessor architecture as well as to a distributed architecture where all decisions are only taken by one site. A system is distributed when the decisions are the result of a consensus among sites exchanging messages.

Distributed programming has to cope with uncertainty resulting from the lack of a common memory and common clock, from the variations of message transfer delays from one site to another as well as from one message to another, and from the existence of an important fault rate. Thus, identical information can never be captured simultaneously at all sites. As the time is one of these pieces of information, the sites are not able to read a common clock simultaneously and define instantaneously whether or not 'they have the same time'.

Computing systems are structured in layers. They all contain an operating system kernelas shown in Figure 1.6. This kernel includes mechanisms for the basic management of the processor, the virtual memory, interrupt handling and communication. More elaborate management policies for these resources and for other resources appear in the higher layers.

Conventional operating systems provide resource allocation and task scheduling, applying global policies in order to optimize the use of resources or to favour the response time of some tasks such as interactive tasks. All tasks are considered as aperiodic: neither their arrival times nor their execution times are known and they have no deadline.

In conventional operating systems the shared resources dynamically allocated to tasks are the main memory and the processor. Program behaviour investigations have indicated that the main memory is the sensitive resource (the most sensitive are demand paging systems with swapping between main memory and disk). Thus memory is allocated first according to allocation algorithms, which are often complicated, and the processor is allocated last. This simplifies processor scheduling since it concerns only the small subset of tasks already granted enough memory (Bawn, 1997; Silberscharz and Galvin, 1998; Tanenbaum, 1994; Tanenbaum and Woodhull, 1997). Conventional operating systems tend to optimize resource utilization, principally the main memory, and they do not give priority to deadline observances. This is a great difference with real-time operating systems.

*Real-time operating systems*   In real-time systems, resources other than the processor are often statically allocated to tasks at their creation. In particular, time should not be wasted in dynamic memory allocation. Real-time files and databases are not stored on disks but reside in main memory; this avoids the non-deterministic disk track seeking and data access. Input–output management is important since the connections with the controlled process are various. Therefore, the main allocation parameter is processor time and this gives importance to the kernel and leads to it being named

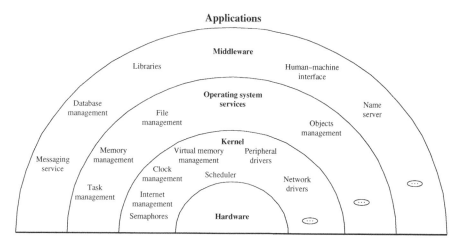

**Figure 1.6**   Structure of a conventional system

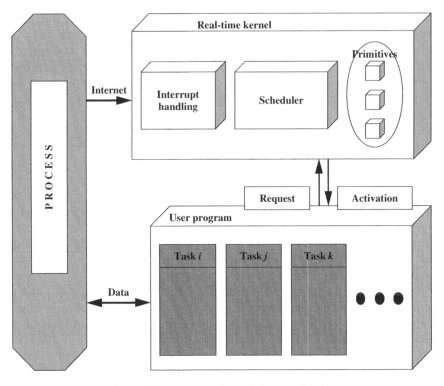

**Figure 1.7**   Schema of a real-time application

the real-time operating system (Figure 1.7). Nevertheless, conventional operating system services are needed by real-time applications that have additional requirements such as, for example, management of large data sets, storing and implementing programs on the computer also used for process control or management of local network interconnection. Thus, some of these conventional operating systems have been reengineered in order to provide a reentrant and interruptible kernel and to lighten the task structure and communication. This has led to real-time Unix implementations. The market seems to be showing a trend towards real-time systems proposing a Posix standard interface (Portable Operating System Interface for Computer Environments; international standardization for Unix-like systems).

## 1.2   Basic Concepts for Real-Time Task Scheduling

### 1.2.1   Task description

*Real-time task model*

Real-time tasks are the basic executable entities that are scheduled; they may be periodic or aperiodic, and have soft or hard real-time constraints. A task model has been defined with the main timing parameters. A task is defined by chronological parameters denoting delays and by chronometric parameters denoting times. The model includes primary and dynamic parameters. Primary parameters are (Figure 1.8):

- $r$, task release time, i.e. the triggering time of the task execution request.

- $C$, task worst-case computation time, when the processor is fully allocated to it.

- $D$, task relative deadline, i.e. the maximum acceptable delay for its processing.

- $T$, task period (valid only for periodic tasks).

- when the task has hard real-time constraints, the relative deadline allows computation of the absolute deadline $d = r + D$. Transgression of the absolute deadline causes a timing fault.

The parameter $T$ is absent for an aperiodic task. A periodic task is modelled by the four previous parameters. Each time a task is ready, it releases a periodic request. The successive release times (also called request times, arrival times or ready times) are request release times at $r_k = r_0 + kT$, where $r_0$ is the first release and $r_k$ the $k + 1$th release; the successive absolute deadlines are $d_k = r_k + D$. If $D = T$, the periodic task has a relative deadline equal to period. A task is well formed if $0 < C \leq D \leq T$.

The quality of scheduling depends on the exactness of these parameters, so their determination is an important aspect of real-time design. If the durations of operations like task switching, operating system calls, interrupt processing and scheduler execution cannot be neglected, the design analysis must estimate these durations and add them

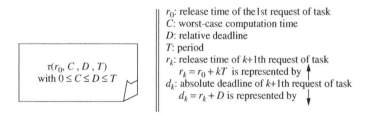

$r_0$: release time of the 1st request of task
$C$: worst-case computation time
$D$: relative deadline
$T$: period
$r_k$: release time of $k+1$th request of task
   $r_k = r_0 + kT$ is represented by ↑
$d_k$: absolute deadline of $k+1$th request of task
   $d_k = r_k + D$ is represented by ↓

$\tau(r_0, C, D, T)$
with $0 \leq C \leq D \leq T$

*Note*: for periodic task with $D = T$ (deadline equal to period) deadline at next release time is represented by ↕

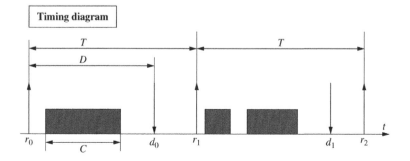

**Figure 1.8**  Task model

to the task computation times. That is why a deterministic behaviour is required for the kernel, which should guarantee maximum values for these operations.

Other parameters are derived:

- $u = C/T$ is the processor utilization factor of the task; we must have $u \leq 1$.

- $ch = C/D$ is the processor load factor; we must have $ch \leq 1$.

The following dynamic parameters help to follow the task execution:

- $s$ is the start time of task execution.

- $e$ is the finish time of task execution.

- $D(t) = d - t$ is the residual relative deadline at time $t$: $0 \leq D(t) \leq D$.

- $C(t)$ is the pending execution time at time $t$: $0 \leq C(t) \leq C$.

- $L = D - C$ is the nominal laxity of the task (it is also called slack time)and it denotes the maximum lag for its start time $s$ when it has sole use of the processor.

- $L(t) = D(t) - C(t)$ is the residual nominal laxity of the task at time $t$ and it denotes the maximum lag for resuming its execution when it has sole use of the processor; we also have $L(t) = D + r - t - C(t)$.

- $TR = e - r$ is the task response time; we have $C \leq TR \leq D$ when there is no time fault.

- $CH(t) = C(t)/D(t)$ is the residual load; $0 \leq CH(t) \leq C/T$ (by definition, if $e = d$, $CH(e) = 0$).

Figure 1.9 shows the evolution of $L(t)$ and $D(t)$ according to time.

Periodic tasks are triggered at successive request release times and return to the passive state once the request is completed. Aperiodic tasks may have the same behaviour if they are triggered more than once; sometimes they are created at release time.

Once created, a task evolves between two states: passive and triggered. Processor and resource sharing introduces several task states (Figure 1.10):

- *elected*: a processor is allocated to the task; $C(t)$ and $D(t)$ decrease, $L(t)$ does not decrease.

- *blocked*: the task waits for a resource, a message or a synchronization signal; $L(t)$ and $D(t)$ decrease.

- *ready*: the task waits for election: in this case, $L(t)$ and $D(t)$ decrease.

- *passive*: the task has no current request.

- *non-existing*: the task is not created.

### *Other task characteristics*

In addition to timing parameters of the task model, tasks are described by other features.

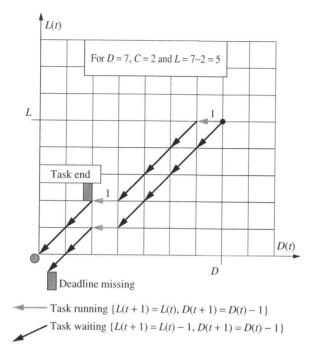

**Figure 1.9**   Dynamic parameter evolution

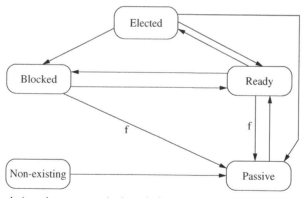

f: evolution when a request is aborted after a timing fault (missing deadline)

**Figure 1.10**   Task states

*Preemptive or non-preemptive task*    Some tasks, once elected, should not be stopped before the end of their execution; they are called *non-preemptive* tasks. For example, a non-preemptive task is necessary to handle direct memory access (DMA) input–output or to run in interrupt mode. Non-preemptive tasks are often called *immediate* tasks. On the contrary, when an elected task may be stopped and reset to the ready state in order to allocate the processor to another task, it is called a *preemptive* task.

*Dependency of tasks*     Tasks may interact according to a partial order that is fixed or caused by a message transmission or by explicit synchronization. This creates precedence relationships among tasks. Precedence relationships are known before execution, i.e. they are static, and can be represented by a static precedence graph (Figure 1.11). Tasks may share other resources than the processor and some resources may be exclusive or critical, i.e. they must be used in mutual exclusion. The sequence of instructions that a task has to execute in mutual exclusion is called a critical section. Thus, only one task is allowed to run its critical section for a given resource (Figure 1.12).

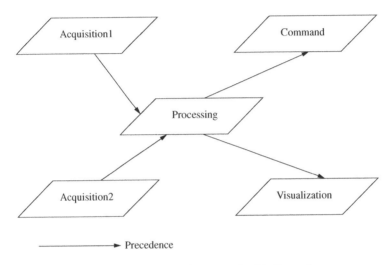

**Figure 1.11**    A precedence graph with five tasks

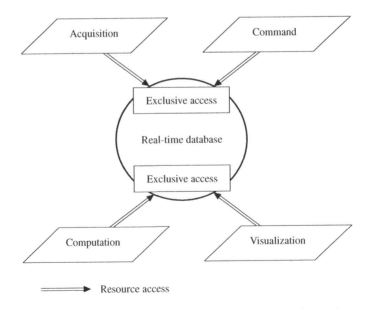

**Figure 1.12**    Example of a critical resource shared by four tasks

Resource sharing induces a dynamic relationship when the resource use order depends on the task election order. The relationships can be represented by an allocation graph. When the tasks have static and dynamic dependencies which may serialize them, the notion of global response time, or end-to-end delay, is used. This is the time elapsed between the release time of the task reactive to the process stimulus and the finish time of the last task that commands the actuators in answer to the stimulus. Tasks are independent when they have no precedence relationships and do not share critical resources.

*Maximum jitter*    Sometimes, periodic requests must have regular start times or response times. This is the case of periodic data sampling, a proportional integral derivative (PID) control loop or continuous emission of audio and video streams. The difference between the start times of two consecutive requests, $s_i$ and $s_{i+1}$, is the start time jitter. A maximum jitter, or absolute jitter, is defined as $|s_{i+1} - (s_i + T)| \leq Gmax$. The maximum response time jitter is similarly defined.

*Urgency*    The task deadline allows the specification of the urgency of data provided by this task. Two tasks with equal urgency are given the same deadline.

*Importance (criticality)*    When some tasks of a set are able to overcome timing faults and avoid their propagation, the control system may suppress the execution of some tasks. The latter must be aware of which tasks to suppress first or, on the other hand, which tasks are essential for the application and should not be suppressed. An importance parameter is introduced to specify the criticality of a task. Two tasks with equal urgency (thus having the same deadline) can be distinguished by different importance values.

*External priority*    The designer may fix a constant priority, called external priority. In this simplified form, all scheduling decisions are taken by an off-line scheduler or by *a priori* rules (for example, the clock management task or the backup task in the event of power failure must run immediately).

## 1.2.2 Scheduling: definitions, algorithms and properties

In a real-time system, tasks have timing constraints and their execution is bounded to a maximum delay that has to be respected imperatively as often as possible. The objective of scheduling is to allow tasks to fulfil these timing constraints when the application runs in a nominal mode. A schedule must be predictable, i.e. it must be *a priori* proven that all the timing constraints are met in a nominal mode. When malfunctions occur in the controlled process, some alarm tasks may be triggered or some execution times may increase, overloading the application and giving rise to timing faults. In an overload situation, the objective of scheduling is to allow some tolerance, i.e. to allow the execution of the tasks that keep the process safe, although at a minimal level of service.

### *Task sets*

A real-time application is specified by means of a set of tasks.

*Progressive or simultaneous triggering*   Application tasks are simultaneously triggered when they have the same first release time, otherwise they are progressively triggered. Tasks simultaneously triggered are also called *in phase* tasks.

*Processor utilization factor*   The processor utilization factor of a set of $n$ periodic tasks is:

$$U = \sum_{i=1}^{n} \frac{C_i}{T_i} \tag{1.1}$$

*Processor load factor*   The processor load factor of a set of $n$ periodic tasks is:

$$CH = \sum_{i=1}^{n} \frac{C_i}{D_i} \tag{1.2}$$

*Processor laxity*   Because of deadlines, neither the utilization factor nor the load factor is sufficient to evaluate an overload effect on timing constraints. We introduce $LP(t)$, the processor laxity at $t$, as the maximal time the processor may remain idle after $t$ without causing a task to miss its deadline. $LP(t)$ varies as a function of $t$. For all $t$, we must have $LP(t) \geq 0$. To compute the laxity, the assignment sequence of tasks to the processor must be known, and then the conditional laxity $LC_i(t)$ of each task $i$ must be computed:

$$LC_i(t) = D_i - \sum C_j(t) \tag{1.3}$$

where the sum in $j$ computes the pending execution time of all the tasks (including task $i$) that are triggered at $t$ and that precede task $i$ in the assignment sequence. The laxity $LP(t)$ is the smallest value of conditional laxity $LC_i(t)$.

*Processor idle time*   The set of time intervals where the processor laxity is strictly positive, i.e. the set of spare intervals, is named the processor idle time. It is a function of the set of tasks and of their schedule.

### Task scheduling definitions

Scheduling a task set consists of planning the execution of task requests in order to meet the timing constraints:

- of all tasks when the system runs in the nominal mode;

- of at least the most important tasks (i.e. the tasks that are necessary to keep the controlled process secure), in an abnormal mode.

An abnormal mode may be caused by hardware faults or other unexpected events. In some applications, additional performance criteria are sought, such as minimizing the response time, reducing the jitter, balancing the processor load among several sites, limiting the communication cost, or minimizing the number of late tasks and messages or their cumulative lag.

The scheduling algorithm assigns tasks to the processor and provides an ordered list of tasks, called the planning sequence or the schedule.

## Scheduling algorithms taxonomy

*On-line or off-line scheduling*   Off-line scheduling builds a complete planning sequence with all task set parameters. The schedule is known before task execution and can be implemented efficiently. However, this static approach is very rigid; it assumes that all parameters, including release times, are fixed and it cannot adapt to environmental changes.

On-line scheduling allows choosing at any time the next task to be elected and it has knowledge of the parameters of the currently triggered tasks. When a new event occurs the elected task may be changed without necessarily knowing in advance the time of this event occurrence. This dynamic approach provides less precise statements than the static one since it uses less information, and it has higher implementation overhead. However, it manages the unpredictable arrival of tasks and allows progressive creation of the planning sequence. Thus, on-line scheduling is used to cope with aperiodic tasks and abnormal overloading.

*Preemptive or non-preemptive scheduling*   In preemptive scheduling, an elected task may be preempted and the processor allocated to a more urgent task or one with higher priority; the preempted task is moved to the ready state, awaiting later election on some processor. Preemptive scheduling is usable only with preemptive tasks. Non-preemptive schedulingdoes not stop task execution. One of the drawbacks of non-preemptive scheduling is that it may result in timing faults that a preemptive algorithm can easily avoid. In uniprocessor architecture, critical resource sharing is easier with non-preemptive scheduling since it does not require any concurrent access mechanism for mutual exclusion and task queuing. However, this simplification is not valid in multiprocessor architecture.

*Best effort and timing fault intolerance*   With soft timing constraints, the scheduling uses a best effort strategy and tries to do its best with the available processors. The application may tolerate timing faults. With hard time constraints, the deadlines must be guaranteed and timing faults are not tolerated.

*Centralized or distributed scheduling*   Scheduling is centralized when it is implemented on a centralized architecture or on a privileged site that records the parameters of all the tasks of a distributed architecture. Scheduling is distributed when each site defines a local scheduling after possibly some cooperation between sites leading to a global scheduling strategy. In this context some tasks may be assigned to a site and migrate later.

## Scheduling properties

*Feasible schedule*   A scheduling algorithm results in a schedule for a task set. This schedule is feasible if all the tasks meet their timing constraints.

*Schedulable task set*   A task set is schedulable when a scheduling algorithm is able to provide a feasible schedule.

*Optimal scheduling algorithm*   An algorithm is optimal if it is able to produce a feasible schedule for any schedulable task set.

*Schedulability test* A schedulability test allows checking of whether a periodic task set that is submitted to a given scheduling algorithm might result in a feasible schedule.

*Acceptance test* On-line scheduling creates and modifies the schedule dynamically as new task requests are triggered or when a deadline is missed. A new request may be accepted if there exists at least a schedule which allows all previously accepted task requests as well as this new candidate to meet their deadlines. The required condition is called an acceptance test. This is often called a guarantee routine since if the tasks respect their worst-case computation time (to which may be added the time waiting for critical resources), the absence of timing faults is guaranteed. In distributed scheduling, the rejection of a request by a site after a negative acceptance test may lead the task to migrate.

*Scheduling period (or major cycle or hyper period)* The validation of a periodic and aperiodic task set leads to the timing analysis of the execution of this task set. When periodic tasks last indefinitely, the analysis must go through infinity. In fact, the task set behaviour is periodic and it is sufficient to analyse only a validation period or pseudo-period, called the scheduling period, the schedule length or the hyper period (Grolleau and Choquet-Geniet, 2000; Leung and Merrill, 1980). The scheduling period of a task set starts at the earliest release time, i.e. at time $t = \text{Min}\{r_{i,0}\}$, considering all tasks of the set. It ends at a time which is a function of the least common multiple (LCM) of periods $(T_i)$, the first release times of periodic tasks and the deadlines of aperiodic tasks:

$$\text{Max}\{r_{i,0}, (r_{j,0} + D_j)\} + 2 \cdot LCM(T_i) \tag{1.4}$$

where $i$ varies in the set of periodic task indexes, and $j$ in the set of aperiodic task indexes.

## Implementation of schedulers

Scheduling implementation relies on conventional data structures.

*Election table* When the schedule is fixed before application start, as in static off-line scheduling, this definitive schedule may be stored in a table and used by the scheduler to decide which task to elect next.

*Priority queuing list* On-line scheduling creates dynamically a planning sequence, the first element of which is the elected task (in a $n$-processor architecture, the $n$ first elements are concerned). This sequence is an ordered list; the ordering relationship is represented by keys; searching and suppression point out the minimal key element; a new element is inserted in the list according to its key ordering. This structure is usually called a heap sorted list or a priority ordered list (Weiss, 1994).

*Constant or varying priority* The element key, called priority when elements are tasks, is a timing parameter or a mix of parameters of the task model. It remains constant when the parameter is not variable, such as computation time, relative deadline, period or external priority. It is variable when the parameter changes during task execution, such as pending computation time, residual laxity, or when it is modified from one request to another, such as the release time or absolute deadline. The priority value or sorting key may be the value of the parameter used or, if the range of values is too large, a one-to-one function from this parameter to a subset of integers. This subset is usually called the priority set. The size of this priority set may be fixed *a priori* by hardware architecture or by the operating system kernel. Coding the priority with a fixed bit-size and using special machine instruction allows the priority list management to be made faster.

*Two-level scheduling*   When scheduling gets complex, it is split into two parts. One elaborates policy (high-level or long-term decisions, facing overload with task suppression, giving preference to some tasks for a while in hierarchical scheduling). The other executes the low-level mechanisms (election of a task in the subset prepared by the high-level scheduler, short-term choices which reorder this subset). A particular case is distributed scheduling, which separates the local scheduling that copes with the tasks allocated to a site and the global scheduling that assigns tasks to sites and migrates them. The order between local and global is another choice whose cost must be appraised: should tasks be settled *a priori* in a site and then migrate if the site becomes overloaded, or should all sites be interrogated about their reception capacity before allocating a triggered task?

## 1.2.3   Scheduling in classical operating systems

### Scheduling objectives in a classical operating system

In a multitasking system, scheduling has two main functions:

- maximizing processor usage, i.e. the ratio between active time and idle time. Theoretically, this ratio may vary from 0% to 100%; in practice, the observed rate varies between 40% and 95%.

- minimizing response time of tasks, i.e. the time between task submission time and the end of execution. At best, response time may be equal to execution time, when a task is elected immediately and executed without preemption.

The success of both functions may be directly appraised by computing the processing ratio and the mean response time, but other evaluation criteria are also used. Some of them are given below:

- evaluating the task waiting time, i.e. the time spent in the ready state;

- evaluating the processor throughput, i.e. the average number of completed tasks during a time interval;

- computing the total execution time of a given set of tasks;

- computing the average response time of a given set of tasks.

### Main policies

The scheduling policy decides which ready task is elected. Let us describe below some of the principal policies frequently used in classical operating systems.

*First-come-first-served scheduling policy*    This policy serves the oldest request, without preemption; the processor allocation order is the task arrival order. Tasks with short computation time may be penalized when a task with a long computation time precedes them.

*Shortest first scheduling policy*    This policy aims to correct the drawback mentioned above. The processor is allocated to the shortest computation time task, without preemption. This algorithm is the non-preemptive scheduling algorithm that minimizes the mean response time. It penalizes long computation tasks. It requires estimating the computation time of a task, which is usually unknown. A preemptive version of this policy is called 'pending computation time first': the elected task gives back the processor when a task with a shorter pending time becomes ready.

*Round-robin scheduling policy*    A time slice, which may be fixed, for example between 10 ms and 100 ms, is given as a quantum of processor allocation. The processor is allocated in turn to each ready task for a period no longer than the quantum. If the task ends its computation before the end of the quantum, it releases the processor and the next ready task is elected. If the task has not completed its computation before the quantum end, it is preempted and it becomes the last of the ready task set (Figure 1.13). A round-robin policy is commonly used in time-sharing systems. Its performance heavily relies on the quantum size. A large quantum increases response times, while too small a quantum increases task commutations and then their cost may no longer be neglected.

*Constant priority scheduling policy*    A constant priority value is assigned to each task and at any time the elected task is always the highest priority ready task (Figure 1.14). This algorithm can be used with or without preemption. The drawback of this policy is that low-priority tasks may starve forever. A solution is to 'age' the priority of waiting ready tasks, i.e. to increase the priority as a function of waiting time. Thus the task priority becomes variable.

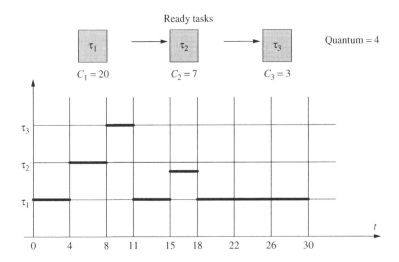

**Figure 1.13**   Example of Round-Robin scheduling

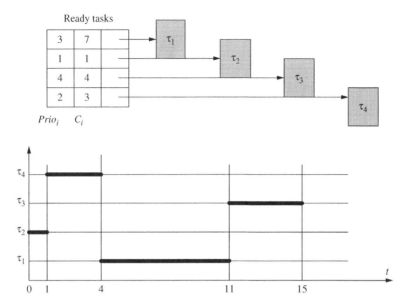

**Figure 1.14**  Example of priority scheduling (the lower the priority index, the higher is the task priority)

*Multilevel priority scheduling policy*    In the policies above, ready tasks share a single waiting list. We choose now to define several ready task lists, each corresponding to a priority level; this may lead to $n$ different priority lists varying from 0 to $n - 1$. In a given list, all tasks have the same priority and are first-come-first-served without preemption or in a round-robin fashion. The quantum value may be different from one priority list to another. The scheduler serves first all the tasks in list 0, then all the tasks in list 1 as long as list 0 remains empty, and so on. Two variants allow different evolution of the task priorities:

- Task priorities remain constant all the time. At the end of the quantum, a task that is still ready is reentered in the waiting list corresponding to its priority value.

- Task priorities evolve dynamically according to the service time given to the task. Thus a task elected from list $x$, and which is still ready at the end of its quantum, will not reenter list $x$, but list $x + 1$ of lower priority, and so on. This policy tries to minimize starvation risks for low-priority tasks by progressively lowering the priority of high-priority tasks (Figure 1.15).

*Note*: none of the preceding policies fulfils the two objectives of real-time scheduling, especially because none of them integrates the notion of task urgency, which is represented by the relative deadline in the model of real-time tasks.

## 1.2.4  Illustrating real-time scheduling

Let us introduce the problem of real-time scheduling by a tale inspired by La Fontaine, the famous French fabulist who lived in the 17th century. The problem is to control

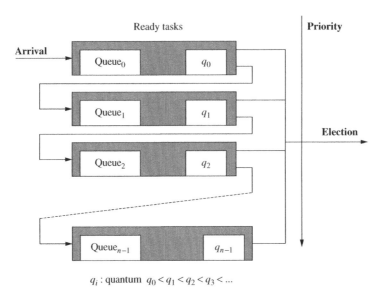

$q_i$ : quantum $q_0 < q_1 < q_2 < q_3 < \dots$

**Figure 1.15** Example of multilevel priority scheduling

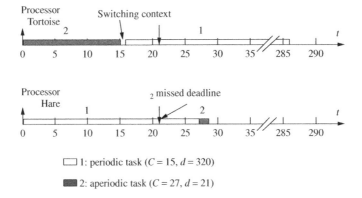

☐ 1: periodic task ($C = 15$, $d = 320$)

■ 2: aperiodic task ($C = 27$, $d = 21$)

**Figure 1.16** Execution sequences with two different scheduling algorithms and two different processors (the Hare and the Tortoise)

a real-time application with two tasks $\tau_1$ and $\tau_2$. The periodic task $\tau_1$ controls the engine of a mobile vehicle. Its period as well as its relative deadline is 320 seconds. The sporadic task $\tau_2$ has to react to steering commands before a relative deadline of 21 seconds. Two systems are proposed by suppliers.

The Tortoise system has a processor whose speed is 1 Mips, a task switching overhead of 1 second and an earliest deadline scheduler. The periodic task computation is 270 seconds; the sporadic task requires 15 seconds. The Hare system has the advantage of being very efficient and of withdrawing resource-sharing contention. It has a processor whose speed is 10 Mips, a task switching overhead of (almost) 0 and a first-in-first-out non-preemptive scheduler. So, with this processor, the periodic task $\tau_1$ computation is 27 seconds; the sporadic task $\tau_2$ requires 1.5 seconds.

An acceptance trial was made by one of our students as follows. Just after the periodic task starts running, the task is triggered. The Tortoise respects both deadlines while the Hare generates a timing fault for the steering command (Figure 1.16). The explanation is a trivial exercise for the reader of this book and is an illustration that scheduling helps to satisfy timing constraints better than system efficiency.

The first verse of La Fontaine's tale, named the Hare and the Tortoise, is 'It is no use running; it is better to leave on time' (La Fontaine, Le lièvre et la tortue, Fables VI, 10, Paris, 17th century).

# 2

# Scheduling of Independent Tasks

This chapter deals with scheduling algorithms for independent tasks. The first part of this chapter describes four basic algorithms: rate monotonic, inverse deadline, earliest deadline first, and least laxity first. These algorithms deal with homogeneous sets of tasks, where tasks are either periodic or aperiodic. However, real-time applications often require both types of tasks. In this context, periodic tasks usually have hard timing constraints and are scheduled with one of the four basic algorithms. Aperiodic tasks have either soft or hard timing constraints. The second part of this chapter describes scheduling algorithms for such hybrid task sets.

There are two classes of scheduling algorithms:

- Off-line scheduling algorithms: a scheduling algorithm is used off-line if it is executed on the entire task set before actual task activation. The schedule generated in this way is stored in a table and later executed by a dispatcher. The task set has to be fixed and known *a priori*, so that all task activations can be calculated off-line. The main advantage of this approach is that the run-time overhead is low and does not depend on the complexity of the scheduling algorithm used to build the schedule. However, the system is quite inflexible to environmental changes.

- On-line scheduling: a scheduling algorithm is used on-line if scheduling decisions are taken at run-time every time a new task enters the system or when a running task terminates. With on-line scheduling algorithms, each task is assigned a priority, according to one of its temporal parameters. These priorities can be either fixed priorities, based on fixed parameters and assigned to the tasks before their activation, or dynamic priorities, based on dynamic parameters that may change during system evolution. When the task set is fixed, task activations and worst-case computation times are known *a priori*, and a schedulability test can be executed off-line. However, when task activations are not known, an on-line guarantee test has to be done every time a new task enters the system. The aim of this guarantee test is to detect possible missed deadlines.

This chapter deals only with on-line scheduling algorithms.

## 2.1  Basic On-Line Algorithms for Periodic Tasks

Basic on-line algorithms are designed with a simple rule that assigns priorities according to temporal parameters of tasks. If the considered parameter is fixed, i.e. request rate or deadline, the algorithm is static because the priority is fixed. The priorities are assigned to tasks before execution and do not change over time. The basic algorithms with fixed-priority assignment are rate monotonic (Liu and Layland, 1973) and inverse deadline or deadline monotonic (Leung and Merrill, 1980). On the other hand, if the scheduling algorithm is based on variable parameters, i.e. absolute task deadlines, it is said to be dynamic because the priority is variable. The most important algorithms in this category are earliest deadline first (Liu and Layland, 1973) and least laxity first (Dhall, 1977; Sorenson, 1974).

The complete study (analysis) of a scheduling algorithm is composed of two parts:

- the optimality of the algorithm in the sense that no other algorithm of the same class (fixed or variable priority) can schedule a task set that cannot be scheduled by the studied algorithm.

- the off-line schedulability test associated with this algorithm, allowing a check of whether a task set is schedulable without building the entire execution sequence over the scheduling period.

## 2.1.1  Rate monotonic scheduling

For a set of periodic tasks, assigning the priorities according to the rate monotonic (RM) algorithm means that tasks with shorter periods (higher request rates) get higher priorities.

### *Optimality of the rate monotonic algorithm*

As we cannot analyse all the relationships among all the release times of a task set, we have to identify the worst-case combination of release times in term of schedulability of the task set. This case occurs when all the tasks are released simultaneously. In fact, this case corresponds to the critical instant, defined as the time at which the release of a task will produce the largest response time of this task (Buttazzo, 1997; Liu and Layland, 1973).

As a consequence, if a task set is schedulable at the critical instant of each one of its tasks, then the same task set is schedulable with arbitrary arrival times. This fact is illustrated in Figure 2.1. We consider two periodic tasks with the following parameters $\tau_1$ ($r_1$, 1, 4, 4) and $\tau_2$ (0, 10, 14, 14). According to the RM algorithm, task $\tau_1$ has high priority. Task $\tau_2$ is regularly delayed by the interference of the successive instances of the high priority task $\tau_1$. The analysis of the response time of task $\tau_2$ as a function of the release time $r_1$ of task $\tau_1$ shows that it increases when the release times of tasks are closer and closer:

- if $r_1 = 4$, the response time of task $\tau_2$ is equal to 12;

- if $r_1 = 2$, the response time of task $\tau_2$ is equal to 13 (the same response time holds when $r_1 = 3$ and $r_1 = 1$);

- if $r_1 = r_2 = 0$, the response time of task $\tau_2$ is equal to 14.

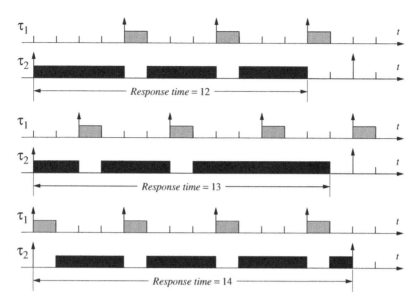

**Figure 2.1**  Analysis of the response time of task $\tau_2$ (0, 10, 14, 14) as a function of the release time of task $\tau_1(r_1, 1, 4, 4)$

In this context, we want to prove the optimality of the RM priority assignment algorithm. We first demonstrate the optimality property for two tasks and then we generalize this result for an arbitrary set of $n$ tasks.

Let us consider the case of scheduling two tasks $\tau_1$ and $\tau_2$ with $T_1 < T_2$ and their relative deadlines equal to their periods ($D_1 = T_1$, $D_2 = T_2$). If the priorities are not assigned according to the RM algorithm, then the priority of task $\tau_2$ may be higher than that of task $\tau_1$. Let us consider the case where task $\tau_2$ has a priority higher than that of $\tau_1$. At time $T_1$, task $\tau_1$ must be completed. As its priority is the low one, task $\tau_2$ has been completed before. As shown in Figure 2.2, the following inequality must be satisfied:

$$C_1 + C_2 \leq T_1 \qquad (2.1)$$

Now consider that the priorities are assigned according to the RM algorithm. Task $\tau_1$ will receive the high priority and task $\tau_2$ the low one. In this situation, we have to distinguish two cases in order to analyse precisely the interference of these two tasks

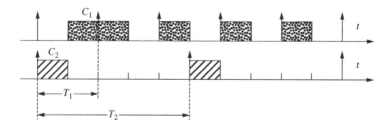

**Figure 2.2**  Execution sequence with two tasks $\tau_1$ and $\tau_2$ with the priority of task $\tau_2$ higher than that of task $\tau_1$

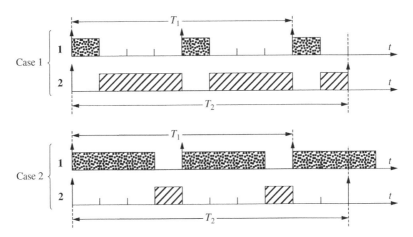

**Figure 2.3**  Execution sequence with two tasks $\tau_1$ and $\tau_2$ with the priority of task $\tau_1$ higher than that of task $\tau_2$ (RM priority assignment)

(Figure 2.3). $\beta = \lfloor T_2/T_1 \rfloor$ is the number of periods of task $\tau_1$ entirely included in the period of task $\tau_2$. The first case (case 1) corresponds to a computational time of task $\tau_1$ which is short enough for all the instances of task $\tau_1$ to complete before the second request of task $\tau_2$. That is:

$$C_1 \leq T_2 - \beta \cdot T_1 \tag{2.2}$$

In case 1, as shown in Figure 2.3, the maximum of the execution time of task $\tau_2$ is given by:

$$C_{2,\max} = T_2 - (\beta + 1) \cdot C_1 \tag{2.3}$$

That can be rewritten as follows:

$$C_2 + (\beta + 1) \cdot C_1 \leq T_2 \tag{2.4}$$

The second case (case 2) corresponds to a computational time of task $\tau_1$ which is large enough for the last request of task $\tau_1$ not to be completed before the second request of task $\tau_2$. That is:

$$C_1 \geq T_2 - \beta \cdot T_1 \tag{2.5}$$

In case 2, as shown in Figure 2.3, the maximum of the execution time of task $\tau_2$ is given by:

$$C_{2,\max} = \beta \cdot (T_1 - C_1) \tag{2.6}$$

That can be rewritten as follows:

$$\beta \cdot C_1 + C_2 \leq \beta \cdot T_1 \tag{2.7}$$

In order to prove the optimality of the RM priority assignment, we have to show that the inequality (2.1) implies the inequalities (2.4) or (2.7). So we start with the assumption that $C_1 + C_2 \leq T_1$, demonstrated when the priority assignment is not done

according to the RM algorithm. By multiplying both sides of (2.1) by $\beta$, we have:
$\beta \cdot C_1 + \beta \cdot C_2 \leq \beta \cdot T_1$

Given that $\beta = \lfloor T_2/T_1 \rfloor$ is greater than 1 or equal to 1, we obtain:

$$\beta \cdot C_1 + C_2 \leq \beta \cdot C_1 + \beta \cdot C_2 \leq \beta \cdot T_1$$

By adding $C_1$ to each member of this inequality, we get $(\beta + 1) \cdot C_1 + C_2 \leq \beta \cdot T_1 + C_1$.

By using the inequality (2.2) previously demonstrated in case 1, we can write $(\beta + 1) \cdot C_1 + C_2 \leq T_2$. This result corresponds to the inequality (2.4), so we have proved the following implication, which demonstrates the optimality of RM priority assignment in case 1:

$$C_1 + C_2 \leq T_1 \Rightarrow (\beta + 1) \cdot C_1 + C_2 \leq T_2 \tag{2.8}$$

In the same manner, starting with the inequality (2.1), we multiply by $\beta$ each member of this inequality and use the property $\beta \geq 1$. So we get $\beta \cdot C_1 + C_2 \leq \beta \cdot T_1$. This result corresponds to the inequality (2.7), so we have proved the following implication, which demonstrates the optimality of RM priority assignment in case 2:

$$C_1 + C_2 \leq T_1 \Rightarrow \beta \cdot C_1 + C_2 \leq \beta \cdot T_1 \tag{2.9}$$

In conclusion, we have proved that, for a set of two tasks $\tau_1$ and $\tau_2$ with $T_1 < T_2$ with relative deadlines equal to periods $(D_1 = T_1, D_2 = T_2)$, if the schedule is feasible by an arbitrary priority assignment, then it is also feasible by applying the RM algorithm. This result can be extended to a set of $n$ periodic tasks (Buttazzo, 1997; Liu and Layland, 1973).

### Schedulability test of the rate monotonic algorithm

We now study how to calculate the least upper bound $U_{\max}$ of the processor utilization factor for the RM algorithm. This bound is first determined for two periodic tasks $\tau_1$ and $\tau_2$ with $T_1 < T_2$ and again $D_1 = T_1$ and $D_2 = T_2$:

$$U_{\max} = \frac{C_1}{T_1} + \frac{C_{2,\max}}{T_2}$$

In case 1, we consider the maximum execution time of task $\tau_2$ given by the equality (2.3). So the processor utilization factor, denoted by $U_{\max,1}$, is given by:

$$U_{\max,1} = 1 - \frac{C_1}{T_2} \cdot \left[ (\beta + 1) - \frac{T_2}{T_1} \right] \tag{2.10}$$

We can observe that the processor utilization factor is monotonically decreasing in $C_1$ because $[(\beta + 1) - (T_2/T_1)] > 0$. This function of $C_1$ goes from $C_1 = 0$ to the limit between the two studied cases given by the inequalities (2.2) and (2.5). Figure 2.4 depicts this function.

In case 2, we consider the maximum execution time of task $\tau_2$ given by the equality (2.6). So the processor utilization factor $U_{\max,2}$ is given by:

$$U_{\max,2} = \beta \cdot \frac{T_1}{T_2} + \frac{C_1}{T_2} \cdot \left[ \frac{T_2}{T_1} - \beta \right] \tag{2.11}$$

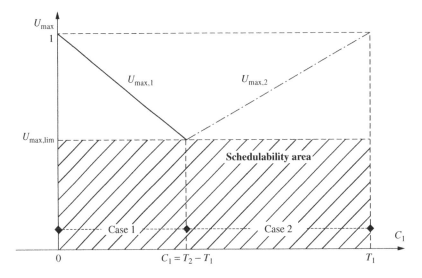

**Figure 2.4**   Analysis of the processor utilization factor function of $C_1$

We can observe that the processor utilization factor is monotonically increasing in $C_1$ because $[T_2/T_1 - \beta] > 0$. This function of $C_1$ goes from the limit between the two studied cases given by the inequalities (2.2) and (2.5) to $C_1 = T_1$. Figure 2.4 depicts this function.

The intersection between these two lines corresponds to the minimum value of the maximum processor utilization factor that occurs for $C_1 = T_2 - \beta \cdot T_1$. So we have:

$$U_{max,lim} = \frac{\alpha^2 + \beta}{\alpha + \beta}$$

where $\alpha = T_2/T_1 - \beta$ with the property $0 \leq \alpha < 1$.

Under this limit $U_{max,lim}$, we can assert that the task set is schedulable. Unfortunately, this value depends on the parameters $\alpha$ and $\beta$. In order to get a couple $\langle \alpha, \beta \rangle$ independent bound, we have to find the minimum value of this limit. Minimizing $U_{max,lim}$ over $\alpha$, we have:

$$\frac{dU_{max,lim}}{d\alpha} = \frac{(\alpha^2 + 2\alpha\beta - \beta)}{(\alpha + \beta)^2}$$

We obtain $dU_{max,lim}/d\alpha = 0$ for $\alpha^2 + 2\alpha\beta - \beta = 0$, which has an acceptable solution for $\alpha$ : $\alpha = \sqrt{\beta(1 + \beta)} - \beta$

Thus, the least upper bound is given by $U_{max,lim} = 2 \cdot [\sqrt{\beta(1 + \beta)} - \beta]$.

For the minimum value of $\beta = 1$, we get:

$$U_{max,lim} = 2 \cdot [2^{1/2} - 1] \approx 0.83$$

And, for any value of $\beta$, we get an upper value of 0.83:

$$\forall \beta, \, U_{max,lim} = 2 \cdot \{[\beta(1 + \beta)]^{1/2} - \beta\} \leq 0.83$$

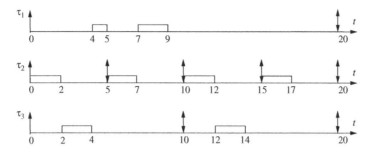

**Figure 2.5**   Example of a rate monotonic schedule with three periodic tasks: $\tau_1$ (0, 3, 20, 20), $\tau_2$ (0, 2, 5, 5) and $\tau_3$ (0, 2, 10, 10)

We can generalize this result for an arbitrary set of $n$ periodic tasks, and we get a sufficient schedulability condition (Buttazzo, 1997; Liu and Layland, 1973).

$$U = \sum_{i=1}^{n} \frac{C_i}{T_i} \leq n \cdot (2^{1/n} - 1) \tag{2.12}$$

This upper bound converges to $\ln(2) = 0.69$ for high values of $n$. A simulation study shows that for random task sets, the processor utilization bound is 88% (Lehoczky et al., 1989). Figure 2.5 shows an example of an RM schedule on a set of three periodic tasks for which the relative deadline is equal to the period: $\tau_1$ (0, 3, 20, 20), $\tau_2$ (0, 2, 5, 5) and $\tau_3$ (0, 2, 10, 10). Task $\tau_2$ has the highest priority and task $\tau_1$ has the lowest priority. The schedule is given within the major cycle of the task set, which is the interval [0, 20]. The three tasks meet their deadlines and the processor utilization factor is $3/20 + 2/5 + 2/10 = 0.75 < 3(2^{1/3} - 1) = 0.779$.

Due to priority assignment based on the periods of tasks, the RM algorithm should be used to schedule tasks with relative deadlines equal to periods. This is the case where the sufficient condition (2.12) can be used. For tasks with relative deadlines not equal to periods, the inverse deadline algorithm should be used (see Section 2.1.2).

Another example can be studied with a set of three periodic tasks for which the relative deadline is equal to the period: $\tau_1$ (0, 20, 100, 100), $\tau_2$ (0, 40, 150, 150) and $\tau_3$ (0, 100, 350, 350). Task $\tau_1$ has the highest priority and task $\tau_3$ has the lowest priority. The major cycle of the task set is $LCM(100, 150, 350) = 2100$. The processor utilization factor is:

$$20/100 + 40/150 + 100/350 = 0.75 < 3(2^{1/3} - 1) = 0.779.$$

So we can assert that this task set is schedulable; all the three tasks meet their deadlines. The free time processor is equal to 520 over the major cycle. Although the scheduling sequence building was not useful, we illustrate this example in the Figure 2.6, but only over a tiny part of the major cycle.

## 2.1.2   Inverse deadline (or deadline monotonic) algorithm

Inverse deadline allows a weakening of the condition which requires equality between periods and deadlines in static-priority schemes. The inverse deadline algorithm assigns

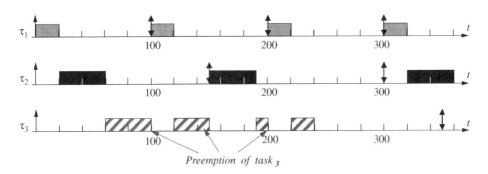

*Preemption of task $_3$*

**Figure 2.6**   Example of a rate monotonic schedule with three periodic tasks: $\tau_1$ (0, 20, 100, 100), $\tau_2$ (0, 40, 150, 150) and $\tau_3$ (0, 100, 350, 350)

priorities to tasks according to their deadlines: the task with the shortest relative deadline is assigned the highest priority. Inverse deadline is optimal in the class of fixed-priority assignment algorithms in the sense that if any fixed-priority algorithm can schedule a set of tasks with deadlines shorter than periods, than inverse deadline will also schedule that task set. The computation given in the previous section can be extended to the case of two tasks with deadlines shorter than periods, scheduled with inverse deadline. The proof is very similar and is left to the reader. For an arbitrary set of $n$ tasks with deadlines shorter than periods, a sufficient condition is:

$$\sum_{i=1}^{n} \frac{C_i}{D_i} \leq n(2^{1/n} - 1) \tag{2.13}$$

Figure 2.7 shows an example of an inverse deadline schedule for a set of three periodic tasks: $\tau_1(r_0 = 0, C = 3, D = 7, T = 20)$, $\tau_2(r_0 = 0, C = 2, D = 4, T = 5)$ and $\tau_3(r_0 = 0, C = 2, D = 9, T = 10)$. Task $\tau_2$ has the highest priority and task $\tau_3$ the lowest. Notice that the sufficient condition (2.13) is not satisfied because the processor load factor is 1.15. However, the task set is schedulable; the schedule is given within the major cycle of the task set.

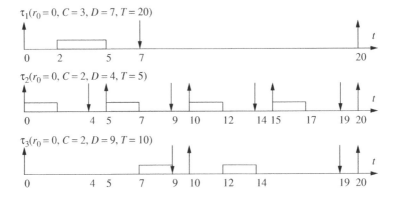

**Figure 2.7**   Inverse deadline schedule

## 2.1.3 Algorithms with dynamic priority assignment

With dynamic priority assignment algorithms, priorities are assigned to tasks based on dynamic parameters that may change during task execution. The most important algorithms in this category are *earliest deadline first* (Liu and Layland, 1973) and *least laxity first* (Dhall, 1977; Sorenson, 1974).

### Earliest deadline first algorithm

The earliest deadline first (EDF) algorithm assigns priority to tasks according to their absolute deadline: the task with the earliest deadline will be executed at the highest priority. This algorithm is optimal in the sense of feasibility: if there exists a feasible schedule for a task set, then the EDF algorithm is able to find it.

It is important to notice that a necessary and sufficient schedulability condition exists for periodic tasks with deadlines equal to periods. A set of periodic tasks with deadlines equal to periods is schedulable with the EDF algorithm if and only if the processor utilization factor is less than or equal to 1:

$$\sum_{i=1}^{n} \frac{C_i}{T_i} \leq 1 \qquad (2.14)$$

A hybrid task set is schedulable with the EDF algorithm if (sufficient condition):

$$\sum_{i=1}^{n} \frac{C_i}{D_i} \leq 1 \qquad (2.15)$$

A necessary condition is given by formula (2.14). The EDF algorithm does not make any assumption about the periodicity of the tasks; hence it can be used for scheduling periodic as well as aperiodic tasks.

Figure 2.8 shows an example of an EDF schedule for a set of three periodic tasks $\tau_1(r_0 = 0, C = 3, D = 7, 20 = T)$, $\tau_2(r_0 = 0, C = 2, D = 4, T = 5)$ and $\tau_3(r_0 = 0, C = 1, D = 8, T = 10)$. At time $t = 0$, the three tasks are ready to execute and the

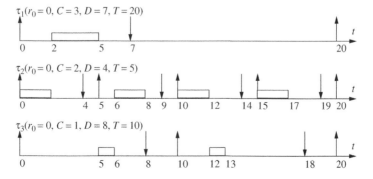

**Figure 2.8** EDF schedule

task with the smallest absolute deadline is $\tau_2$. Then $\tau_2$ is executed. At time $t = 2$, task $\tau_2$ completes. The task with the smallest absolute deadline is now $\tau_1$. Then $\tau_1$ executes. At time $t = 5$, task $\tau_1$ completes and task $\tau_2$ is again ready. However, the task with the smallest absolute deadline is now $\tau_3$, which begins to execute.

### *Least laxity first algorithm*

The least laxity first (LLF) algorithm assigns priority to tasks according to their relative laxity: the task with the smallest laxity will be executed at the highest priority. This algorithm is optimal and the schedulability of a set of tasks can be guaranteed using the EDF schedulability test.

When a task is executed, its relative laxity is constant. However, the relative laxity of ready tasks decreases. Thus, when the laxity of the tasks is computed only at arrival times, the LLF schedule is equivalent to the EDF schedule. However if the laxity is computed at every time $t$, more context-switching will be necessary.

Figure 2.9 shows an example of an LLF schedule on a set of three periodic tasks $\tau_1(r_0 = 0, C = 3, D = 7, T = 20)$, $\tau_2(r_0 = 0, C = 2, D = 4, T = 5)$ and $\tau_3(r_0 = 0, C = 1, D = 8, T = 10)$. Relative laxity of the tasks is only computed at task arrival times. At time $t = 0$, the three tasks are ready to execute. Relative laxity values of the tasks are:

$$L(\tau_1) = 7 - 3 = 4; \qquad L(\tau_2) = 4 - 2 = 2; \qquad L(\tau_3) = 8 - 1 = 7$$

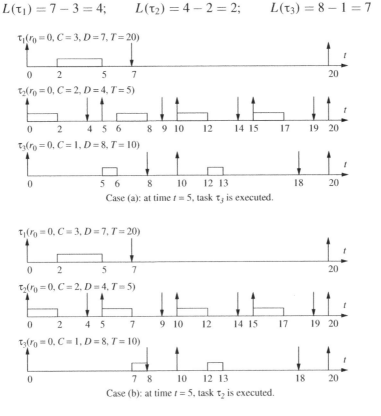

Case (a): at time $t = 5$, task $\tau_3$ is executed.

Case (b): at time $t = 5$, task $\tau_2$ is executed.

**Figure 2.9**  *Least Laxity First* schedules

Thus the task with the smallest relative laxity is $\tau_2$. Then $\tau_2$ is executed. At time $t = 5$, a new request of task $\tau_2$ enters the system. Its relative laxity value is equal to the relative laxity of task $\tau_3$. So, task $\tau_3$ or task $\tau_2$ is executed (Figure 2.9).

### Examples of jitter

Examples of jitters as defined in Chapter 1 can be observed with the schedules of the basic scheduling algorithms. Examples of release jitter can be observed for task $\tau_3$ with the inverse deadline schedule and for tasks $\tau_2$ and $\tau_3$ with the EDF schedule. Examples of finishing jitter will be observed for task $\tau_3$ with the schedule of Exercise 2.4, Question 3.

## 2.2 Hybrid Task Sets Scheduling

The basic scheduling algorithms presented in the previous sections deal with homogeneous sets of tasks where all tasks are periodic. However, some real-time applications may require aperiodic tasks. Hybrid task sets contain both types of tasks. In this context, periodic tasks usually have hard timing constraints and are scheduled with one of the four basic algorithms. Aperiodic tasks have either soft or hard timing constraints. The main objective of the system is to guarantee the schedulability of all the periodic tasks. If the aperiodic tasks have soft time constraints, the system aims to provide good average response times (best effort algorithms). If the aperiodic tasks have hard deadlines, the system aim is to maximize the guarantee ratio of these aperiodic tasks.

### 2.2.1 Scheduling of soft aperiodic tasks

We present the most important algorithms for handling soft aperiodic tasks. The simplest method is background scheduling, but it has quite poor performance. Average response time of aperiodic tasks can be improved through the use of a server (Sprunt et al., 1989). Finally, the slack stealing algorithm offers substantial improvements for aperiodic response time by 'stealing' processing time from periodic tasks (Chetto and Delacroix, 1993, Lehoczky et al., 1992).

### Background scheduling

Aperiodic tasks are scheduled in the background when there are no periodic tasks ready to execute. Aperiodic tasks are queued according to a first-come-first-served strategy.

Figure 2.10 shows an example in which two periodic tasks $\tau_1 (r_0 = 0, C = 2, T = 5)$ and $\tau_2 (r_0 = 0, C = 2, T = 10)$ are scheduled with the RM algorithm while three aperiodic tasks $\tau_3 (r = 4, C = 2)$, $\tau_4 (r = 10, C = 1)$ and $\tau_5 (r = 11, C = 2)$ are executed in the background. Idle times of the RM schedule are the intervals [4, 5], [7, 10], [14, 15] and [17, 20]. Thus the aperiodic task $\tau_3$ is executed immediately and finishes during the following idle time, that is between times $t = 7$ and $t = 8$. The aperiodic task

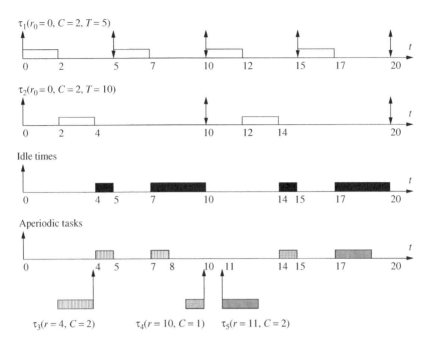

**Figure 2.10**   Background scheduling

$\tau_4$ enters the system at time $t = 10$ and waits until the idle time [14, 15] to execute. And finally, the aperiodic task $\tau_5$ is executed during the last idle time [17, 20].

The major advantage of background scheduling is its simplicity. However, its major drawback is that, for high loads due to periodic tasks, response time of aperiodic requests can be high.

### Task servers

A server is a periodic task whose purpose is to serve aperiodic requests. A server is characterized by a period and a computation time called *server capacity*. The server is scheduled with the algorithm used for the periodic tasks and, once it is active, it serves the aperiodic requests within the limit of its capacity. The ordering of aperiodic requests does not depend on the scheduling algorithm used for periodic tasks.

Several types of servers have been defined. The simplest server, called *polling server*, serves pending aperiodic requests at regular intervals equal to its period. Other types of servers (*deferrable server, priority exchange server, sporadic server*) improve this basic polling service technique and provide better aperiodic responsiveness. This section only presents the polling server, deferrable server and sporadic server techniques. Details about the other kinds of servers can be found in Buttazzo (1997).

*Polling server*   The polling server becomes active at regular intervals equal to its period and serves pending aperiodic requests within the limit of its capacity. If no aperiodic requests are pending, the polling server suspends itself until the beginning of its next period and the time originally reserved for aperiodic requests is used by periodic tasks.

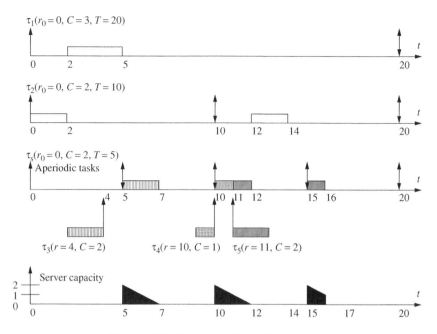

**Figure 2.11**  Example of a polling server $\tau_s$

Figure 2.11 shows an example of aperiodic service obtained using a polling server. The periodic task set is composed of three tasks, $\tau_1 (r_0 = 0, C = 3, T = 20)$, $\tau_2 (r_0 = 0, C = 2, T = 10)$ and $\tau_s (r_0 = 0, C = 2, T = 5)$. $\tau_s$ is the task server: it has the highest priority because it is the task with the smallest period. The three periodic tasks are scheduled with the RM algorithm . The processor utilization factor is: $3/20 + 2/10 + 2/5 = 0.75 < 3(2^{1/3} - 1) = 0.779$.

At time $t = 0$, the processor is assigned to the polling server. However, since no aperiodic requests are pending, the server suspends itself and its capacity is lost for aperiodic tasks and used by periodic ones. Thus, the processor is assigned to task $\tau_2$, then to task $\tau_1$. At time $t = 4$, task $\tau_3$ enters the system and waits until the beginning of the next period of the server ($t = 5$) to execute. The entire capacity of the server is used to serve the aperiodic task. At time $t = 10$, the polling server begins a new period and immediately serves task $\tau_4$, which just enters the system. Since only half of the server capacity has been used, the server serves task $\tau_5$, which arrives at time $t = 11$. Task $\tau_5$ uses the remaining server capacity and then it must wait until the next period of the server to execute to completion. Only half of the server capacity is consumed and the remaining half is lost because no other aperiodic tasks are pending.

The main drawback of the polling server technique is the following: when the polling server becomes active, it suspends itself until the beginning of its next period if no aperiodic requests are pending and the time reserved for aperiodic requests is discarded. So, if aperiodic tasks enter the system just after the polling server suspends itself, they must wait until the beginning of the next period of the server to execute.

*Deferrable server*    The deferrable server is an extension of the polling server which improves the response time of aperiodic requests. The deferrable server looks like the polling server. However, the deferrable server preserves its capacity if no aperiodic requests are pending at the beginning of its period. Thus, an aperiodic request that enters the system just after the server suspends itself can be executed immediately. However, the deferrable server violates a basic assumption of the RM algorithm: a periodic task must execute whenever it is the highest priority task ready to run, otherwise a lower priority task could miss its deadline. So, the behaviour of the deferrable server results in a lower upper bound of the processor utilization factor for the periodic task set, and the schedulability of the periodic task set is guaranteed under the RM algorithm if:

$$U \leq \ln\left(\frac{U_s + 2}{2U_s + 1}\right) \qquad U_s = \frac{C_s}{T_s} \qquad U = \sum_{i \in TP} \frac{C_i}{T_i} \qquad (2.16)$$

$U_s$ is the processor utilization factor of the deferrable server $\tau_s(C_s, T_s)$. $U$ is the processor utilization factor of the periodic task set. $TP$ is the periodic task index set.

*Sporadic server*     The sporadic server is another server technique which improves the response time of aperiodic requests without degrading the processor utilization factor of the periodic task set. Like the deferrable server, the sporadic server preserves its capacity until an aperiodic request occurs; however, it differs in the way it replenishes this capacity. Thus, the sporadic server does not recover its capacity to its full value at the beginning of each new period, but only after it has been consumed by aperiodic task executions. More precisely, the sporadic server replenishes its capacity each time $t_R$ it becomes active and its capacity is greater than 0. The replenishment time is set to $t_R$ plus the server period. The replenishment amount is set to the capacity consumed within the interval $t_R$ and the time when the sporadic server becomes idle or its capacity has been exhausted.

Figure 2.12 shows an example of aperiodic service obtained using a sporadic server. The periodic task set is composed of three tasks, $\tau_1(r_0 = 0, C = 3, T = 20)$, $\tau_2(r_0 = 0, C = 2, T = 10)$ and $\tau_s(r_0 = 0, C = 2, T = 5)$. $\tau_s$ is the task server. The aperiodic task set is composed of three tasks $\tau_3(r = 4, C = 2)$, $\tau_4(r = 10, C = 1)$ and $\tau_5(r = 11, C = 2)$. At time $t = 0$, the server becomes active and suspends itself because there are no pending aperiodic requests. However, it preserves its full capacity. At time $t = 4$, task $\tau_3$ enters the system and is immediately executed within the interval $[4, 6]$. The capacity of the server is entirely used to serve the aperiodic task. As the server has executed, the replenishment time is set to time $t_R = 4 + 5 = 9$. The replenishment amount is set to 2. At time $t = 9$, the server replenishes its capacity; however, it suspends itself since no aperiodic requests are pending. At time $t = 10$, task $\tau_4$ enters the system and is immediately executed. At time $t = 11$, task $\tau_5$ enters the system and it is executed immediately too. It consumes the remaining server capacity. The replenishment time is computed again and set to time $t_R = 15$. Task $\tau_5$ is executed to completion when the server replenishes its capacity, i.e. within the interval $[15, 16]$. At time $t = 20$, the sporadic server will replenish its capacity with an amount of 1, consumed by task $\tau_5$.

The replenishment rule used by the sporadic server compensates for any deferred execution so that the sporadic server exhibits a behaviour equivalent to one or more periodic tasks. Thus, the schedulability of the periodic task set can be guaranteed under the RM algorithm without degrading the processor utilization bound.

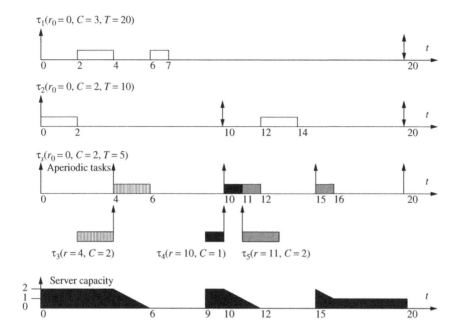

**Figure 2.12**   Example of a sporadic server

There is also a dynamic version of the sporadic server based on EDF scheduling (Spuri and Buttazzo, 1994, 1996). This version differs from the static version based on RM scheduling in the way the server capacity is re-initialized. In particular, the server capacity replenishment time is set so that a deadline can be assigned to each server execution. More details related to this technique can be found in Buttazzo (1997).

### Slack stealing and joint scheduling techniques

These two techniques are quite similar and both use the laxity of the periodic tasks to schedule aperiodic tasks. With the first method, called *slack stealing*, the tasks are scheduled with the RM algorithm. With the second method, called *joint scheduling*, the tasks are scheduled with the EDF algorithm.

Unlike the server techniques, these techniques do not require the use of a periodic task for aperiodic task service. Rather, each time an aperiodic request enters the system, time for servicing this request is made by 'stealing' processing time from the periodic tasks without causing deadline missing. So, the laxity of the periodic tasks is used to schedule aperiodic requests as soon as possible.

With the joint scheduling technique, a fictive deadline *fd* is defined for each aperiodic task so that the aperiodic task gets the shortest response time possible. *fd* is set to the earlier time *t*, for which the amount of processing time of the task is equal to the processor idle time while all pending task deadlines are met.

Figure 2.13 shows an example of aperiodic service obtained using the slack stealing technique. The periodic task set is composed of two tasks $\tau_1 (r_0 = 0, C = 2, T = 5)$ and $\tau_2 (r_0 = 0, C = 2, T = 10)$. The aperiodic task set is composed of three tasks

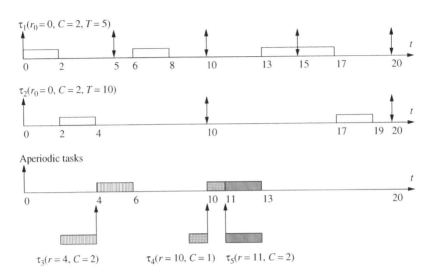

**Figure 2.13** Example of slack stealing schedule

$\tau_3(r = 4, C = 2)$, $\tau_4(r = 10, C = 1)$ and $\tau_5(r = 11, C = 2)$. At time $t = 4$, the aperiodic task enters the system. The laxity of task $\tau_1$, which will become active at time $t = 5$, is equal to 3; the execution of task $\tau_1$ can be delayed until time $t = 6$ and the aperiodic task can be executed within the interval [4, 6]. Similarly, the third request of the periodic task $\tau_1$ can delay its execution until time $t = 13$ so that the aperiodic tasks $\tau_4$ and $\tau_5$ are executed as soon as they enter the system. Notice that the aperiodic tasks have the smallest possible response times.

Figure 2.14 shows an example of aperiodic service obtained with the joint scheduling technique. The periodic task set is composed of two tasks $\tau_1(r_0 = 0, C = 2, D = 4, T = 5)$ and $\tau_2(r_0 = 0, C = 1, D = 8, T = 10)$ and is scheduled with the

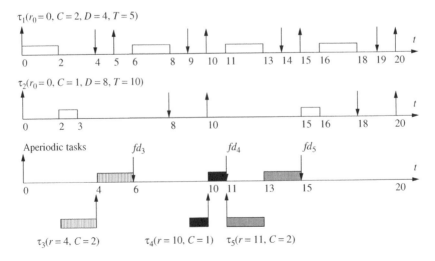

**Figure 2.14** Example of schedule using the joint scheduling technique

EDF algorithm. The aperiodic task set is composed of three tasks $\tau_3(r = 4, C = 2)$, $\tau_4(r = 10, C = 1)$ and $\tau_5(r = 11, C = 2)$. At time $t = 4$, the aperiodic task $\tau_3$ enters the system. The laxity of task $\tau_1$, which will become active at time $t = 5$, is equal to 2; the execution of task $\tau_1$ can be delayed until time $t = 6$ and the aperiodic task can be executed within the interval $[4, 6]$. So the fictive deadline $fd$ is set to 6 for the aperiodic task $\tau_3$.

Similarly, the third request of the periodic task $\tau_1$ can delay its execution until time $t = 11$ so that the aperiodic request $\tau_4$ is executed as soon as it enters the system. The fictive deadline assigned to task $\tau_4$ is equal to 11. Task $\tau_5$, which enters the system at $t = 11$, cannot be executed until completion of the third request of $\tau_1$. It is executed in the interval $[13, 15]$. Thus the fictive deadline assigned to task $\tau_5$ is equal to 15. Notice that with the joint scheduling technique, the aperiodic tasks again have the smallest possible response times.

## 2.2.2  Hard aperiodic task scheduling

If an aperiodic task is associated with a critical event which can be characterized by a minimum inter-arrival time between consecutive instances, the aperiodic task can be mapped onto a periodic task and scheduled with the periodic task set (Nassor and Bres, 1991; and Sprunt et al., 1989). However, it is not always possible to bound *a priori* the maximum arrival rate of some events. Moreover, mapping the aperiodic tasks onto periodic tasks guarantees the timing constraints of all the tasks but results in poor processor utilization. If the maximum arrival rate of some events cannot be bounded *a priori*, an on-line guarantee of each aperiodic request can be done (Chetto et al., 1990a). Each time a new aperiodic task enters the system, an acceptance test is executed to verify whether the request can be scheduled within its deadline and without jeopardizing the deadlines of periodic tasks and previously accepted aperiodic tasks. If the test is negative, the aperiodic request is rejected.

In the next sections, we present two main acceptance techniques for aperiodic tasks. Notice that these two policies always guarantee the periodic task deadlines: in an overload situation, the rejected task is always the newly arrived aperiodic task. This rejection assumes that the real-time system is a distributed system within which distributed scheduling is attempted to assign the rejected task to an underloaded processor (Stankovic 1985). *Spring* (Stankovic and Ramamritham, 1989) is a real-time distributed operating system where such dynamic guarantees and distributed scheduling are used. The second technique is optimal; it means that an aperiodic task which can be guaranteed is never rejected.

### Background scheduling of aperiodic tasks

The principle of this technique consists in scheduling aperiodic tasks in the background when there are no periodic tasks ready to execute according to the EDF algorithm. So, this technique looks like the background scheduling strategy presented in Section 2.2.1. However, the aperiodic requests have hard timing constraints and as they are accepted, they are queued according to a strict increasing order of deadlines. Thus, each time a new aperiodic request enters the system, an on-line acceptance test is executed as follows:

- The acceptance test algorithm computes the amount of processor idle time between the arrival time of the aperiodic task and its deadline. This amount of idle time must be at least equal to the computation time requested by the newly arrived aperiodic task.

- If there is enough idle time to execute the aperiodic task within its deadline, the acceptance test verifies that the execution of the new task does not jeopardize the guarantee of previously accepted tasks that have a later deadline and that have not yet completed.

If there is not enough idle time or if the acceptance of the new task would jeopardize the guarantee of previously accepted tasks, the new task is rejected. Otherwise it is accepted and added to the set of accepted aperiodic tasks according to its deadline.

Figure 2.15 shows an example of this guarantee strategy for a task set composed of:

- three periodic tasks: $\tau_1(r_0 = 0, C = 3, D = 7, T = 20)$, $\tau_2(r_0 = 0, C = 2, D = 4, T = 5)$, $\tau_3(r_0 = 0, C = 1, D = 8, T = 10)$.

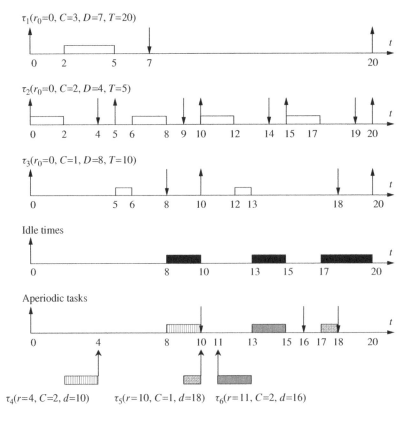

**Figure 2.15** Background scheduling of aperiodic tasks

- three aperiodic tasks: $\tau_4(r = 4, C = 2, d = 10)$, $\tau_5(r = 10, C = 1, d = 18)$, $\tau_6(r = 11, C = 2, d = 16)$.

Within the major cycle of the EDF schedule, the idle times of the processor are the intervals [8, 10], [13, 15] and [17, 20]. The three aperiodic tasks $\tau_4$, $\tau_5$ and $\tau_6$ can be guaranteed and executed within the idle times of the processor.

At time $t = 4$, task $\tau_4$ enters the system. The amount of idle time between its arrival time and its deadline is given by the interval [8, 10]. It is equal to the computation time of the task. As there are no previously accepted aperiodic requests, the aperiodic task $\tau_4$ is accepted.

At time $t = 10$, task $\tau_5$ enters the system. The amount of idle time between its arrival time and its deadline is equal to 3. It is greater than the computation time of the task. As there are no previously accepted aperiodic requests which have not completed (the task $\tau_4$ completes its execution at time $t = 10$), the aperiodic task $\tau_4$ is accepted.

At time $t = 11$, task $\tau_6$ enters the system. The amount of idle time between its arrival time and its deadline is equal to 2. It is just equal to the computation time of the task. However, task $\tau_5$, which has previously been accepted, has not yet begun its execution and it has a greater deadline than $\tau_6$. So, the acceptance test must verify that the acceptance of task $\tau_6$ does not jeopardize the guarantee of task $\tau_5$. Task $\tau_6$ will be executed first and will complete at time $t = 15$. Task $\tau_5$ will be executed within the idle time [17, 18]. Then both tasks can meet their deadlines. The aperiodic task $\tau_6$ is accepted.

### *Joint scheduling of aperiodic and periodic tasks*

This second acceptance test for aperiodic tasks looks like the technique we presented in Section 2.2.1 where soft aperiodic requests were jointly scheduled with the periodic tasks. The laxity of the periodic tasks and of the previously accepted aperiodic tasks is used to schedule a newly arrived aperiodic task within its deadline.

Thus, each time a new aperiodic task enters the system, a new EDF schedule is built with a task set which is composed of the periodic requests, the previously accepted requests and the new request. If this schedule meets all the deadlines, then the new request is accepted. Otherwise it is rejected.

Figure 2.16 shows an example of this strategy for a task set composed of the same tasks as for the previous example. The three aperiodic tasks $\tau_4$, $\tau_5$ and $\tau_6$ can be jointly scheduled with the periodic tasks.

At time $t = 4$, task $\tau_4$ enters the system. A new EDF schedule is built with a task set composed of the ready periodic tasks $\tau_1$ $(C(4) = 1, d = 7)$ and $\tau_3$, the next requests of the periodic tasks and the aperiodic task $\tau_4$. Within this schedule, all the deadlines are met. Task $\tau_4$ will be executed between times $t = 8$ and $t = 10$.

At time $t = 10$, the aperiodic task $\tau_5$ enters the system. A new EDF schedule is built with a task set composed of the next requests of the periodic tasks $\tau_2$ and $\tau_3$ and the aperiodic task $\tau_5$. Within this schedule, all the deadlines are met. Task $\tau_5$ will be executed between times $t = 13$ and $t = 14$.

At time $t = 11$, task $\tau_6$ enters the system. A new EDF schedule is built with a task set composed of the ready periodic tasks $\tau_2$ $(C(11) = 1, d = 14)$ and $\tau_3$, the next requests of the periodic task $\tau_2$ and the aperiodic task $\tau_5$ and $\tau_6$. Figure 2.16 shows the resulting schedule.

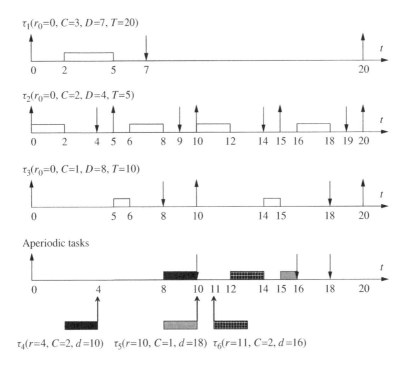

$\tau_1(r_0=0, C=3, D=7, T=20)$

$\tau_2(r_0=0, C=2, D=4, T=5)$

$\tau_3(r_0=0, C=1, D=8, T=10)$

Aperiodic tasks

$\tau_4(r=4, C=2, d=10)$   $\tau_5(r=10, C=1, d=18)$   $\tau_6(r=11, C=2, d=16)$

**Figure 2.16**   Example of joint scheduling of periodic and aperiodic tasks

## 2.3   Exercises

### 2.3.1   Questions

---

*Exercise 2.1:*   *Task set schedulability*

Consider the four following preemptive scheduling algorithms:

- the rate monotonic algorithm (RM), which assigns fixed priority to tasks according to their periods:

- the inverse deadline algorithm (ID), which assigns fixed priority to tasks according to their relative deadlines;

- the earliest deadline first algorithm (EDF), which assigns dynamic priority to tasks according to their absolute deadlines;

- the least laxity first algorithm (LLF), which assigns dynamic priority to tasks according to their relative laxity.

Consider a task set $\tau$ composed of the following three periodic tasks $\{\tau_1, \tau_2, \tau_3\}$:

*Continued on page 43*

---

---

_Continued from page 42_

- $\tau_1 (r_0 = 0, C = 1, D = 3, T = 3)$

- $\tau_2 (r_0 = 0, C = 1, D = 4, T = 4)$

- $\tau_3 (r_0 = 0, C = 2, D = 3, T = 6)$

**Q1** Compute the processor utilization factor and the major cycle of the task set.

**Q2** Build the schedule of the task set under the four scheduling algorithms RM, ID, EDF and LLF.

---

**_Exercise 2.2:  Aperiodic task schedulability_**

Consider the task set $\tau$ composed of the following three periodic tasks:

- $\tau_1 (r_0 = 0, C = 1, D = 4, T = 4)$

- $\tau_2 (r_0 = 0, C = 2, D = 6, T = 6)$

- $\tau_3 (r_0 = 0, C = 2, D = 8, T = 8)$

_1. Schedulability of the task set $\tau$_

**Q1** The task set is scheduled with the RM algorithm. Compute the processor utilization factor and verify the schedulability of the task set. Compute the major cycle of the task set and build the corresponding schedule. What can you conclude?

**Q2** The task set is scheduled with the EDF algorithm. Verify the schedulability under the EDF algorithm. Compute the major cycle of the task set and build the corresponding schedule. What can you conclude? What are the idle times of the processor?

_2. Schedulability with aperiodic tasks_

 Consider the hybrid task set composed of the periodic task set $\tau$ and the following aperiodic requests:

- case a: $\tau_4 (r = 9, C = 2, D = 6)$

- case b: $\tau_4 (r = 9, C = 2, D = 10)$

A server is a periodic task whose purpose is to service aperiodic requests. The new task set is $\tau' = \tau + \{\tau_s\}$. $\tau_s (r_0 = 0, C = 1, D = 6, T = 6)$ is the task server.

**Q3** Compute the processor utilization factor of the task set $\tau'$. Compute the major cycle of the task set.

_Continued on page 44_

*Continued from page 43*

**Q4**  Verify the schedulability under the RM algorithm. Build the RM schedule. What can you conclude?

**Q5**  Verify the schedulability under the EDF algorithm. Build the EDF schedule. What can you conclude?

---

***Exercise 2.3:   Hard aperiodic task scheduling under the EDF algorithm***

Consider a task set $\tau$ composed of the following three periodic tasks:

- $\tau_1(r_0 = 0, C = 5, D = 25, T = 30)$
- $\tau_2(r_0 = 0, C = 10, D = 40, T = 50)$
- $\tau_3(r_0 = 0, C = 20, D = 55, T = 75)$

The task set is scheduled with the EDF algorithm.

**Q1**  Verify the schedulability under the EDF algorithm. Build the corresponding schedule. What are the idle times of the processor?

Consider the following aperiodic tasks:

- $\tau_4(r = 40, C = 10, D = 15)$
- $\tau_5(r = 70, C = 15, D = 35)$
- $\tau_6(r = 100, C = 20, D = 40)$
- $\tau_7(r = 105, C = 5, D = 25)$
- $\tau_8(r = 120, C = 5, D = 15)$

**Q2**  Can these requests be guaranteed in the idle times of the processor?

---

***Exercise 2.4:   Soft aperiodic task scheduling under the RM algorithm***

Consider a task set $\tau$ composed of the following three periodic tasks:

- $\tau_1(r_0 = 0, C = 5, T = 30)$
- $\tau_2(r_0 = 0, C = 10, T = 50)$
- $\tau_3(r_0 = 0, C = 25, T = 75)$

*Continued on page 45*

---

*Continued from page 44*

**Q1** Compute the major cycle of the task set. Verify the schedulability under the RM algorithm. Build the schedule.

Consider the following aperiodic tasks:

- $\tau_4(r = 5, C = 12)$
- $\tau_5(r = 40, C = 7)$
- $\tau_6(r = 105, C = 20)$

**Q2** The aperiodic tasks are scheduled in background. Compute the response times of tasks $\tau_4$, $\tau_5$ and $\tau_6$.

**Q3** The aperiodic tasks are scheduled with a server. The server capacity is set to 5 and its period is set to 25. Verify the schedulability of the new task set. Build the schedule. Consider that the server is a polling server. Compute the response times of tasks $\tau_4$, $\tau_5$ and $\tau_6$.

---

## 2.3.2 Answers

---

*Exercise 2.1:*  *Task set schedulability*

**Q1**  $U = 0.33 + 0.25 + 0.33 = 0.92$
Major cycle $= [0, \text{LCM}(3, 4, 6)] = [0, 12]$

**Q2** Figure 2.17 shows the schedules under the RM, EDF, ID and LLF algorithms.

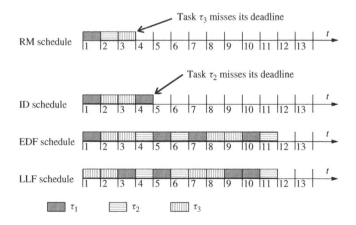

**Figure 2.17**  Schedules under the RM, ID, EDF and LLF algorithms

***Exercise 2.2:    Aperiodic task schedulability***

**Q1**   $U = 0.25 + 0.33 + 0.25 = 0.83. n(2^{1/n} - 1) = 0.78(n = 3)$. The schedulability test is not verified.
Major cycle $= [0, 24]$. Figure 2.18 shows the schedule under the RM algorithm.

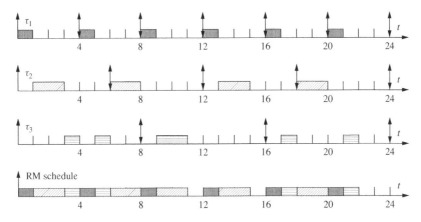

**Figure 2.18**   Schedule under the RM algorithm

**Q2**   We can verify that $U \leq 1$. So the task set is schedulable under the EDF algorithm. The schedule (Figure 2.19) under the EDF algorithm is the same as the schedule under the RM algorithm. The processor is idle within the following intervals: $[11, 12]$, $[15, 16]$, $[22, 24]$.

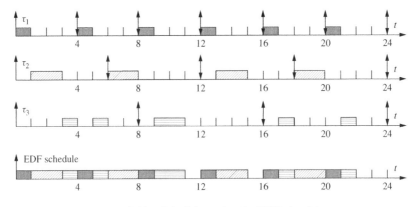

**Figure 2.19**   Schedule under the EDF algorithm

**Q3**   $U = 1$. Major cycle $= [0, 24]$.

_____ *Continued on page 47*_____

*Continued from page 46*

**Q4** The schedulability test is not verified because $U = 1$. To conclude about the task set schedulability, the schedule has to be built within the major cycle of the task set. Figure 2.20 shows the schedule under the RM algorithm.

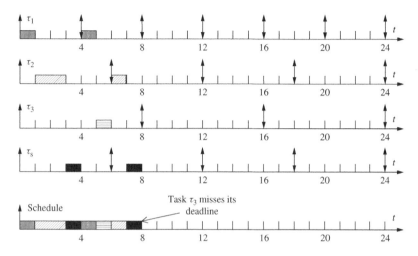

**Figure 2.20** RM schedule of Exercise 2.4, Q4

**Q5** As $U$ is equal to 1, the task set is schedulable under EDF. Figure 2.21 shows the schedule under the EDF algorithm during the major cycle.

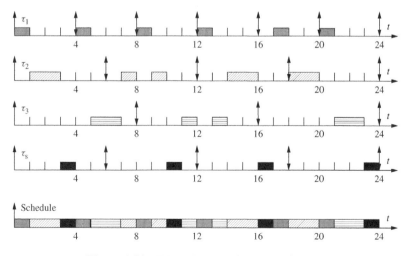

**Figure 2.21** EDF schedule of Exercise 2.2, Q5

*Continued on page 48*

_Continued from page 46_

- case a: $\tau_4(r = 9, C = 2, D = 6)$ : $\tau_4$ can not be guaranteed

- case b: $\tau_4(r = 9, C = 2, D = 10)$ : $\tau_4$ is guaranteed

---

### Exercise 2.3:   Hard aperiodic task scheduling under the EDF algorithm

**Q1**   $0.2 + 0.25 + 0.36 = 0.8 < 1$. In consequence, the task set is schedulable under EDF.

Figure 2.22 shows the schedule.

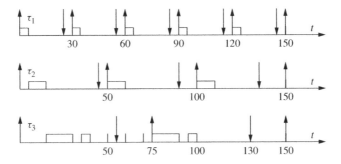

**Figure 2.22**   EDF schedule of Exercise 2.3, Q1

The processor is idle during the intervals [40, 50], [65, 75], [110, 120] and [125, 150].

**Q2**   Task $\tau_4$ is accepted and executes during the idle time [40, 50]. Task $\tau_5$ is rejected because there is not enough idle time to guarantee its deadline. Task $\tau_6$ is accepted and it is executed during the idle times [110, 120] and [125, 140]. Task $\tau_7$ is accepted:

- The task can be guaranteed if it is executed within the idle time [110, 115].

- The acceptance of task $\tau_7$ does not jeopardize the guarantee of task $\tau_6$, which has not yet executed to completion.

Task $\tau_8$ is rejected:

- The task can be guaranteed if it executes within the idle time [125, 130].

- However, the acceptance of task $\tau_8$ jeopardizes the guarantee of task $\tau_6$, which has not been yet executed to completion ($C_6(t) = 15$).

*Exercise 2.4:* **Soft aperiodic task scheduling under the RM algorithm**

**Q1** The major cycle $= [0, \text{LCM}(30, 50, 75)] = [0, 150]$.
$U = 5/30 + 10/50 + 25/75 = 0.7 < 0.78$: the task set is schedulable.
Figure 2.23 shows the schedule.

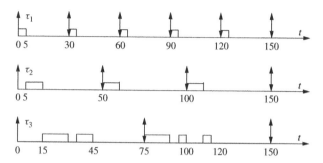

**Figure 2.23** RM schedule of Exercise 2.4, Q1

**Q2** The processor is idle within the following intervals: [45, 50], [65, 75], [115, 120] and [125, 150].
Task $\tau_4$ is executed during time intervals [45, 50] and [65, 72]. Its response time is equal to $72 - 5 = 67$.
Task $\tau_5$ is executed during time intervals [72, 75] and [115, 119]. Its response time is equal to $119 - 40 = 79$.
Task $\tau_6$ is executed during time intervals [119, 120] and [125, 144]. Its response time is equal to $144 - 105 = 39$.

**Q3** The schedulability test is not verified. The schedule built within the major cycle shows that all the tasks meet their deadlines. Figure 2.24 shows the schedule.

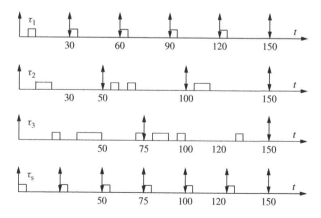

**Figure 2.24** RM schedule of Exercise 2.4, Q3

_Continued on page 50_

*Continued from page 49*

The response time of $\tau_4$ is equal to $77 - 5 = 72$.
The response time of $\tau_5$ is equal to $104 - 40 = 64$.
The response time of $\tau_6$ is equal to $200 - 105 = 95$.

# 3

# Scheduling of Dependent Tasks

In the previous chapter, we assumed that tasks were independent, i.e. with no relationships between them. But in many real-time systems, inter-task dependencies are necessary for realizing some control activities. In fact, this inter-task cooperation can be expressed in different ways: some tasks have to respect a processing order, data exchanges between tasks, or use of various resources, usually in exclusive mode. From a behavioural modelling point of view, there are two kinds of typical dependencies that can be specified on real-time tasks:

- precedence constraints that correspond to synchronization or communication among tasks;

- mutual exclusion constraints to protect shared resources. These critical resources may be data structures, memory areas, external devices, registers, etc.

## 3.1 Tasks with Precedence Relationships

The first type of constraint is the precedence relationship among real-time tasks. We define a precedence constraint between two tasks $\tau_i$ and $\tau_j$, denoted by $\tau_i \rightarrow \tau_j$, if the execution of task $\tau_i$ precedes that of task $\tau_j$. In other words, task $\tau_j$ must await the completion of task $\tau_i$ before beginning its own execution.

As the precedence constraints are assumed to be implemented in a deterministic manner, these relationships can be described through a graph where the nodes represent tasks and the arrows express the precedence constraint between two nodes, as shown in Figure 3.1. This precedence acyclic graph represents a partial order on the task set. If task $\tau_i$ is connected by a path to task $\tau_j$ in the precedence graph then $\tau_i \rightarrow \tau_j$. A general problem concerns tasks related by complex precedence relationships where $n$ successive instances of a task can precede one instance of another task, or one instance of a task precedes $m$ instances of another task. Figure 3.2 gives an example where the rates of the communicating tasks are not equal.

To facilitate the description of the precedence constraint problem, we only consider the case of simple precedence constraint, i.e. if a task $\tau_i$ has to communicate the result of its processing to another task $\tau_j$, these tasks have to be scheduled in such a way that the execution of the $k$th instance of task $\tau_i$ precedes the execution of the $k$th instance of task $\tau_j$. Therefore, these tasks have the same rate (i.e. $T_i = T_j$). So all tasks belonging to a connected component of the precedence graph must have the same period. On the graph represented in Figure 3.1, tasks $\tau_1$ to $\tau_5$ have the same period and tasks $\tau_6$ to $\tau_9$ also have the same period. If the periods of the tasks are different, these tasks will run

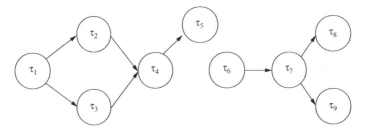

**Figure 3.1**    Example of two precedence graphs related to a set of nine tasks

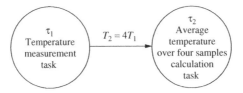

**Figure 3.2**    Example of a generalized precedence relationship between two tasks with different periods

at the lowest rate sooner or later. As a consequence the task with the shortest period will miss its deadline. We do not consider cyclical asynchronous message buffers.

An answer to the first question was given by Blazewicz (1977): if we have to get $\tau_i \rightarrow \tau_j$, then the task parameters must be in accordance with the following rules:

- $r_j \geq r_i$
- $Prio_i \geq Prio_j$ in accordance with the scheduling algorithm

In the rest of this chapter, we are interested in the validation context. This problem can be studied from two points of view: execution and validation. First, in the case of preemptive scheduling algorithms based on priority, the question is: which modification of the task parameters will lead to an execution that respects the precedence constraints? Second, is it possible to validate *a priori* the schedulability of a dependent task set?

### 3.1.1 Precedence constraints and fixed-priority algorithms (RM and DM)

The rate monotonic scheduling algorithm assigns priorities to tasks according to their periods. In other words, tasks with shorter period get higher priorities. Respecting this rule, the goal is to modify the task parameters in order to take account of precedence constraints, i.e. to obtain an independent task set with modified parameters. The basic idea of these modifications is that a task cannot start before its predecessors and cannot preempt its successors. So if we have to get $\tau_i \rightarrow \tau_j$, then the release time and the priority of task parameters must be modified as follows:

- $r_j^* \geq \text{Max}(r_j, r_i^*)$ $r_i^*$ is the modified release time of task $\tau_i$
- $Prio_i \geq Prio_j$ in accordance with the RM algorithm

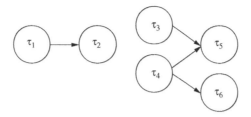

**Figure 3.3**  Precedence graphs of a set of six tasks

**Table 3.1**  Example of priority mapping taking care of precedence constraints and using the RM scheduling algorithm

| Task | $\tau_1$ | $\tau_2$ | $\tau_3$ | $\tau_4$ | $\tau_5$ | $\tau_6$ |
|------|------|------|------|------|------|------|
| Priority | 6 | 5 | 4 | 3 | 2 | 1 |

It is important to notice that, as all tasks of a precedence graph share the same period, according to RM policy there is a free choice concerning the priorities that we use to impose the precedence order. Let us consider a set of six tasks with simultaneous release times and two graphs describing their precedence relationships (Figure 3.3). The priority mapping, represented in Table 3.1, handles the precedence constraint and meets the RM algorithm rule.

The deadline monotonic scheduling algorithm assigns priorities to tasks according to their relative deadline $D$ (tasks with shorter relative deadline get higher priorities). The modifications of task parameters are close to those applied for RM scheduling except that the relative deadline is also changed in order to respect the priority assignment. So if $\tau_i \rightarrow \tau_j$, then the release time, the relative deadline and the priority of the task parameters must be modified as follows:

- $r_j^* \geq \text{Max}(r_j, r_i^*)$ $r_i^*$ is the modified release time of task $\tau_i$
- $D_j^* \geq \text{Max}(D_j, D_i^*)$ $D_i^*$ is the modified relative deadline of task $\tau_i$
- $Prio_i \geq Prio_j$ in accordance with the DM scheduling algorithm

This modification transparently enforces the precedence relationship between two tasks.

## 3.1.2  Precedence constraints and the earliest deadline first algorithm

In the case of the earliest deadline first algorithm, the modification of task parameters relies on the deadline $d$. So the rules for modifying release times and deadlines of tasks are based on the following observations (Figure 3.4) (Blazewicz, 1977; Chetto et al., 1990).

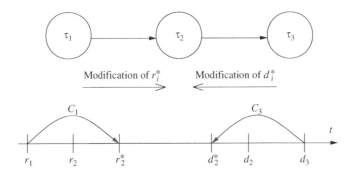

**Figure 3.4**   Modifications of task parameters in the case of EDF scheduling

First, if we have to get $\tau_i \rightarrow \tau_j$, the release time $r_j^*$ of task $\tau_j$ must be greater than or equal to its initial value or to the new release times $r_i^*$ of its immediate predecessors $\tau_i$ increased by their execution times $C_i$:

$$r_j^* \geq \text{Max}((r_i^* + C_i), r_j)$$

Then, if we have to get $\tau_i \rightarrow \tau_j$, the deadline $d_i^*$ of task $\tau_i$ has to be replaced by the minimum between its initial value $d_i$ or by the new deadlines $d_j^*$ of the immediate successors $\tau_j$ decreased by their execution times $C_j$:

$$d_i^* \geq \text{Min}((d_j^* - C_j), d_i)$$

Procedures that modify the release times and the deadlines can be implemented in an easy way as shown by Figure 3.4. They begin with the tasks that have no predecessors for modifying their release times and with those with no successors for changing their deadlines.

### 3.1.3 Example

Let us consider a set of five tasks whose parameters $(r_i, C_i, d_i)$ are indicated in Table 3.2. Note that all the tasks are activated simultaneously except task $\tau_2$. Their precedence graph is depicted in Figure 3.5. As there is one precedence graph linking

**Table 3.2**   Set of five tasks and the modifications of parameters according to the precedence constraints (4 is the highest priority)

| Task | Initial task parameters | | | Modifications to use RM | | Modifications to use EDF | |
|---|---|---|---|---|---|---|---|
| | $r_i$ | $C_i$ | $d_i$ | $r_i^*$ | $Prio_i$ | $r_i^*$ | $d_i^*$ |
| $\tau_1$ | 0 | 1 | 5 | 0 | 3 | 0 | 3 |
| $\tau_2$ | 5 | 2 | 7 | 5 | 4 | 5 | 7 |
| $\tau_3$ | 0 | 2 | 5 | 0 | 2 | 1 | 5 |
| $\tau_4$ | 0 | 1 | 10 | 5 | 1 | 7 | 9 |
| $\tau_5$ | 0 | 3 | 12 | 5 | 0 | 8 | 12 |

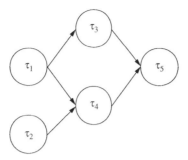

**Figure 3.5**  Precedence graph linking five tasks

all the tasks of the application, we assume that all these tasks have the same rate. Table 3.2 also shows the modifications of task parameters in order to take account of the precedence constraints in both RM and EDF scheduling.

Let us note that, in the case of RM scheduling, only the release time parameters are changed and the precedence constraint is enforced by the priority assignment. Under EDF scheduling, both parameters $(r_i, d_i)$ must be modified.

## 3.2  Tasks Sharing Critical Resources

This section describes simple techniques that can handle shared resources for dynamic preemptive systems. When tasks are allowed to access shared resources, their access needs to be controlled in order to maintain data consistency. Let us consider a critical resource, called $R$, shared by two tasks $\tau_1$ and $\tau_2$. We want to ensure that the sequences of statements of $\tau_1$ and $\tau_2$, which perform on $R$, are executed under mutual exclusion. These pieces of code are called critical sections or critical regions. Specific mechanisms (such as semaphore, protected object or monitor), provided by the real-time kernel, can be used to create critical sections in a task code. It is important to note that, in a non-preemptive context, this problem does not arise because by definition a task cannot be preempted during a critical section. In this chapter, we consider a preemptive context in order to allow fast response time for high-priority tasks which correspond to high-safety software.

Let us consider again the small example with two tasks $\tau_1$ and $\tau_2$ sharing one resource $R$. Let us assume that task $\tau_1$ is activated first and uses resource $R$, i.e. enters its critical section. Then the second task $\tau_2$, having a higher priority than $\tau_1$, asks for the processor. Since the priority of task $\tau_2$ is greater, preemption occurs, task $\tau_1$ is blocked and task $\tau_2$ starts its execution. However, when task $\tau_2$ wants access to the shared resource $R$, it is blocked due to the mutual exclusion process. So task $\tau_1$ can resume its execution. When task $\tau_1$ finishes its critical section, the higher priority task $\tau_2$ can resume its execution and use resource $R$. This process can lead to an uncontrolled blocking time of task $\tau_2$. On the contrary, to meet hard real-time requirements, an application must be controlled by a scheduling algorithm that can always guarantee a predictable system response time. The question is how to ensure a predictable response time of real-time tasks in a preemptive scheduling mechanism with resource constraints.

## 3.2.1  Assessment of a task response time

In this section, we consider on-line preemptive scheduling where the priorities are fixed and assigned to tasks. We discuss the upper bound of the response time of a task $\tau_0$ which has a worst-case execution time $C_0$. Let us assume now that the utilization factor of the processor is low enough to permit the task set, including $\tau_0$, to be schedulable whatever the blocking time due to the shared resources.

In the first step, we suppose that the tasks are independent, i.e. without any shared resource. If task $\tau_0$ has the higher priority, it is obvious that the response time $TR_0$ of this task $\tau_0$ is equal to its execution time $C_0$. On the other hand, when task $\tau_0$ has an intermediate priority, the upper bound of the response can also be evaluated easily as a function of the tasks with a priority higher than that of task $\tau_0$, denoted $\tau_{\text{HPT}}$:

- Where all tasks are periodic with the same period or aperiodic, we obtain:

$$TR_0 \leq C_0 + \sum_{i \in \text{HPT}} C_i \tag{3.1}$$

- Where all tasks are periodic with different periods, we obtain:

$$TR_0 \leq C_0 + \sum_{i \in \text{HPT}} \left\lceil \frac{T_0}{T_i} \right\rceil C_i \tag{3.2}$$

In the second step, we consider a task set sharing resources. The assumptions are the following. Concerning task dispatching or resource access, the management of all the queues is done according to the task priorities. Moreover, we assume that the overhead due to kernel mechanisms (resource access, task queuing, context switches) is negligible. Of course, these overheads can be taken into account as an additional term of task execution times.

Now, in the context of a set with $n+1$ tasks and $m$ resources, let us calculate the upper bound of the response time of task $\tau_0$ (i) when it does and (ii) when it does not hold the highest priority. First, when task $\tau_0$ has the highest priority of the task set, its execution can be delayed only by the activated tasks which have a lower priority and use the same $m_0$ shared resources. This situation has to be analysed for two cases:

- Case I: The $m_0$ shared resources are held by at least $m_0$ tasks as shown in Figure 3.6, where task $\tau_j$ holds resource $R_1$ requested by task $\tau_0$. It is important to notice that task $\tau_i$ waiting for resource $R_1$ is preempted by task $\tau_0$ due to the priority ordering management of queues. Let $CR_{i,q}$ denote the maximum time the task $\tau_i$ uses resource $R_q$, $CR_{\text{max},q}$ the maximum of $CR_{i,q}$ over all tasks $\tau_i$, $CR_{i,\text{max}}$ the maximum of $CR_{i,q}$ over all resources $R_q$, and finally $CR_{\text{max}}$ the maximum of $CR_{i,q}$ over all tasks and resources. As a consequence, the upper bound of the response time of task $\tau_0$ is given by:

$$TR_0 \leq C_0 + \sum_{i=1}^{m_0} CR_{i,\text{max}} \tag{3.3}$$

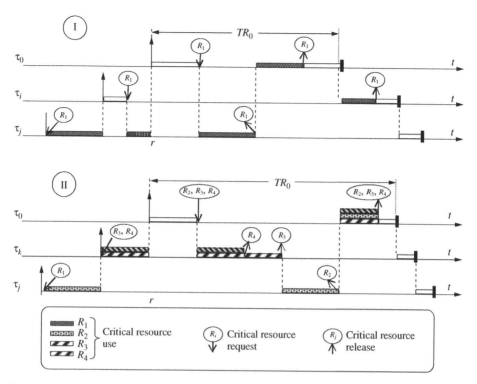

**Figure 3.6** Response time of the highest priority task sharing critical resources: Case I: two lower priority tasks sharing a critical resource with task $\tau_0$. Case II: two lower priority tasks sharing three critical resources with task $\tau_0$

In the worst case, for this set ($n$ other tasks using the $m$ resources, with $n < m$), the response time is at most:

$$TR_0 \leq C_0 + m \cdot CR_{\max} \tag{3.4}$$

Or more precisely, we get:

$$TR_0 \leq C_0 + \sum_{i=1}^{m} CR_{i,\max} \tag{3.5}$$

- Case II: The $m_0$ shared resources are held by $n_1$ tasks with $n_1 < m_0$, as shown in Figure 3.6, where tasks $\tau_k$ and $\tau_j$ hold resources $R_2$, $R_3$ and $R_4$ requested by $\tau_0$. We can notice that, at least, one task holds two resources. If we assume that the critical sections of a task are properly nested, the maximum critical section duration of a task using several resources is given by the longest critical section. So the response time of task $\tau_0$ is upper-bounded by:

$$TR_0 \leq C_0 + n_1 \cdot CR_{\max} \tag{3.6}$$

Or more precisely, we get:

$$TR_0 \leq C_0 + \sum_{q=1}^{n_1} CR_{\max,q} \tag{3.7}$$

In the worst case, for this set ($n$ other tasks and $m$ resources, with $n < m$), the response time of task $\tau_0$ is at most:

$$TR_0 \leq C_0 + n \cdot CR_{\max} \tag{3.8}$$

Or more precisely, we get:

$$TR_0 \leq C_0 + \sum_{q=1}^{n} CR_{\max,q} \tag{3.9}$$

To sum up, an overall expression of the response time for the highest priority task in a real-time application composed of $n + 1$ tasks and $m$ resources is given by the following inequality:

$$TR_0 \leq C_0 + \inf(n, m) \cdot CR_{\max} \tag{3.10}$$

Let us consider now that task $\tau_0$ has an intermediate priority. The task set includes $n_1$ tasks having a higher priority level (HPT set) and $n_2$ tasks which have a lower priority level and share $m$ critical resources with task $\tau_0$. This case is depicted in Figure 3.7 with the following specific values: $n_1 = 1, n_2 = 2$ and $m = 3$. With the assumption that the $n_2$ lower priority tasks haves dependencies only with $\tau_0$, and not with the $n_1$ higher priority tasks, it should be possible to calculate the upper bound of the response time of task $\tau_0$ by combining inequalities (3.2) and (3.10). The response time is:

$$TR_0 \leq C_0 + \inf(n_1, m) \cdot CR_{\max} + \sum_{i \in \text{HPT}} \left\lceil \frac{T_0}{T_i} \right\rceil C_i \tag{3.11}$$

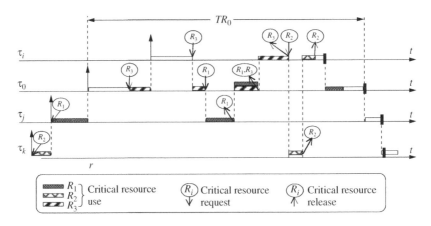

**Figure 3.7**   Response time of task sharing critical resources: $Prio_i > Prio_0 > Prio_j > Prio_k$

However, this computation of the upper bound of each task relies on respect for the assumptions concerning the scheduling rules. In particular, for a preemptive scheduling algorithm with fixed priority, there is an implicit condition of the specification that must be inviolable: at its activation time, a task $\tau_0$ must run as soon as all the higher priority tasks have finished their execution and all the lower priority tasks using critical resources, requested by $\tau_0$, have released the corresponding critical sections. In fact two scheduling problems can render this assumption false: the priority inversion phenomenon and deadlock.

## 3.2.2 Priority inversion phenomenon

In preemptive scheduling that is driven by fixed priority and where critical resources are protected by a mutual exclusion mechanism, the priority inversion phenomenon can occur (Kaiser, 1981; Rajkumar, 1991; Sha et al., 1990). In order to illustrate this problem, let us consider a task set composed of four tasks $\{\tau_1, \tau_2, \tau_3, \tau_4\}$ having decreasing priorities. Tasks $\tau_2$ and $\tau_4$ share a critical resource $R_1$, the access of which is mutually exclusive. Let us focus our attention on the response time of task $\tau_2$. The scheduling sequence is shown in Figure 3.8. The lowest priority task $\tau_4$ starts its execution first and after some time it enters a critical section using resource $R_1$. When task $\tau_4$ is in its critical section, the higher priority task $\tau_2$ is released and preempts task $\tau_4$. During the execution of task $\tau_2$, task $\tau_3$ is released. Nevertheless, task $\tau_3$, having a lower priority than task $\tau_2$, must wait. When task $\tau_2$ needs to enter its critical section, associated with the critical resource $R_1$ shared with task $\tau_4$, it finds that the corresponding resource $R_1$ is held by task $\tau_4$. Thus it is blocked. The highest priority task able to execute is task $\tau_3$. So task $\tau_3$ gets the processor and runs.

During this execution, the highest priority task $\tau_1$ awakes. As a consequence task $\tau_3$ is suspended and the processor is allocated to task $\tau_1$. At the end of execution of task $\tau_1$, task $\tau_3$ can resume its execution until it reaches the end of its code. Now, only the lowest priority task $\tau_4$, preempted in its critical section, can execute again. It resumes

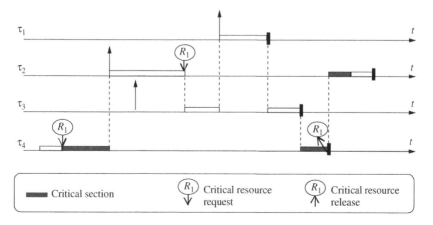

**Figure 3.8**  Example of priority inversion phenomenon

its execution until it releases critical resource $R_1$ required by the higher priority task $\tau_2$. Then, this task can resume its execution by holding critical resource $R_1$ necessary for its activity.

It is of great importance to analyse this simple example precisely. The maximum blocking time that task $\tau_2$ may experience depends on the duration of the critical sections of the lower priority tasks sharing a resource with it, such as task $\tau_4$, and on the other hand on the execution times of higher priority tasks, such as task $\tau_1$. These two kinds of increase of the response time of task $\tau_2$ are completely consistent with the scheduling rules. But, another task, $\tau_3$, which has a lower priority and does not share any critical resource with task $\tau_2$, participates in the increase of its blocking time. This situation, called *priority inversion*, contravenes the scheduling specification and can induce deadline missing as can be seen in the example given in Section 9.2. In this case the blocking time of each task cannot be bounded unless a specific protocol is used and it can lead to uncontrolled response time of each task.

### 3.2.3 Deadlock phenomenon

When tasks share the same set of two or more critical resources, then a deadlock situation can occur and, as a consequence, the real-time application fails. The notion of deadlock is better illustrated by the following simple example (Figure 3.9a).

Let us consider two tasks $\tau_1$ and $\tau_2$ that use two critical resources $R_1$ and $R_2$. $\tau_1$ and $\tau_2$ access $R_1$ and $R_2$ in reverse order. Moreover, the priority of task $\tau_1$ is greater than that of task $\tau_2$. Now, suppose that task $\tau_2$ executes first and locks resource $R_1$.

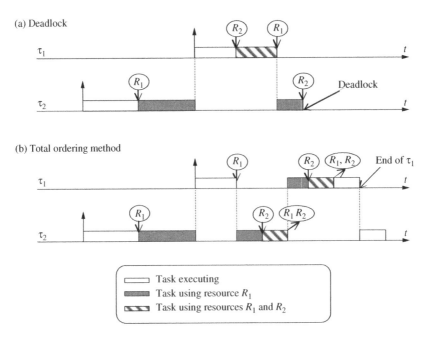

**Figure 3.9** (a) Example of the deadlock phenomenon. (b) Solution for deadlock prevention by imposing a total ordering on resource access

During the critical section of task $\tau_2$ using resource $R_1$, task $\tau_1$ awakes and preempts task $\tau_2$ before it can lock the second resource $R_2$. Task $\tau_1$ needs resource $R_2$ first, which is free, and it locks it. Then task $\tau_1$ needs resource $R_1$, which is held by task $\tau_2$. So task $\tau_2$ resumes and asks for resource $R_2$, which is not free. The final result is that task $\tau_2$ is in possession of resource $R_1$ but is waiting for resource $R_2$ and task $\tau_1$ is in possession of resource $R_2$ but is waiting for resource $R_1$. Neither task $\tau_1$ nor task $\tau_2$ will release the resource until its pending request is satisfied. This situation leads to a deadlock of both tasks. This situation can be extended to more than two tasks with a circular resource access order and leads to a chained blocking.

Deadlock is a serious problem for critical real-time applications. Solutions must be found in order to prevent deadlock situations, as classically done for operating systems (Bacon, 1997; Silberschatz and Galvin, 1998; Tanenbaum, 1994; Tanenbaum and woodhull, 1997). One method is to impose a total ordering of the critical resource accesses (Havender, 1968). It is not always possible to apply this technique, because it is necessary to know all the resources that a task will need during its activity. This is why this method is called static prevention (Figure 3.9b). Another technique that can be used on-line is known as the banker's algorithm (Haberman, 1969), and requires that each task declares beforehand the maximum number of resources that it may hold simultaneously.

Other methods to cope with deadlocks are based on detection and recovering processes (for example by using a watchdog timer). The use of a watchdog timer allows detection of inactive tasks: this may be a deadlock, or the tasks may be waiting for external signals. Then, the technique for handling the deadlock is to reset the tasks involved in the detected deadlock or, in an easier way, the whole task set. This method, used very often when the deadlock situation is known to occur infrequently, is not acceptable for highly critical systems.

## 3.2.4 Shared resource access protocols

Scheduling of tasks that share critical resources leads to some problems in all computer science applications:

- synchronization problems between tasks and particularly the priority inversion situation when they share mutually exclusive resources;

- deadlock and chained blocking problems.

In real-time systems, a simple method to cope with these problems is the reservation and pre-holding of resources at the beginning of task execution. However, such a technique leads to a low utilization factor of resources, so some resource access protocols have been designed to avoid such drawbacks and also to bound the maximum response time of tasks.

Different protocols have been developed for preventing the priority inversion in the RM or EDF scheduling context. These protocols permit the upper bound of the blocking time due to the critical resource access for each task $\tau_i$ to be determined. This is called $B_i$. This maximum blocking duration is then integrated into the schedulability tests of classical scheduling algorithms like RM and EDF (see Chapter 2). This integration is simply obtained by considering that a task $\tau_i$ has an execution time equal to $C_i +$ $B_i$. Some of these resource access protocols also prevent the deadlock phenomenon (Rajkumar, 1991).

### Priority inheritance protocol

The basic idea of the priority inheritance protocol is to dynamically change the priority of some tasks (Kaiser, 1981; Sha et al., 1990). So a task $\tau_i$, which is using a critical resource inside a critical section, gets the priority of any task $\tau_j$ waiting for this resource if the priority of task $\tau_j$ is higher than that of task $\tau_i$. Consequently, task $\tau_i$ is scheduled at a higher level than its initial level of priority. This new context leads to freeing of the critical resource earlier and minimizes the waiting time of the higher priority task $\tau_j$. The priority inheritance protocol does not prevent deadlock, which has to be avoided by using the techniques discussed above. However, the priority inheritance protocol has to be used for task code with correctly nested critical sections. In this case, the protocol is applied in a recursive manner. This protocol of priority inheritance has been implemented in the real-time operating system DUNE-IX (Banino et al., 1993).

Figure 3.10 gives an example of this protocol for a task set composed of three tasks $\{\tau_1, \tau_2, \tau_3\}$ having decreasing priorities and two critical resources $\{R_1, R_2\}$. Task $\tau_1$ uses resource $R_1$, task $\tau_2$ resource $R_2$, and task $\tau_3$ both resources $R_1$ and $R_2$. Task $\tau_3$ starts running first and takes successively resources $R_1$ and $R_2$. Later task $\tau_2$ awakes and preempts task $\tau_3$ in its nested critical section. When task $\tau_2$ requires resource $R_2$, it is blocked by task $\tau_3$, thus task $\tau_3$ gets the priority of task $\tau_2$. We say that task $\tau_3$ inherits the priority of task $\tau_2$. Then, in the same manner, task $\tau_1$ awakes and preempts task $\tau_3$ in its critical section. When task $\tau_1$ requests resource $R_1$, it is blocked by task $\tau_3$, consequently task $\tau_3$ inherits the priority of task $\tau_1$. So task $\tau_3$ continues its execution with the highest priority of the task set. When $\tau_3$ releases resources $R_2$ and then $R_1$, it resumes its original priority. Immediately, the higher priority task $\tau_1$, waiting for a resource, preempts task $\tau_3$ and gets the processor. The end of the execution sequence follows the classical rules of scheduling.

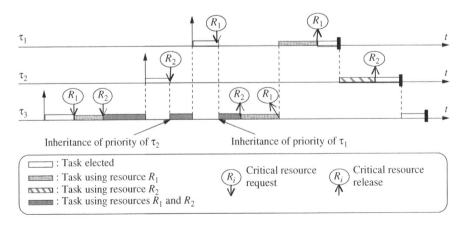

**Figure 3.10**   Example of application of priority inheritance protocol

When the priority inheritance protocol is used, it is possible to evaluate the upper bound of the blocking time of each task. Under this protocol, a task $\tau_i$ can be blocked at most by $n$ critical sections of lower priority tasks or by $m$ critical sections corresponding to resources shared with lower priority tasks (Buttazzo, 1997; Klein et al., 1993; Rajkumar, 1991). That is:

$$B_i \leq \inf(n, m) \cdot CR_{\max} \qquad (3.12)$$

As we can see in Figure 3.10, task $\tau_2$ is at most delayed by the longest critical section of task $\tau_3$ (recall that several critical sections used by a task must be correctly nested. In the example, $R_1$ is released after $R_2$).

### Priority ceiling protocol

The basic idea of this protocol is to extend the preceding protocol in order to avoid deadlocks and chained blocking by preventing a task from entering in a critical section that leads to blocking it (Chen and Lin, 1990; Sha et al., 1990). To do so, each resource is assigned a priority, called *priority ceiling*, equal to the priority of the highest priority task that can use it. The priority ceiling is similar to a threshold. In the same way as in the priority inheritance protocol, a task $\tau_i$, which is using a critical resource inside a critical section, gets the priority of any task $\tau_j$ waiting for this resource if the priority of task $\tau_j$ is higher than that of $\tau_i$. Consequently, task $\tau_i$ is scheduled at a higher level than its initial level of priority and the waiting time of the higher priority task $\tau_j$ is minimized. Moreover, in order to prevent deadlocks, when a task requests a resource, the resource is allocated only if it is free and if the priority of this task is strictly greater than the highest priority ceiling of resources used by other tasks. This rule provides early blocking of tasks that may cause deadlock and guarantees that future higher priority tasks get their resources.

Figure 3.11 gives an example of this protocol for a task set composed of three tasks $\{\tau_1, \tau_2, \tau_3\}$ with decreasing priorities and two critical resources $\{R_1, R_2\}$. Task $\tau_1$ uses resource $R_1$, task $\tau_2$ resource $R_2$, and task $\tau_3$ both resources $R_1$ and $R_2$. Task

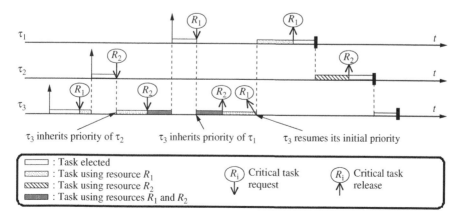

**Figure 3.11** Example of application of the priority ceiling protocol

$\tau_3$ starts running first and takes resource $R_1$, which is free. The priority ceiling of resource $R_1$ (respectively $R_2$) is the priority of task $\tau_1$ (respectively $\tau_2$). Later task $\tau_2$ awakes and preempts task $\tau_3$ given that its priority is greater than the current priority of task $\tau_3$. When task $\tau_2$ requests resource $R_2$, it is blocked by the protocol because its priority is not strictly greater than the priority ceiling of held resource $R_1$. Since task $\tau_2$ is waiting, task $\tau_3$ inherits the priority of task $\tau_2$ and resumes its execution. In the same way, task $\tau_1$ awakes and preempts task $\tau_3$ given that its priority is greater than that of task $\tau_3$. When task $\tau_1$ requests resource $R_1$, it is blocked by the protocol because its priority is not strictly greater than the priority ceiling of used resource $R_1$. And, since task $\tau_1$ is waiting, task $\tau_3$ inherits the priority of $\tau_1$ and resumes its execution. When task $\tau_3$ exits the critical sections of both resources $R_2$ and then $R_1$, it resumes its original priority and it is immediately preempted by the waiting highest priority task, i.e task $\tau_1$. The end of the execution sequence follows the classical rules of scheduling.

Initially designed for fixed-priority scheduling algorithms, such as rate monotonic, this protocol has been extended by Chen and Lin (1990) to variable-priority scheduling algorithms, such as earliest deadline first. In this context, the priority ceiling is evaluated at each modification of the ready task list that is caused by activation or completion of tasks. This protocol has been implemented in the real-time operating system Mach at Carnegie Mellon University (Nakajima et al., 1993; Tokuda and Nakajima, 1991).

It is important to notice that this protocol needs to know *a priori* all the task priorities and all the resources used by each task in order to assign priority ceilings. Moreover, we can outline that the properties of this protocol are true only in a one-processor context. When the priority ceiling protocol is used, it is possible to evaluate the upper bound of the blocking time of each task. Under this protocol, a task $\tau_i$ can be blocked at most by the longest critical section of a lower priority task that is using a resource of priority ceiling less than or equal to the priority of that task $\tau_i$ (Buttazzo, 1997; Klein et al., 1993; Rajkumar, 1991).

The priority ceiling protocol is the so-called original priority ceiling protocol (Burns and Wellings, 2001). A slightly different priority ceiling protocol, called the immediate priority ceiling protocol (Burns and Wellings, 2001), takes a more straightforward approach and raises the priority of a process as soon as it locks a resource rather than only when it is actually blocking a higher priority process. The worst-case behaviour of the two ceiling protocols is identical.

### Stack resource policy

The stack resource protocol extends the preceding protocol in two ways: it allows the use of multi-unit resources and can be applied with a variable-priority scheduling algorithm like earliest deadline first (Baker, 1990). In addition to the classical priority, each task is assigned a new parameter $\pi$, called level of preemption, which is related to the time devoted for its execution (i.e $\pi$ is inversely proportional to its relative deadline $D$). This level of preemption is such that a task $\tau_i$ cannot preempt a task $\tau_j$ unless $\pi(\tau_i) > \pi(\tau_j)$. The current level of preemption of the system is determined as a function of the resource access. Then a task cannot be elected if its level of preemption is lower than this global level of preemption. The application of this rule points out that the main difference between the priority ceiling protocol and the stack resource policy is the time at which a task is blocked. With the priority ceiling protocol, a task is blocked when it wants to use a resource, and with the stack resource policy, a task is blocked as soon as it wants to get the processor. A complete and precise presentation of this protocol can be found in Buttazzo (1997) and Stankovic et al. (1998).

## 3.2.5 Conclusions

Table 3.3 summarizes comparative studies that have been done between the different shared-resource protocols (Buttazzo, 1997). These protocols do not all try to avoid the priority inversion phenomenon, but they attempt to minimize the blocking time of high-priority tasks, induced by this fact. The upper bound of task blocking times, which can be evaluated according to a given protocol, is then included in the schedulability tests of the task set.

First, two general comments can be made about the three protocols studied to manage shared resources in a preemptive scheduling context:

- Whereas the ceiling priority and stack resource protocols can be used for aperiodic and/or periodic tasks, the priority inheritance protocol is applied only for a periodic task set if we want to evaluate the upper bound of the blocking time according to equation (3.12).

- The stack resource protocol induces the lowest proportion of context switches in the execution sequence thanks to its earliest task blocking system.

The computation of the response time of any task, done in Section 3.2.1, has shown how the explicit specifications of the scheduling algorithm are important and then the implementation fits in correctly with these specifications. No assumption has been made about deadlock prevention in Section 3.2.1. Once again, the explicit specification of this particularly crucial phenomenon can be presented in two ways:

- The specification itself takes into account the deadlock prevention and gives a deadlock-free off-line solution. This leads to the imposition of precise rules of programming either on resource use (global allocation or total ordering method) or on task concurrency management (a unique global critical section is defined for each task).

**Table 3.3** Evaluation summary of protocols preventing deadlocks and priority inversion

| Protocol | Scheduling algorithm | Deadlock prevention | Blocking time calculation |
|---|---|---|---|
| Priority inheritance protocol | RM EDF | No | $\min(n, m) \cdot CR_{max}$ |
| Priority ceiling protocol | RM | Yes (in uniprocessor context) | $CR_{max}$ |
| Dynamic priority ceiling protocol | EDF | Yes (in uniprocessor context) | $CR_{max}$ |
| Stack resource Protocol | RM EDF | Yes (in uniprocessor context) | $CR_{max}$ |

- The specification indicates only that the prevention of deadlock has to be taken into account by an on-line method whatever the shared resource managing protocol. This leads to implementation of an on-line algorithm like the banker's algorithm or the priority ceiling protocol.

To compare both methods, the banker's algorithm and the priority ceiling protocol, consider two tasks $\tau_1$ and $\tau_2$ where $\tau_2$ has a higher priority than $\tau_1$. Task $\tau_1$ first uses resource $R_1$, then uses both resources $R_1$ and $R_2$ in a nested fashion. Task $\tau_2$ first uses resource $R_2$, then it uses both resources $R_1$ and $R_2$ in a nested fashion. Let us assume that $\tau_2$ is awakened during the critical section of $\tau_1$ corresponding to resource $R_1$. The execution sequences, obtained for both algorithms, are the following:

- Under the banker's algorithm, task $\tau_2$ preempts task $\tau_1$ as it has a higher priority and runs until it requests resource $R_2$. Task $\tau_2$ is blocked by the banker's algorithm because it knows that task $\tau_1$ will need resource $R_2$ in the future (in this context the algorithm holds the list of all the resources used by any task). Consequently $\tau_1$ resumes its execution and, after a while, uses both resources $R_1$ and $R_2$. Then, when resource $R_2$ is free, $\tau_2$ resumes its execution by using $R_2$ and then both resources $R_1$ and $R_2$.

- Under the immediate priority ceiling protocol, resources $R_1$ and $R_2$ get the priority of task $\tau_2$. Similarly, $\tau_1$ inherits the priority of task $\tau_2$ when it attempts to use resource $R_1$. As a consequence, task $\tau_1$ is not preempted by task $\tau_2$ as long as task $\tau_1$ uses resources $R_1$ and $R_2$. So when task $\tau_1$ releases resources $R_1$ and $R_2$, task $\tau_1$ resumes its initial priority and task $\tau_2$ can begin its execution.

From this example, we can notice:

- Resources are used in the correct order for preventing deadlock.

- With the banker's algorithm, task $\tau_2$ begins its execution before it requests resource $R_2$. So there is more task context switching than with the use of the priority ceiling protocol.

- In a multiprocessor execution context, the results would be quite different. For the priority ceiling protocol, both tasks $\tau_1$ and $\tau_2$ are executed concurrently with the same priority and this situation can lead to a deadlock. By using the banker's algorithm, the behaviour is correct and identical to the one-processor behaviour.

If intermediate priority tasks exist other than tasks $\tau_1$ and $\tau_2$, the priority inheritance technique works well in the case of the priority ceiling protocol. On the other hand, the banker's algorithm can lead to a priority inversion unless a transitive priority inheritance is realized (quite possible since the banker's algorithm holds all the needed parameters). The banker's algorithm prescribes that, when resources are released, all waiting tasks should be examined for resource allocation. If the highest priority waiting task is examined solely, in a strict fixed-priority service, this can lead to a deadlock. However, a safe solution exists by examining the highest priority waiting task and only some subset of low-priority waiting tasks (Kaiser and Pradat-Peyre, 1998). In conclusion, we can say that no algorithm answers properly to the problem of scheduling shared resource access in all cases (uniprocessor and multiprocessor). There is no known solution guaranteeing a behaviour that is simultaneously free of deadlock and constraints. This is a general problem for concurrent systems.

Since, typically, the number of resources is low and since one knows quite well the use of critical resources by an off-line analysis, it is better to separate the two problems: deadlock and the priority inversion phenomenon. Then the use of critical resources is treated according to a total ordering method on the access of critical resources. The inversion priority is taken into account by one of the studied algorithms. Moreover, the total ordering technique on resource access allows the use of any protocol preventing priority inversion, which is often imposed by the real-time kernel.

# 3.3 Exercises

In addition to the following exercises, the reader will find three complete and real examples, explained and described in detail, in Chapter 9.

## 3.3.1 Questions

*Exercise 3.1:* **Scheduling with precedence constraints**

*1. Earliest deadline first scheduling of a task set*
Consider five independent periodic tasks described by the classical parameters given in Table 3.4.

**Table 3.4** Example of a task set

| Task | $r_i$ | $C_i$ | $D_i$ | $T_i$ |
|------|-------|-------|-------|-------|
| $\tau_1$ | 0 | 3 | 12 | 12 |
| $\tau_2$ | 0 | 2 | 11 | 11 |
| $\tau_3$ | 0 | 3 | 12 | 12 |
| $\tau_4$ | 0 | 1 | 11 | 11 |
| $\tau_5$ | 0 | 2 | 9 | 9 |

**Q1** Compute the processor utilization factor $U$ of this task set. Verify the schedulability under the EDF algorithm. Calculate the scheduling period of this task set. Compute the number of idle times of the processor in this scheduling cycle. Finally, construct the schedule obtained under the EDF algorithm for the first 20 time units.

*2. Scheduling with precedence constraints*
Referring to the previous task set, we suppose now that tasks are dependent and linked by precedence constraints presented in the graph of Figure 3.12. In order to take into account these relationships between tasks in an EDF scheduling context, one has to modify the task parameters $r$ and $D$ (or $d$) as presented

*Continued on page 68*

_Continued from page 67_

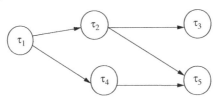

**Figure 3.12**  Example of precedence constraints between five tasks

in Section 3.1. If we have to get $\tau_i \rightarrow \tau_j$, the parameters must be modified according to the following equations:

- $r_j^* \geq \text{Max}((r_i^* + C_i), r_j)$
- $d_i^* \geq \text{Min}((d_j^* - C_j), d_i)$

**Q2**  Compute the new parameters $r^*$ and $d^*$ for handling the precedence constraints. Then construct the schedule obtained under the EDF algorithm for the first 20 time units with these modified parameters. Conclude.

---

_**Exercise 3.2:   Scheduling with shared critical resources**_

Consider three dependent tasks $\tau_1$, $\tau_2$ and $\tau_3$. The tasks $\tau_1$ and $\tau_3$ share a critical resource $R$. In order to describe this task set with the critical sections of task $\tau_1$ and $\tau_3$, we add new parameters that specify the computation time $C_t$:

- $C_t^\alpha$: task duration before entering the critical section,
- $C_t^\beta$: critical section duration,
- $C_t^\gamma$: task duration after the critical section.

Of course, we have $C_t = C_t^\alpha + C_t^\beta + C_t^\gamma$. So the task set is described by the classical parameters given in Table 3.5. As assumed, each task in a critical section can be preempted by a higher priority task which does not need this resource.

**Table 3.5**  Example of a task set sharing a critical resource, Exercise 3.2

| Task | $r_t$ | $C_t$ | $D_t$ | $T_t$ | $C_t^\alpha$ | $C_t^\beta$ | $C_t^\gamma$ |
|------|-------|-------|-------|-------|--------------|-------------|--------------|
| $\tau_1$ | 0 | 2 | 6 | 6 | 1 | 1 | 0 |
| $\tau_2$ | 0 | 2 | 8 | 8 | 2 | 0 | 0 |
| $\tau_3$ | 0 | 4 | 12 | 12 | 0 | 4 | 0 |

**Q1**  Construct the schedule obtained under the RM algorithm for the scheduling period. Indicate clearly on the graphical representation the time at which a priority inversion phenomenon occurs between $\tau_1$ and $\tau_2$.

_Continued on page 69_

_Continued from page 68_

**Q2** In order to prevent this priority inversion phenomenon, apply the priority inheritance protocol. Construct the new schedule obtained under the RM algorithm for the scheduling period. Indicate clearly on the graphical representation the time at which the task $\tau_2$ is blocked, avoiding the priority inversion phenomenon.

---

**_Exercise 3.3: Application with precedence constraints and critical resources_**

In this exercise, we analyse the schedulability of an application for which we introduce the constraints in a progressive way. First the tasks are considered independent, then a critical resource is shared by two tasks and finally dependent with precedence constraints.

_1. Periodic and independent tasks_
Consider three independent periodic tasks described by the classical parameters given in Table 3.6.

**Q1** Compute the processor utilization factor $U$ of this task set. Discuss the schedulability under the RM algorithm. Calculate the scheduling period of this task set. Compute the duration of idle times of the processor in this scheduling period. Finally, construct the schedule obtained under the RM algorithm.

**Table 3.6**  Task parameters, Exercise 3.3, Q1

| Task | $r_t$ | $C_t$ | $D_t$ | $T_t$ |
|------|-------|-------|-------|-------|
| $\tau_1$ | 0 | 2 | 6 | 6 |
| $\tau_2$ | 0 | 2 | 8 | 8 |
| $\tau_3$ | 0 | 4 | 12 | 12 |

The computation time of the task $\tau_3$ is now equal to 5. Thus the task set is characterized by the parameters given in Table 3.7.

**Table 3.7**  Task parameters, Exercise 3.3, Q2

| Task | $r_i$ | $C_i$ | $D_i$ | $T_i$ |
|------|-------|-------|-------|-------|
| $\tau_1$ | 0 | 2 | 6 | 6 |
| $\tau_2$ | 0 | 2 | 8 | 8 |
| $\tau_3$ | 0 | 5 | 12 | 12 |

**Q2** Compute the new processor utilization factor of this task set. Discuss the schedulability under the RM algorithm. Compute the duration of idle times of the processor in the major cycle. Finally, construct the schedule obtained under the RM algorithm.

_Continued on page 70_

*Continued from page 69*

In order to improve the schedulability of the new task set, the first release time of some tasks can be modified. In this case, the critical instant, defined for a task set where all the initial release times are equal, is avoided.

Consider an initial release time of 3 for the task $\tau_3$. So the task set parameters are given in Table 3.8.

**Table 3.8**   Task parameters, Exercise 3.3, Q3

| Task | $r_i$ | $C_i$ | $D_i$ | $T_i$ |
|------|-------|-------|-------|-------|
| $\tau_1$ | 0 | 2 | 6 | 6 |
| $\tau_2$ | 0 | 2 | 8 | 8 |
| $\tau_3$ | 3 | 5 | 12 | 12 |

**Q3**   Calculate the scheduling period of this task set. Construct the schedule obtained under the RM algorithm of this modified task set.

Another way to improve the schedulability of a task set is to use a powerful priority assignment algorithm, such as EDF. So we consider the previous task set, managed by the EDF algorithm, described by Table 3.9.

**Table 3.9**   Task parameters, Exercise 3.3, Q4

| Task | $r_i$ | $C_i$ | $D_i$ | $T_i$ |
|------|-------|-------|-------|-------|
| $\tau_1$ | 0 | 2 | 6 | 6 |
| $\tau_2$ | 0 | 2 | 8 | 8 |
| $\tau_3$ | 0 | 5 | 12 | 12 |

**Q4**   Compute the processor utilization factor $U$ of this task set. Discuss the schedulability under the EDF algorithm. Construct the schedule obtained under the EDF algorithm.

*2. Periodic tasks sharing critical resources*
Consider three dependent periodic tasks described by the classical parameters given in Table 3.10. What we can notice about this task set is that the tasks have different initial release times and two tasks share a critical resource, named $R$ in Table 3.10, during their whole execution time.

**Table 3.10**   Task parameters, Exercise 3.3, Q5 and Q6

| Task | $r_i$ | $C_i$ | $D_i$ | $T_i$ |
|------|-------|-------|-------|-------|
| $\tau_1$ | 1 | 2 ($R$) | 6 | 6 |
| $\tau_2$ | 1 | 2 | 8 | 8 |
| $\tau_3$ | 0 | 5 ($R$) | 12 | 12 |

*Continued on page 71*

*Continued from page 69*

**Q5** Compute the processor utilization factor $U$ of this task set. Discuss the schedulability under the EDF algorithm. Calculate the scheduling period of this task set. Construct the schedule obtained under the EDF algorithm considering no particular critical resource management except the mutual exclusion process. Indicate on the graphical representation the time at which a priority inversion phenomenon occurs.

**Q6** In order to prevent the priority inversion phenomenon, we apply the priority inheritance protocol. Construct the new schedule obtained under the EDF algorithm and the priority inheritance resource protocol until time $t = 25$. Indicate clearly on the graphical representation the time at which the task $\tau_3$ inherits a higher priority, thus avoiding the priority inversion phenomenon.

*3. Periodic tasks with precedence constraints*

Consider four dependent periodic tasks described by the parameters given in Table 3.11.

**Table 3.11**  Task parameters, Exercise 3.3, Q7

| Task | $r_i$ | $C_i$ | $D_i$ | $T_i$ |
|------|-------|-------|-------|-------|
| $\tau_1$ | 0 | 2 | 6  | 6  |
| $\tau_2$ | 0 | 2 | 8  | 8  |
| $\tau_3$ | 0 | 4 | 12 | 12 |
| $\tau_4$ | 0 | 1 | 12 | 12 |

**Q7** Compute the processor utilization factor $U$ of this task set. Discuss the schedulability under the EDF algorithm. Calculate the scheduling period of this task set. Give the execution sequence obtained under the EDF algorithm considering independent tasks.

The precedence constraint between tasks $\tau_3$ and $\tau_4$ is presented as a precedence graph in Figure 3.13 (task $\tau_4$ must be executed before task $\tau_3$). In order to take into account this relationship between tasks in an EDF scheduling context, one has to modify the task parameters $r$ and $D$ (or $d$) as presented in Section 3.1. If we have to get $\tau_i \rightarrow \tau_j$, the parameters will be modified according to the following equations:

- $r_j^* \geq \mathrm{Max}((r_i^* + C_i), r_j)$
- $d_i^* \geq \mathrm{Min}(d_j^* - C_j), d_i)$

**Figure 3.13**  Precedence graph

**Q8** Compute the new parameters $r^*$ and $d^*$ for handling the precedence constraints. Compute the scheduling period of this task set. Then construct the schedule obtained under the EDF algorithm for the first 25 time units with these modified parameters. Conclude.

## 3.3.2  Answers

---

*Exercise 3.1:  Scheduling with precedence constraints*

**Q1**  The processor utilization factor is the sum of the processor utilization factors of all the tasks. That is: $u_1 = 3/12 = 0.25$, $u_2 = 2/11 = 0.182$, $u_3 = 3/12 = 0.25$, $u_4 = 1/11 = 0.091$, $u_5 = 2/9 = 0.222$.
Then, the processor utilization factor is: $U = 0.995$.
Given that a set of periodic tasks, having a relative deadline $D$ equal to the period $T$, is schedulable with the EDF algorithm if and only if $U \leq 1$, the considered task set is schedulable.
The scheduling period of a set of periodic tasks is the least common multiplier of all periods, i.e.: $H = \text{LCM}(\{T_1, T_2, T_3, T_4, T_5\}) = 396$.
The number $N_i$ of idle times of the processor is given by this equation: $N_i = H(1 - U) = 2$.
The scheduling sequence is represented in Figure 3.14.

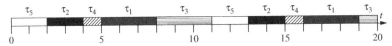

**Figure 3.14**  Scheduling sequence of five independent tasks under the EDF algorithm

**Q2**  In order to take into account the precedence constraints given in Figure 3.12, the new task parameters are obtained by modifying release times and deadlines. The computations for modifying release times begin with the task which has no predecessors, i.e. task $\tau_1$, and for changing deadlines with the task with no successors, i.e. task $\tau_5$. So the deadlines become:

$$d_5^* = \min\{d_5, \min\{\emptyset\}\} = 9$$

$$d_4^* = \min\{d_4, \min\{d_5^* - C_5\}\} = 7$$

$$d_3^* = \min\{d_3, \min\{\emptyset\}\} = 12$$

$$d_2^* = \min\{d_2, \min\{d_3^* - C_3, d_5^* - C_5\}\} = 7$$

$$d_1^* = \min\{d_1, \min\{d_2^* - C_2, d_4^* - C_4\}\} = 5$$

and the release times become:

$$r_1^* = \min\{r_1, \min\{\emptyset\}\} = 0$$

$$r_2^* = \min\{r_2, \min\{r_1^* + C_1\}\} = 3$$

$$r_3^* = \min\{r_3, \min\{r_2^* + C_2\}\} = 5$$

$$r_4^* = \min\{r_4, \min\{r_1 + C_1\}\} = 3$$

$$r_5^* = \min\{r_5, \min\{r_2^* + C_2, r_4^* + C_4\}\} = 5$$

*Continued on page 73*

*Continued from page 72*

The scheduling sequence is represented in Figure 3.15. We can verify that the tasks meet their deadlines and precedence constraints.

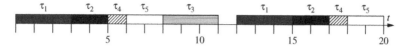

**Figure 3.15** Scheduling sequence of five dependent tasks under the EDF algorithm

---

*Exercise 3.2:* *Scheduling with shared critical resources*

**Q1** The schedule is given in Figure 3.16. At time $t = 7$, task $\tau_1$ is blocked because task $\tau_3$ uses the critical resource. Thus, task $\tau_3$ runs anew. However, at time $t = 8$, task $\tau_3$ is preempted by task $\tau_2$, which has a higher priority. Thus, there is a priority inversion during two time units.

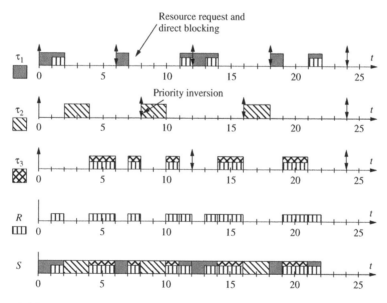

**Figure 3.16** Scheduling sequence under the RM algorithm showing a priority inversion phenomenon

**Q2** In order to prevent the priority inversion phenomenon, we use the priority inheritance protocol. The schedule is given in Figure 3.17. At time $t = 7$, when task $\tau_1$ requests the critical resource used by task $\tau_3$, it is blocked.

*Continued on page 74*

*Continued from page 73*

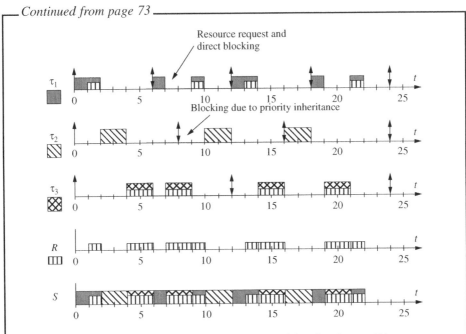

**Figure 3.17**   Scheduling sequence under the RM algorithm showing a valid management of a critical resource with the priority inheritance protocol

Thus, task $\tau_3$ inherits the priority of $\tau_1$ and resumes its execution. The execution of task $\tau_2$ is now delayed until time $t = 10$ and it runs after task $\tau_1$.

---

***Exercise 3.3:   Application with precedence constraints and critical resources***

*1. Periodic and independent tasks*

**Q1**   The processor utilization factor is the sum of the processor utilization factors of all the tasks. That is: $u_1 = 0.33$, $u_2 = 0.25$, $u_3 = 0.33$.
The processor utilization factor is then: $U = 11/12 = 0.916$.
Given that a set of periodic tasks, having relative deadline $D$ equal to period $T$, is schedulable with the RM algorithm if $U \leq n(2^{1/n} - 1) = 0.78(n = 3)$, the schedulability test is not verified. The schedule sequence has to be built over the scheduling period in order to test the schedulability.
The scheduling period of a set of periodic tasks is the least common multiplier of all periods, i.e.: $H = \text{LCM}(\{T_1, T_2, T_3, \}) = 24$.
The duration of idle times of the processor is 2. It is given by $(1 - U)H$.
The scheduling sequence, according to the RM algorithm priority assignment, is represented in Figure 3.18. This task set is schedulable.

*Continued on page 75*

_Continued from page 74_

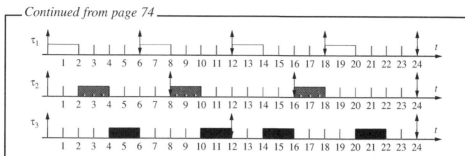

**Figure 3.18** Scheduling sequence of three independent tasks under the RM algorithm

**Q2** The processor utilization factor is now equal to 1 and the number of idle times of the processor is 0. So the RM schedulability test is not verified. The schedule sequence has to be built over the scheduling period in order to test the schedulability. The scheduling sequence, according to the RM algorithm priority assignment, is represented in Figure 3.19. This task set is not schedulable because task $\tau_3$ misses its deadline at time 12.

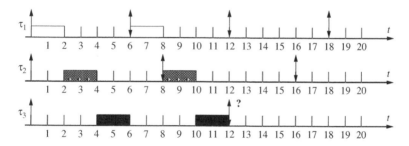

**Figure 3.19** Scheduling sequence of three independent tasks under the RM algorithm

**Q3** The scheduling period of the periodic task set is given by equation (1.4), i.e.:

$$H = \text{Max}\{r_i\} + 2 \cdot \text{LCM}(\{T_1, T_2, T_3\}) = 3 + 2 \times 24 = 51$$

The scheduling sequence, according to the RM algorithm priority assignment, is represented in Figure 3.20. This task set is schedulable.

**Q4** The processor utilization factor is equal to 1. Given that a set of periodic tasks, with relative deadlines equal to periods, is schedulable with the EDF algorithm if and only if $U \leq 1$, the task set is schedulable. The schedule sequence is represented in Figure 3.21.

_Continued on page 76_

*Continued from page 74*

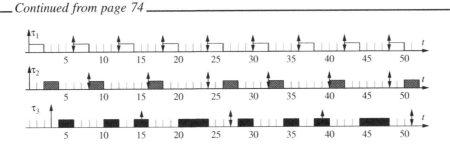

**Figure 3.20** Scheduling sequence of three independent tasks with different initial release times under the RM algorithm

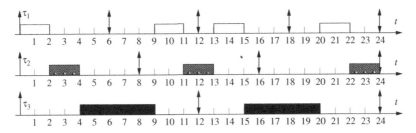

**Figure 3.21** Scheduling sequence of three independent tasks under the EDF algorithm

*2. Periodic tasks sharing critical resources*

**Q5** The processor utilization factor is equal to 1. Given that a set of independent periodic tasks, with relative deadlines equal to periods, is schedulable with the EDF algorithm if and only if $U \leq 1$, the task set is schedulable. But as the tasks are not independent, we cannot conclude that before doing a simulation. The schedule sequence is represented in Figure 3.22. Due to

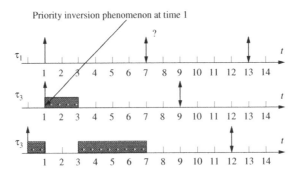

**Figure 3.22** Scheduling sequence of three dependent tasks under the EDF algorithm showing a priority inversion phenomenon

*Continued on page 76*

_Continued from page 74_

the mutual exclusion process, a priority inversion phenomenon occurs at time 1 by task $\tau_2$. This leads to missing of the deadline of task $\tau_1$.

**Q6** In order to prevent the priority inversion phenomenon, we use the priority inheritance protocol. Similarly to the sequence of Figure 3.22, when $\tau_1$ wants to take the critical resource, used by task $\tau_3$, task $\tau_1$ is blocked. But $\tau_3$ inherits the priority of $\tau_1$ and $\tau_3$ resumes its execution. The execution of task $\tau_2$ is now delayed and it runs after task $\tau_1$. This valid execution is shown in Figure 3.23.

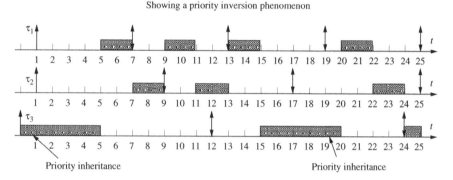

**Figure 3.23** Scheduling sequence under the EDF algorithm showing the correct management of a critical resource with the priority inheritance protocol

_3. Periodic tasks with precedence constraints_

**Q7** The processor utilization factor is equal to 1. So the EDF schedulability test is verified. The scheduling period of the periodic task set is the least common multiplier of all periods, i.e.: $H = \text{LCM}(\{T_1, T_2, T_3, T_4\}) = 24$. The valid schedule sequence with the EDF priority assignment algorithm is represented in Figure 3.24. The execution sequence is valid in terms of respect for deadlines, but this sequence does not fit with the precedence sequence studied after.

**Q8** The computations for modifying release times begin with the tasks which have no predecessors, i.e. $\tau_4$, and those for changing deadlines with the tasks without any successors, i.e. $\tau_3$. So the deadline of task $\tau_4$ becomes:

$$d_4^* = \min\{d_4, \min\{d_3^* - C_3\}\} = 8 (d_3 \text{ is not changed})$$

and the release time of task $\tau_3$ becomes:

$$r_3^* = \min\{r_3, \min\{r_4^* + C_4\}\} = 1 (r_4 \text{ is not changed})$$

_Continued on page 76_

*Continued from page 75*

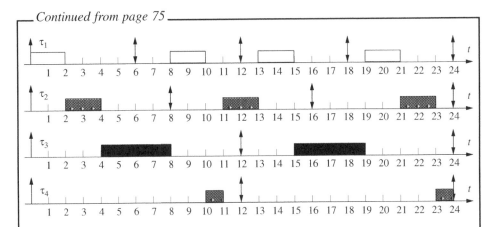

**Figure 3.24** Scheduling sequence of four tasks with precedence constraints under EDF, Exercise 3.3, Q7

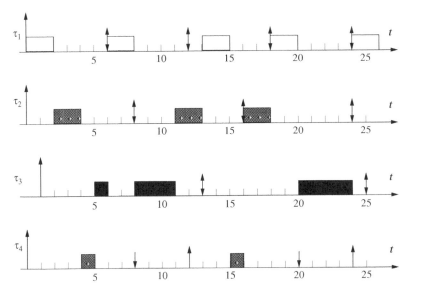

**Figure 3.25** Scheduling sequence of four dependent tasks under EDF, Exercise 3.3, Q8

The scheduling period is now given by equation (1.4), i.e.:

$$H = \text{Max}\{r_i\} + 2 \cdot \text{LCM}(\{T_1, T_2, T_3, T_4\}) = 1 + 2 \cdot 24 = 49$$

The scheduling sequence is represented in Figure 3.25. We can verify that the tasks respect deadlines and precedence constraints. It is important to notice that the modifications of $r_i$ and $d_i$ are sufficient, but not necessary. It is possible to find quite easily another schedule that respects precedence constraints.

# 4

# Scheduling Schemes
# for Handling Overload

## 4.1 Scheduling Techniques in Overload Conditions

This chapter presents several techniques to solve the problem of scheduling real-time tasks in overload conditions. In such situations, the computation time of the task set exceeds the time available on the processor and then deadlines can be missed. Even when applications and the real-time systems have been properly designed, lateness can occur for different reasons, such as missing a task activation signal due to a fault of a device, or the extension of the computation time of some tasks due to concurrent use of shared resources. Simultaneous arrivals of aperiodic tasks in response to some exceptions raised by the system can overload the processor too. If the system is not designed to handle overloads, the effects can be catastrophic and some paramount tasks of the application can miss their deadlines. Basic algorithms such as EDF and RM exhibit poor performance during overload situations and it is not possible to control the set of late tasks. Moreover, with these two algorithms, one missed deadline can cause other tasks to miss their deadlines: this phenomenon is called the *domino effect*.

Several techniques deal with overload to provide deadline missing tolerance. The first algorithms deal with periodic task sets and allow the system to handle variable computation times which cannot always be bounded. The other algorithms deal with hybrid task sets where tasks are characterized with an importance value. All these policies handle task models which allow recovery from deadline missing so that the results of a late task can be used.

## 4.2 Handling Real-Time Tasks with Varying Timing Parameters

A real-time system typically manages many tasks and relies on its scheduler to decide when and which task has to be executed. The scheduler, in turn, relies on knowledge about each task's computational time, dependency relationships and deadline supplied by the designer to make the scheduling decisions. This works quite well as long as the execution time of each task is fixed (as in Chapters 2 and 3). Such a rigid framework is a reasonable assumption for most real-time control systems, but it can be too restrictive for other applications. The schedule based on fixed parameters may not work if the environment is dynamic. In order to handle a dynamic environment, an execution scheduling of real-time system must be flexible.

For example, in multimedia systems, timing constraints can be more flexible and dynamic than control theory usually permits. Activities such as voice or image treatments (sampling, acquisition, compression, etc.) are performed periodically, but their execution rates or execution times are not as strict as in control applications. If a task manages compressed frames, the time for coding or decoding each frame can vary significantly depending on the size or the complexity of the image. Therefore, the worst-case execution time of a task can be much greater than its mean execution time. Since hard real-time tasks are guaranteed based on their worst-case execution times, multimedia activities can cause a waste of processor resource, if treated as rigid hard real-time tasks.

Another example is related to a radar system where the number of objects to be monitored may vary from time to time. So the processor load may change due to the increase of execution duration of a task related to the number of objects. Sometimes it can be advantageous for a real-time computation not to pursue the highest possible precision so that the time and resources saved can be used by other tasks.

In order to provide theoretical support for applications, much work has been done to deal with tasks with variable computation times. We can distinguish three main ways to address this problem:

- specific task model able to integrate a variation of task parameters, such as execution time, period or deadline;

- on-line adaptive model, which calculates the largest possible timing parameters for a task at any time;

- fault-tolerant mechanism based on minimum software, for a given task, which ensures compliance with specified timing requirements in all circumstances.

## 4.2.1  Specific models for variable execution task applications

In the context of specific models for tasks with variable execution times, two approaches have been proposed: statistical rate monotonic scheduling (Atlas and Bestavros, 1998) and the multiframe model for real-time tasks (Mok and Chen, 1997).

The first model, called statistical rate monotonic scheduling, is a generalization of the classical rate monotonic results (see Chapter 2). This approach handles periodic tasks with highly variable execution times. For each task, a quality of service is defined as the probability that in an arbitrary long execution history, a randomly selected instance of this task will meet its deadline. The statistical rate monotonic scheduling consists of two parts: a job admission and a scheduler. The job admission controller manages the quality of service delivered to the various tasks through admit/reject and priority assignment decisions. In particular, it wastes no resource on task instances that will miss their deadlines, due to overload conditions, resulting from excessive variability in execution times. The scheduler is a simple, preemptive and fixed-priority scheduler. This statistical rate monotonic model fits quite well with multimedia applications.

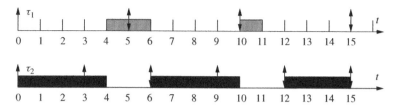

**Figure 4.1**   Execution sequence of an application integrating two tasks: one classical task $\tau_1$ (0, 1, 5, 5) and one multiframe task $\tau_2$ (0, (3, 1), 3, 3)

The second model, called the multiframe model, allows the execution time of a task to vary from one instance to another. In this model, the execution times of successive instances of a task are specified by a finite array of integer numbers rather than a single number which is the worst-case execution time commonly assumed in the classical model. Step by step, the peak utilization bound is derived in a preemptive fixed-priority scheduling policy under the assumption of the execution of the task instance time array. This model significantly improves the utilization processor load. Consider, for example, a set of two tasks with the following four parameters $(r_i, C_i, D_i, T_i)$: a classical task $\tau_1$ (0, 1, 5, 5) and a multiframe task $\tau_2$ (0, (3, 1), 3, 3). The two execution times of the latter task mean that the duration of this task is alternatively 3 and 1. The two durations of task $\tau_2$ can simulate a program with two different paths which are executed alternatively. Figure 4.1 illustrates the execution sequence obtained with this multiframe model and a RM algorithm priority assignment.

## 4.2.2   On-line adaptive model

In the context of the on-line adaptive model, two approaches have been proposed: the elastic task model (Buttazzo et al., 1998) and the scheduling adaptive task model (Wang and Lin, 1994). In the elastic task model, the periods of task are treated as springs, with given elastic parameters: minimum length, maximum length and a rigidity coefficient. Under this framework, periodic tasks can intentionally change their execution rate to provide different quality of service, and the other tasks can automatically adapt their period to keep the system underloaded. This model can also handle overload conditions. It is extremely useful for handling applications such as multimedia in which the execution rates of some computational activities have to be dynamically tuned as a function of the current system state, i.e. oversampling, etc. Consider, for example, a set of three tasks with the following four parameters $(r_i, C_i, D_i, T_i)$: $\tau_1$ (0, 10, 20, 20), $\tau_2$ (0, 10, 40, 40) and $\tau_3$ (0, 15, 70, 70). With these periods, the task set is schedulable by EDF since (see Chapter 2):

$$U = \frac{10}{20} + \frac{10}{40} + \frac{15}{70} = 0.964 < 1$$

If task $\tau_3$ reduces its execution rate to 50, no feasible schedule exists, since the processor load would be greater than 1:

$$U = \frac{10}{20} + \frac{10}{40} + \frac{15}{50} = 1.05 > 1$$

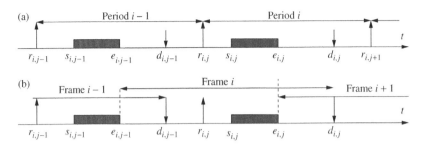

**Figure 4.2**  Comparison between (a) a classical task model and (b) an adaptive task model

However, the system can accept the higher rate of task $\tau_3$ by slightly decreasing the execution of the two other tasks. For instance, if we give a period of 22 for task $\tau_1$ and 45 for task $\tau_2$, we get a processor load lower than 1:

$$U = \frac{10}{22} + \frac{10}{45} + \frac{15}{50} = 0.977 < 1$$

The scheduling adaptive model considers that the deadline of an adaptive task is set to one period interval after the completion of the previous task instance and the release time can be set anywhere before the deadline. The time domain must be divided into frames of equal length. The main goal of this model is to obtain constant time spacing between adjacent task instances. The execution jitter is deeply reduced with this model while it can vary from zero to twice the period with a scheduling of classical periodic tasks. Figure 4.2 shows a comparison between a classical task model and an adaptive task model. The fundamental difference between the two models is in selecting the release times, which can be set anywhere before the deadline depending on the individual requirements of the task. So the deadline is defined as one period from the previous task instance completion.

### 4.2.3  Fault-tolerant mechanism

The basic idea of the fault-tolerant mechanism, based on an imprecise computation model, relies on making available results that are of poorer, but acceptable, quality on a timely basis when results of the desired quality cannot be produced in time. In this context, two approaches have been proposed: the deadline mechanism model (Campbell et al., 1979; Chetto and Chetto, 1991) and the imprecise computation model (Chung et al., 1990). These models are detailed in the next two subsections.

*Deadline mechanism model*

The deadline mechanism model requires each task $\tau_i$ to have a primary program $\tau_i^p$ and an alternate one $\tau_i^a$. The primary algorithm provides a good quality of service which is in some sense more desirable, but in an unknown length of time. The alternate program produces an acceptable result, but may be less desirable, in a known and deterministic length of time. In a controlling system that uses the deadline mechanism, the scheduling algorithm ensures that all the deadlines are met either by the primary program or by alternate algorithms but in preference by primary codes whenever possible.

To illustrate the use of this model, let us consider an avionics application that concerns the space position of a plane during flight. The more accurate method is to use satellite communication for the GPS technique. But the program, corresponding to this function, has an unknown execution duration due to the multiple accesses to that satellite service by many users. On the other hand, it is possible to get quite a good position of the plane by using its previous position, given its speed and its direction during a fixed time step. The first positioning technique with a non-deterministic execution time corresponds to the primary code of this task and the second method, which is less precise, is an alternate code for this task. Of course it is necessary that the precise positioning should be executed from time to time in order to get a good quality of this crucial function. To achieve the goal of this deadline mechanism, two strategies can be applied:

- The first-chance technique schedules the alternate programs first and the primary codes are then scheduled in the remaining times after their associated alternate programs have completed. If the primary program ends before its deadline, its results are used in preference to those of the alternate program.

- The last-chance technique schedules the alternate programs in reserved time intervals at the latest time. Primary codes are then scheduled in the remaining time before their associated alternate programs. By applying this strategy, the scheduler preempts a running primary program to execute the corresponding alternate program at the correct time in order to satisfy deadlines. If a primary program successfully completes, the execution of the associated alternate program is no longer necessary.

To illustrate the first-chance technique, we consider a set of three tasks: two classical tasks $\tau_1$ (0, 2, 16, 16) and $\tau_2$ (0, 6, 32, 32), and a task $\tau_3$ with primary and alternate programs. The alternate code $\tau_i^a$ is defined by the classical fixed parameters (0, 2, 8, 8). The primary program $\tau_i^p$ has various computational durations at each instance; assume that, for the first four instances, the execution times of task $\tau_i^p$ are successively (4, 4, 6, 6). The scheduling is based on an RM algorithm for the three task $\tau_1$, $\tau_2$ and the alternate code $\tau_i^a$. The primary programs $\tau_i^p$ are scheduled with the lowest priority or during the idle time of the processor. Figure 4.3 shows the result of the simulated sequence. We can notice that, globally, the success in executing the primary program is 50%. As we can see, we have the following executions:

- Instance 1: no free time for primary program execution;

- Instance 2: primary program completed;

- Instance 3: not enough free time for primary program execution;

- Instance 4: primary program completed.

In order to illustrate the last-chance technique, we consider a set of three tasks: two classical tasks $\tau_1$ (0, 4, 16, 16) and $\tau_2$ (0, 6, 32, 32), and task $\tau_3$ with primary and

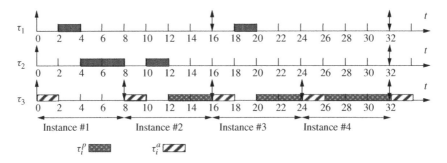

**Figure 4.3**  Execution sequence of an application integrating three tasks: two classical tasks $\tau_1$ and $\tau_2$, and a task $\tau_3$ with primary and alternate programs managed by the first-chance technique

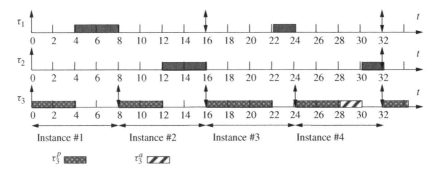

**Figure 4.4**  Execution sequence of an application integrating three tasks: two classical tasks $\tau_1$ and $\tau_2$, and task $\tau_3$ with primary and alternate programs managed by the last-chance technique

alternate programs similar to that defined in the example of the first-chance technique. The alternate code $\tau_i^a$ is defined by (0, 2, 8, 8) and the execution times of primary program $\tau_i^p$ are successively (4, 4, 6, 6) for the first four instances. Figure 4.4 shows the result of the simulated sequence. We can notice that, globally, the success in executing the primary program is 75%. As we can see, we have the following executions:

- Instance 1: no need for alternate program execution, because primary program completes;

- Instance 2: no need for alternate program execution, because primary program completes;

- Instance 3: no need for alternate program execution, because primary program completes;

- Instance 4: primary program is preempted because there is not enough time to complete primary program execution, and the alternate code is executed.

The last-chance technique seems better in terms of quality of service and processor load (no execution of useless alternate programs). Its drawback is the complexity of the scheduler, which has to verify at each step that the remaining time before the deadline of this specific task will permit the processor to execute at least the alternate program.

### *Imprecise computation model*

In the imprecise computation model, a task is logically decomposed into a mandatory part followed by optional parts. The mandatory part of the code must be completed to produce an acceptable result before the deadline of the task. The optional parts refine and improve the results produced by the mandatory part. The error in the task result is further reduced as the optional parts are allowed to execute longer. Many numerical algorithms involve iterative computations to improve precision results.

A typical application is the image synthesis program for virtual simulation devices (training system, video games, etc.). The more the image synthesis program can be executed, the more detailed and real the image will be. When the evolution rate of the image is high, there is no importance in representing details because of the user's visual ability. In the case of a static image, the processor must take time to visualize precise images in order to improve the 'reality' of the image.

To illustrate the imprecise computation model, we have chosen a set of three tasks: two classical tasks $\tau_1$ (0, 2, 16, 16) and $\tau_2$ (0, 6, 32, 32), and an imprecise computation task $\tau_3$ with one mandatory and two optional programs. The mandatory code $\tau_3^m$ is defined by (0, 2, 8, 8). The execution times of the optional programs $\tau_3^{op}$ are successively (2, 2) for the first instance, (2, 4) for the second one, (4, 4) for the third one and (2, 2) for the fourth instance. The scheduling is based on an RM algorithm for the three tasks $\tau_1$, $\tau_2$ and the mandatory code $\tau_3^m$. The optional programs $\tau_3^{op}$ are scheduled with the lowest priority or during the idle time of the processor. Figure 4.5 shows the result of the simulated sequence. We can notice that the success in executing the first optional program is 75% and only 25% in executing the second optional part. As we can see, we have the following executions:

- Instance 1: no free time for optional programs;

- Instance 2: first optional part completes, but the second optional part is preempted;

- Instance 3: only the first optional part completes, but the second optional part is not executed;

- Instance 4: all the optional programs are executed.

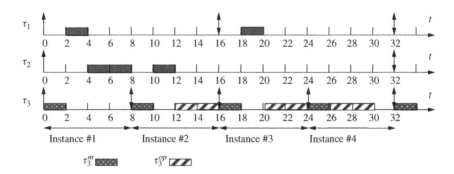

**Figure 4.5** Execution sequence of an application integrating three tasks: two classical tasks $\tau_1$ and $\tau_2$, and a task $\tau_3$ with mandatory and optional programs

# 4.3   Handling Overload Conditions for Hybrid Task Sets

## 4.3.1   Policies using importance value

With the policies presented in this section, each task is characterized by a deadline which defines its urgency and by a value which defines the importance of its execution, with respect to the other tasks of the real-time application. The importance (or criticality) of a task is not related to its deadline; thus, two different tasks which have the same deadline can have different importance values.

Arrivals of new aperiodic tasks in the system in response to an exception may overload the processor. Dynamic guarantee policies, seen in Chapter 2, resorb overload situations by rejecting the newly arriving aperiodic tasks which can not be guaranteed. This rejection assumes that the real-time system is a distributed system where a distributed scheduling policy attempts to assign the rejected task to an underloaded processor (Ramamritham and Stankovic, 1984). However, distributed real-time scheduling introduces large run-time overhead, thus other policies have been defined to use centralized systems. These policies jointly use a dynamic guarantee to predict an overload situation and a rejection policy based on the importance value to resorb the predicted overload situation.

Every time $t$ a new periodic or aperiodic task enters the system, a dynamic guarantee is run to ensure that the newly arriving task can execute without overloading the processor. The dynamic guarantee computes $LP(t)$, the system laxity at time $t$. The system laxity is an evaluation of the maximum fraction of time during which the processor may remain inactive while all the tasks still meet their deadlines. Let $\tau = \{\tau_i(t, C_i(t), d_i)\}, \{i < j \Leftrightarrow d_i < d_j\}$, be the set of tasks which are ready to execute at time $t$, sorted by increasing deadlines. The conditional laxity of task $\tau_i$ is defined as follows:

$$LC_i(t) = D_i - \sum_j C_j(t), d_j \le d_i \tag{4.1}$$

The system laxity is given by:

$$LP(t) = \underset{i}{\text{Min}}\{LC_i(t)\} \tag{4.2}$$

An overload situation is detected as soon as the system laxity $LP(t)$ is less than 0. The late tasks are those whose conditional laxity is negative. The overload value is equal to the absolute value of the system laxity, $|LP(t)|$. The overload is resorbed by a rejection policy based on removing tasks with a deadline smaller than or equal to the late task and having the minimum importance value. Among the policies based on these principles, two classes are discussed hereafter: multimode-based policy and importance value cumulating-based policy.

### *Multimode-based policy*

The aim of this policy is to favour the executions of the tasks with the highest importance value (this means that the favoured tasks are those which undergo fewer timing

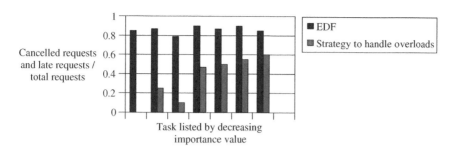

**Figure 4.6** Performance results when a policy handling overloads is used. Tasks are listed by decreasing importance value: $\tau_1$, $\tau_2$, $\tau_3$, $\tau_4$, $\tau_5$, $\tau_6$, $\tau_7$

faults, and which are dropped less frequently) (Delacroix, 1994, 1996; Delacroix and Kaiser, 1998). Figure 4.6 shows the results of this policy (Delacroix, 1994). Simulation experiments have been conducted using a set of three periodic tasks and four aperiodic tasks with a large utilization factor. The task set was first scheduled with the EDF algorithm without a policy to handle overloads, and then with the EDF algorithm and a policy to handle overloads. In the plot shown in Figure 4.6, the number of late requests and the number of cancelled requests is presented for each task, which are listed by decreasing importance value, and for each schedule. As one can see from Figure 4.6, the executions of the aperiodic task $\tau_1$ and of the periodic task $\tau_3$ are clearly favoured when a policy to handle overloads is used. However, all of the tasks have a high deadline missing ratio when they are scheduled with the EDF algorithm alone.

Each task is also characterized by two properties, called *execution properties*, which specify how a task can miss one of its executions. The first property is the *abortion property*: a task can be aborted if its execution can be stopped without being resumed later at the instruction at which it had been stopped. The second property is the *adjournment property*: a task can be adjourned if its request can be completely cancelled; it means the task does not execute and skips its occurrence. When an overload is detected, the executions of the task are dropped following a strict increasing order of importance value. So the tasks with the highest importance values, ready to execute as the overload occurs, are favoured. A recent extension (Delacroix and Kaiser, 1998) describes an adapted model of task, where a task is made up of several execution modes: the *normal mode* is the mode which is executed when the task begins to execute. It takes care of normal execution of the task. The *survival modes* are executed when the task is cancelled by the overload resorption or when it misses its deadline.

The computation time of a survival mode should be short because it only contains specific actions allowing cancelling of tasks in such a way that the application state remains safe. Such specific actions are, for example, release of shared resources, saving of partial computation or cancellation of dependent tasks. Figure 4.7 shows this task model. A task is made up of at most four modes: a normal mode, two survival modes executed when the normal mode is either adjourned or aborted, and a survival mode executed when the task misses its deadline. Each mode is characterized by a worst computation time, an importance value and two execution properties which specify how a mode can be cancelled by the overload resorption mechanism.

```
Task model:
  Task τᵢ is
    Begin
       Normal mode:
          Normal mode actions (C, properties, Imp)
       Abortion survival mode:
          Abortion mode actions (Cab, properties, Imp)
       Adjournment survival mode:
          Adjournment mode actions (Caj, properties, Imp)
       Deadline survival mode:
          Deadline mode actions (Cd, properties, Imp)
    End;


Task example:
  Task τ₁ is
    begin
       Normal mode: (C=10, Adjournable, Abortable, Imp=5)
          Get(Sensor);
          Read(Sensor, Temp);
          Release(Sensor);
          -- computation with Temp value
          Temp := compute();
          -- Temp value is sent to the task τ₂
          Send (Temp, τ₂);
       Abortion mode: (C=3, compulsory execution, Imp=5)
          -- Task τ₂ adjournment
          Release(Sensor);
          Adjourn(τ₂);
       Adjournment mode: (C=2, compulsory execution, Imp=5)
          -- An approximate value is computed with the
             preceding value
          Temp := Old_Temp * approximate_factor;
          Send (temp, τ₂);
    End;
```

**Figure 4.7**  Example of a task with several modes

### Importance value cumulating-based policy

With this policy, the importance value assigned to a task depends on the time at which the task is completed: so, a hard task contributes to a value only if it completes within its deadline (Baruah et al., 1991; Clark, 1990; Jensen et al., 1985; Koren and Shasha, 1992). The performance of these policies is measured by accumulating the values of the tasks which complete within their deadlines. So, as an overload has to be resorbed, the rejection policy aims to maximize this cumulative value, $\beta$, rather than to favour the execution of the most important ready tasks. Several algorithms have been proposed based on this principle. They differ in the way the rejection policy drops tasks to achieve a maximal cumulative value $\beta$. The competitive factor is a parameter that measures the worst-case performance of these algorithms and allows comparison of them. So, an algorithm has a competitive factor $\varphi$, if and only if it can guarantee a cumulative value $\beta$ which is greater than or equal to $\varphi\beta^*$ where $\beta^*$ is the cumulative value achieved by an optimal clairvoyant scheduler. A clairvoyant scheduler is a theoretical abstraction, used as a reference model, that has *a priori* knowledge of the task arrival times.

The algorithm $D_{over}$ (Koren and Shasha, 1992) has the best competitive factor among all the on-line algorithms which follow this principle. When an overload is detected, the importance value $Imp_z$ of the arrival task is compared with the total value $Imp_{priv}$ of all the privileged tasks (i.e. all preempted tasks). If the condition $Imp_z > (1 + \sqrt{k})(Imp_{curr} + Imp_{priv})$ holds, then the new task is executed; otherwise it is rejected. $Imp_{curr}$ is the importance value of the presently running task and $k$ the ratio of the highest value and the lowest value task.

In the RED (robust earliest deadline) algorithm (Buttazzo and Stankovic, 1993), each task is characterized by a relative deadline $D_r$ and a deadline tolerance $M$ which defines a secondary deadline $d_r = r + D_r + M$, where $r$ is the arrival time of the task. Tasks are scheduled based on their primary deadline but accepted based on their secondary deadline. An overload is detected as soon as some tasks miss their secondary deadlines. Then the rejection policy discards the tasks with the least importance value.

### 4.3.2 Example

Consider the following task set composed of:

- two periodic tasks:
  - $\tau_1(r_0 = 0, C = 1, D = 7, T = 10, Imp = 3)$
  - $\tau_2(r_0 = 0, C = 3, D = 4, T = 5, Imp = 1)$
- and four aperiodic tasks:
  - $\tau_3(r = 4, C = 0.2, d = 5, Imp = 4)$
  - $\tau_4(r = 5.5, C = 1, d = 10, Imp = 5)$
  - $\tau_5(r = 6, C = 1, d = 8, Imp = 2)$
  - $\tau_6(r = 7, C = 1.5, d = 9.5, Imp = 6)$

This task set is scheduled by the EDF algorithm. A policy for handling overloads is used. The rejection policy discards the tasks with low importance values. The schedule of the task set is shown within the major cycle of the two periodic tasks, i.e. within the interval [0, 10].

- At time $t = 0$, tasks $\tau_1$ and $\tau_2$ enter the system. Let $A(t)$ be the set of tasks which are ready at time $t$, sorted by increasing deadlines. The overload detection algorithm computes the conditional laxity of each task in the set $A(t)$.

$$A(0) = \{\tau_2(C(0) = 3, d = 4), \tau_1(C(0) = 1, d = 7)\}$$
$$LC_2(t) = 4 - 3 - 0 = 1$$
$$LC_1(t) = 7 - 1 - 3 - 0 = 3$$

There is no overload since all conditional laxities are greater than 0.

- At time $t = 4$, task $\tau_3$ enters the system.

$$A(4) = \{\tau_3(C(4) = 0.2, d = 5)\}$$
$$LC_3(t) = 5 - 4 - 0.2 = 0.8$$

The conditional laxity of the task $\tau_3$ is greater than 0; so there is no overload.

- At time $t = 5$, task $\tau_2$ enters the system.

$$A(5) = \{\tau_2(C(5) = 3, d = 9)\}$$
$$LC_2(t) = 9 - 5 - 3 = 1$$

The conditional laxity of the task $\tau_2$ is greater than 0, so there is no overload.

- At time $t = 5.5$, task $\tau_4$ enters the system.

$$A(5.5) = \{\tau_2(C(5.5) = 2.5, d = 9), \tau_4(C(5.5) = 1, d = 10)\}$$
$$LC_2(t) = 9 - 5.5 - 2.5 = 1$$
$$LC_4(t) = 10 - 5.5 - 1 - 2.5 = 1$$

There is no overload since no conditional laxity is less than 0.

- At time $t = 6$, task $\tau_5$ enters the system.

$$A(6) = \{\tau_5(C(6) = 1, d = 8), \tau_2(C(6) = 2, d = 9), \tau_4(C(6) = 1, d = 10)\}$$
$$LC_5(t) = 8 - 6 - 1 = 1$$
$$LC_2(t) = 9 - 6 - 1 - 2 = 0$$
$$LC_4(t) = 10 - 6 - 1 - 2 - 1 = 0$$

There is no overload since no conditional laxity is less than 0.

- At time $t = 7$, task $\tau_6$ enters the system.

$$A(7) = \{\tau_2(C(7) = 2, d = 9), \tau_6(C(7) = 1.5, d = 9.5), \tau_4(C(7) = 1, d = 10)\}$$
$$LC_2(t) = 9 - 7 - 2 = 0$$
$$LC_6(t) = 9.5 - 7 - 2 - 1.5 = -1$$

The conditional laxity of task $\tau_6$ is negative. So an overload situation is detected. The late task is task $\tau_6$ and the overload value is equal to one computation time. Figure 4.8 shows the overload situation.

To resorb the overload situation, the rejection policy cancels executions of tasks whose deadlines are smaller than or equal to the deadline of the task $\tau_6$ in the set $A(7)$. These cancellations are made following the strict increasing order of importance values and are stopped when the amount of computation time of the cancelled executions is greater than or equal to the overload value. So the rejection policy cancels task $\tau_2$, which has the lowest importance value. The remaining computation time of task $\tau_2$ is equal to 2.

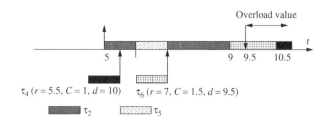

Overload value

$\tau_4 (r = 5.5, C = 1, d = 10)$     $\tau_6 (r = 7, C = 1.5, d = 9.5)$

$\tau_2$     $\tau_5$

**Figure 4.8**   Overload situation at time $t = 7$

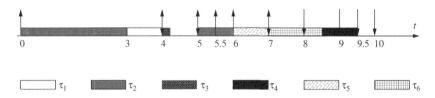

$\tau_1$     $\tau_2$     $\tau_3$     $\tau_4$     $\tau_5$     $\tau_6$

**Figure 4.9**   Schedule resulting from the policy handling overload with importance values

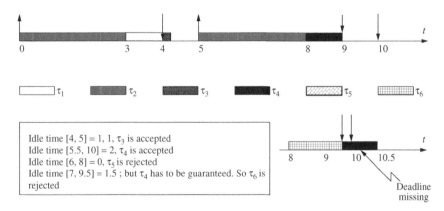

$\tau_1$     $\tau_2$     $\tau_3$     $\tau_4$     $\tau_5$     $\tau_6$

Idle time [4, 5] = 1, 1, $\tau_3$ is accepted
Idle time [5.5, 10] = 2, $\tau_4$ is accepted
Idle time [6, 8] = 0, $\tau_5$ is rejected
Idle time [7, 9.5] = 1.5 ; but $\tau_4$ has to be guaranteed. So $\tau_6$ is rejected

Deadline missing

**Figure 4.10**   Schedule resulting from the guarantee policy without importance value

Then the cancellations are stopped and the overload algorithm verifies that the overload situation is really resorbed:

$$A(7) = \{\tau_6(C(7) = 1.5, d = 9.5), \tau_4(C(7) = 1, d = 10)\}$$

$$LC_6(t) = 9.5 - 7 - 1.5 = 1$$

$$LC_4(t) = 0 - 7 - 1 - 1.5 = 0.5$$

Figure 4.9 shows the resulting schedule within the major cycle of the two periodic tasks. Figure 4.10 shows the schedule, resulting from the first guarantee strategy (see Section 2.2.2) which does not use the importance value.

# 5

# Multiprocessor Scheduling

## 5.1 Introduction

In this chapter, we limit the study to multiprocessor systems with centralized control that are called 'strongly coupled systems'. The main characteristics of such systems are the existence of a common base of time (for global scheduling of events and tasks) and a common memory (for implementing the vector of communication between tasks). Consequently, one has a global view of the state of the system accessible at every moment. In addition to the common memory, which contains the whole of the code and the data shared by the different tasks, the processors can have local memory (stack, cache memory, and so on). These systems present strong analogies with the centralized systems (uniprocessor) while primarily being different by their capacity to implement parallel execution of tasks. In a multiprocessor environment, a scheduling algorithm is valid if all task deadlines are met. This definition, identical to the one used in the uniprocessor context, is extended with the two following conditions:

- a processor can execute only one task at any time;
- a task is treated only by one processor at any time.

The framework of the study presented here is limited to the most common architecture, which is made up of identical processors (identical speed of processing) with an on-line preemptive scheduling. In this book, we do not treat off-line scheduling algorithms, which are often very complex, and not suitable for real-time systems. It is, however, important to note that off-line algorithms are the only algorithms which make it possible to obtain an optimal schedule (by the resolution of optimization problems of linear systems) and to handle some configurations unsolved by an on-line scheduling algorithm.

## 5.2 First Results and Comparison with Uniprocessor Scheduling

The first significant result is a theorem stating the absence of optimality of on-line scheduling algorithms (Sahni, 1979):

**Theorem 5.1:**
An on-line algorithm which builds a feasible schedule for any set of tasks with deadlines within $m$ processors ($m \geq 2$), cannot exist.

From Theorem 5.1, we can deduce that, in general, the centralized-control real-time scheduling on multiprocessors could not be an optimal scheduling. In the case of a set of periodic and independent tasks $\{\tau_i(r_i, C_i, D_i, T_i), i \in [1, n]\}$ to execute on $m$ processors, a second obvious result is:

**Necessary condition:**
The necessary condition of schedulability referring to the maximum load $U_j$ of each processor $j (U_j \leq 1, j \in [1, m])$ is:

$$U = \sum_{j=1}^{m} U_j = \sum_{i=1}^{n} u_i = \sum_{i=1}^{n} \frac{C_i}{P_i} \leq m \tag{5.1}$$

where $u_i$ is the processor utilization factor of task $\tau_i$.

A third result is related to the schedule length, which is identical to that in the uniprocessor environment:

**Theorem 5.2:**
There is a feasible schedule for a set of periodic and independent tasks if and only if there is a feasible schedule in the interval $[r_{min}, r_{max} + \Delta]$ where $r_{min} = Min\{r_i\}$, $r_{max} = Max\{r_i\}$, $\Delta = LCM\{T_i\}$, and $i \in [1, n]$.

LCM($T_i$) means the least common multiple of periods $T_i (i = 1, \ldots, n)$. For instance, the earliest deadline first algorithm, which is optimal in the uniprocessor case, is not optimal in the multiprocessor case. To show that, let us consider the following set of four periodic tasks $\{\tau_1(r_0 = 0, C = 1, D = 2, T = 10), \tau_2(r_0 = 0, C = 3, D = 3, T = 10), \tau_3(r_0 = 1, C = 2, D = 3, T = 10), \tau_4(r_0 = 2, C = 3, D = 3, T = 10)\}$ to execute on two processors, $Proc_1$ and $Proc_2$. The EDF schedule does not respect the deadline of task $\tau_4$, whereas there are feasible schedules as shown in Figure 5.1b.

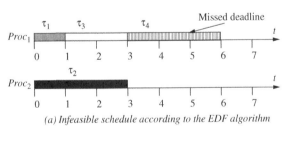

*(a) Infeasible schedule according to the EDF algorithm*

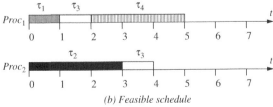

*(b) Feasible schedule*

**Figure 5.1** Example showing that the EDF algorithm is not optimal in the multiprocessor environment

## 5.3 Multiprocessor Scheduling Anomalies

It is very important to stress that some applications, which are executed in a multiprocessor environment, are prone to anomalies at the time of apparently positive changes of parameters. Thus, it was proven that (Graham, 1976):

> **Theorem 5.3:**
> If a task set is optimally scheduled on a multiprocessor with some priority assignment, a fixed number of processors, fixed execution times, and precedence constraints, then increasing the number of processors, reducing computation times, or weakening the precedence constraints can increase the schedule length.

This results implies that if tasks have deadlines, then adding resources (for instance, adding processors) or relaxing constraints can make things worse. The following example can best illustrate why Graham's theorem is true.

Let us consider a set of six tasks that accept preemption but not migration (i.e. the tasks cannot migrate from one processor to another during execution). These tasks have to be executed on two identical processors using a fixed-priority based scheduling algorithm (external priorities of tasks are fixed as indicated by Table 5.1). The

**Table 5.1.** Set of six tasks to highlight anomalies of multiprocessor scheduling

| Task | $r_i$ | $C_i$ | $d_i$ | Priority |
|------|-------|-------|-------|----------|
| $\tau_1$ | 0 | 5 | 10 | 1 (max) |
| $\tau_2$ | 0 | [2, 6] | 10 | 2 |
| $\tau_3$ | 4 | 8 | 15 | 3 |
| $\tau_4$ | 0 | 10 | 20 | 4 |
| $\tau_5$ | 5 | 100 | 200 | 5 |
| $\tau_6$ | 7 | 2 | 22 | 6 (min) |

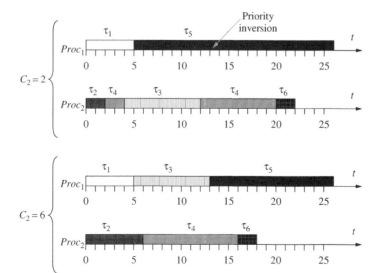

**Figure 5.2** Schedules of the task set presented in Table 5.1 considering the bounds of the computation time of task $\tau_2$

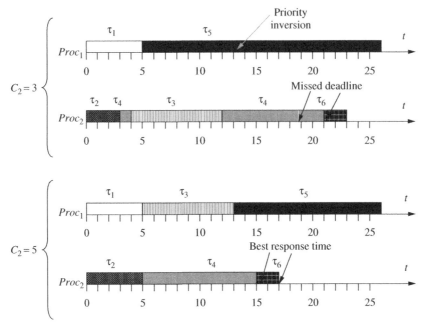

**Figure 5.3** Schedules of the task set presented in Table 5.1 considering two computation times of task $\tau_2$ taken inside the fixed interval

computation time of task $\tau_2$ is in the interval [2, 6]. The current analysis in the uniprocessor environment consists of testing the schedulability of a task set for the bounds of the task computation time interval. The results presented in Figure 5.2 show a feasible schedule for each one of the bounds of the computation time interval $C_2$ with, however, a phenomenon of priority inversion between tasks $\tau_4$ and $\tau_5$ for the weakest computation time of task $\tau_2$.

The schedules, built for two other values of $C_2$ taken in the fixed interval, show the anomalies of multiprocessor scheduling (Figure 5.3): an infeasible schedule for $C_2 = 3$ (missed deadlines for tasks $\tau_4$ and $\tau_6$), and a feasible schedule for $C_2 = 5$ with better performance (lower response time for tasks $\tau_4$ and $\tau_6$).

## 5.4  Schedulability Conditions

### 5.4.1  Static-priority schedulability condition

Here we deal with a static-priority scheduling of systems of $n$ periodic tasks $\{\tau_1, \tau_2, \ldots, \tau_n\}$ on $m$ identical processors ($m \geq 2$). The assumptions are: task migration is permitted (at task start or after it has been preempted) and parallelism is forbidden. Without loss of generality, we assume that $T_i \leq T_{i+1}$ for all $i$, $1 \leq i \leq n$; i.e. the tasks are indexed according to increasing order of periods. Given $u_i$ the processor utilization of each task $\tau_i$, we define the global processor utilization factor $U$ as classically for the one-processor context.

The priority assignment is done according to the following rule (Andersson et al., 2001):

- if $u_i > m/(3m - 2)$ then $\tau_i$ has the highest priority and ties are broken arbitrarily but in a consistent manner (always the same for the successive instances);

- if $u_i \leq m/(3m - 2)$ then $\tau_i$ has the RM priority (the smaller the period, the higher the priority).

With this priority assignment algorithm, we have a sufficient schedulability condition (Andersson et al., 2001):

**Sufficient condition:**
A set of periodic and independent tasks with periods equal to deadlines such that $T_i \geq T_{i+1}$ for $i \in [1, n - 1]$ is schedulable on $m$ identical processors if:

$$U \leq \frac{m^2}{3m - 2} \tag{5.2}$$

Consider an example of a set of five tasks to be scheduled on a platform of three identical unit-speed processors ($m = 3$). The temporal parameters of these tasks are: $\tau_1(r_0 = 0, C = 1, D = 7, T = 7), \tau_2(r_0 = 0, C = 2, D = 15, T = 15), \tau_3(r_0 = 0, C = 9, D = 20, T = 20), \tau_4(r_0 = 0, C = 11, D = 24, T = 24), \tau_5(r_0 = 0, C = 2, D = 25, T = 25)$. The utilization factors of these five tasks are respectively: 0.143, 0.133, 0.45, 0.458 and 0.08. Following the priority assignment rule, we get:

- $u_i > \dfrac{m}{3m - 2} = 0.4286$ for both tasks $\tau_3$ and $\tau_4$

- $u_i \leq \dfrac{m}{3m - 2} = 0.4286$ for the other tasks $\tau_1, \tau_2$ and $\tau_5$

Hence, tasks $\tau_3$ and $\tau_4$ will be assigned the highest priorities and the remaining three tasks will be assigned according to RM priorities. The possible priority assignments are therefore as follows in a decreasing priority order: $\tau_3, \tau_4, \tau_1, \tau_2, \tau_5$ or $\tau_4, \tau_3, \tau_1, \tau_2, \tau_5$.

In this example, the global processor utilization factor $U$ is equal to 1.264 and it is smaller than the limit defined above by the sufficient condition: $m^2/(3m - 2) = 1.286$. So we can assert that this task set is schedulable on a platform of three processors. Figure 5.4 shows a small part of the scheduling period of this task set.

## 5.4.2   Schedulability condition based on task period property

In order to be able to obtain schedulability conditions, the multiprocessor scheduling problem should be restricted. In this case, a particular property of the task period is used to elaborate a specific sufficient condition. If we consider a set of periodic and independent tasks with periods equal to deadlines ($D_i = T_i$), we have a sufficient schedulability condition under the assumption that the previous necessary condition (i.e. (5.1)) is satisfied (Dertouzos and Mok, 1989; Mok and Dertouzos, 1978):

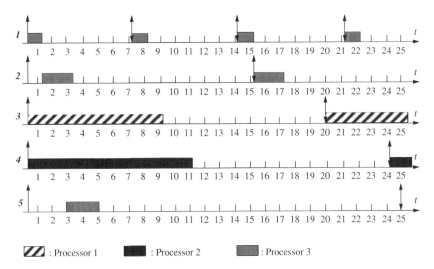

**Figure 5.4**  A set of five periodic tasks to illustrate the sufficient static-priority condition of schedulability

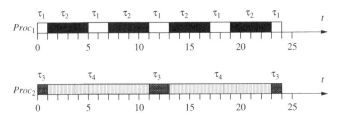

**Figure 5.5**  A set of four periodic tasks to illustrate the sufficient condition of schedulability based on the task period property

**Sufficient condition:**
Let $T'$ be the greatest common divider (GCD) of task periods $T_i$, $u_i$ (equal to $C_i/T_i$) be the processor utilization factor of task $T_i$, and $T''$ be the GCD of $T'$ and the products $T'u_i (i = 1, \ldots, n)$. One sufficient schedulability condition is that $T''$ must be an integer.

The example, shown in Figure 5.5, corresponds to a set of four periodic tasks $\tau_1 (r_0 = 0, C = 2, D = 6, T = 6)$, $\tau_2(r_0 = 0, C = 4, D = 6, T = 6)$, $\tau_3(r_0 = 0, C = 2, D = 2, T = 12)$ and $\tau_4(r_0 = 0, C = 20, D = 24, T = 24)$ to execute on two processors. The processor utilization factor is equal to 2 and the schedule length is equal to 24. $T'$, i.e. $GCD(T_i)$, is equal to 6 and $T''$ is equal to 1. This example illustrates the application of the previous sufficient condition under a processor utilization factor equal to 100% for the two processors.

As the previous condition is only sufficient (but not necessary), one could easily find task sets that do not respect the condition, but that have feasible schedules. For example, let us consider a set of four tasks $\{\tau_1(r_0 = 0, C = 1, D = 2, T = 2), \tau_2(r_0 = 0, C = 2, D = 4, T = 4), \tau_3(r_0 = 0, C = 2, D = 3, T = 3), \tau_4(r_0 = 0, C = 2, D = 6, T = 6)\}$. $GCD(T_i)$ is equal to 1, but $GCD_{i=1,\ldots,4}(T', T'u_i)$ cannot be computed because the products $Tu_i (i = 1, \ldots, 4)$ are not integers. Thus, the considered task set does not meet the sufficient condition. However this task set is schedulable by assigning the first two tasks to one processor and the other two to the other processor.

### 5.4.3 Schedulability condition based on proportional major cycle decomposition

This particular case is more a way to schedule on-line the task set than a schedulability condition. The major cycle is split into intervals corresponding to all the arrival times of tasks. Then the tasks are allocated to a processor for a duration proportional to its processor utilization. This way of building an execution sequence leads to the following condition (which is more complex) (Bertossi and Bonucelli, 1983):

**Sufficient and necessary condition:**
A set of periodic and independent tasks with periods equal to deadlines such that $u_i \geq u_{i+1}$ for $i \in [1, n-1]$ is schedulable on $m$ identical processors if and only if:

$$\text{Max} \left\{ \underset{j \in [1, m-1]}{\text{Max}} \left\{ \frac{1}{j} \sum_{i=1}^{j} u_i \right\}, \quad \frac{1}{m} \sum_{i=1}^{n} u_i \right\} \leq 1 \tag{5.3}$$

Let us consider a set of three tasks $\{\tau_1(r_0 = 0, C = 2, D = 3, T = 3), \tau_2(r_0 = 0, C = 2, D = 4, T = 4), \tau_3(r_0 = 0, C = 3, D = 6, T = 6)\}$ satisfying condition (5.3). Their respective processor utilization factors are $u_1 = 2/3$, $u_2 = 1/2$ and $u_3 = 1/2$. The necessary condition of schedulability (i.e. condition (5.1)) with two processors is quite satisfied since $U = 5/3 < 2$. The inequality of the previous necessary and sufficient condition is well verified: $\text{Max}\{\text{Max}\{(2/3), (7/12)\}, (5/6)\} \leq 1$. Consequently, the set of the three tasks is schedulable on the two processors taking into account the LCM of the periods, which is equal to 12. It is possible to obtain the schedule associated with the two processors by decomposing the time interval $[0, 12]$ into six subintervals corresponding to six release times of the three tasks, i.e. $\{0, 3, 4, 6, 8, 9, 12\}$. Then, a processor is assigned to each task during a period of time proportional to its processor utilization factor $u_i$ and to the time interval considered between two release times of tasks (Figure 5.6). During time interval $[0, 3]$, processors $Proc_1$ and $Proc_2$

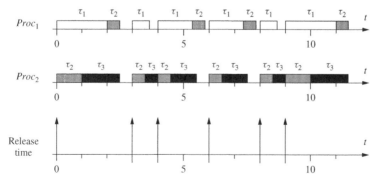

**Figure 5.6** Schedule of a set of three periodic tasks with deadlines equal to periods on two processors: $\{\tau_1(r_0 = 0, C = 2, D = 3, T = 3), \tau_2(r_0 = 0, C = 2, D = 4, T = 4), \tau_3(r_0 = 0, C = 3, D = 6, T = 6)\}$

are allocated to the three tasks as follows: $\tau_1$ is executed for $3 \times 2/3$ time units on $Proc_1$, $\tau_2$ is executed for $3 \times 1/2$ time units on $Proc_1$ and $Proc_2$, and $\tau_3$ is executed for $3 \times 1/2$ time units on $Proc_2$. The two processors are idle for $1/2$ time units. After that, the time interval $[3, 4]$ is considered, and so on. The drawback of this algorithm is that it can generate a prohibitive number of preemptions, leading to a high overhead at run-time.

## 5.5  Scheduling Algorithms

### 5.5.1  Earliest deadline first and least laxity first algorithms

Let us recall that EDF and LLF are optimal algorithms in the uniprocessor environment. We saw that the EDF algorithm was not optimal in the multiprocessor environment. Another interesting property related to the performance of EDF and LLF algorithms has been proven (Dertouzos and Mok, 1989; Nissanke, 1997):

> **Property:**
> A set of periodic tasks that is feasible with the EDF algorithm in a multiprocessor architecture is also feasible with the LLF algorithm.

The reciprocal of this property is not true. The LLF policy, which schedules the tasks according to their dynamic slack times, has a better behaviour than the EDF policy, which schedules tasks according to their dynamic response times, as shown in Figure 5.7 with a set of three periodic tasks $\tau_1(r_0 = 0, C = 8, D = 9, T = 9)$, $\tau_2(r_0 = 0, C = 2, D = 8, T = 8)$ and $\tau_3(r_0 = 0, C = 2, D = 8, T = 8)$ executed on two processors.

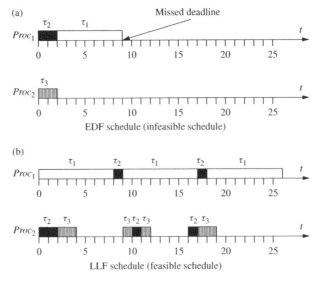

**Figure 5.7**  Example showing the better performance of the LLF algorithm compared to the EDF algorithm

## 5.5.2  Independent tasks with the same deadline

In the particular case of independent tasks having the same deadline and different release times, it is possible to use an optimal on-line algorithm proposed in McNaughtan (1959) and which functions according to the following principle:

**Algorithm:**
Let $C_+$ be the maximum of task computation times, $C_S$ be the sum of the computation times of already started tasks, and $m$ be the number of processors. The algorithm schedules all tasks on the time interval $[0, b]$, where $b = \text{Max}(C_+, \lceil C_S/m \rceil)$, while starting to allocate the tasks on the first processor and, when a task must finish after the bound $b$, it is allocated to the next processor. The allocation of the tasks is done according to decreasing order of computation times. This rule is applied for each new task activation.

Let us consider a set of tasks to execute on three processors once before the deadline $t = 10$. Each task is defined by its release and computation times: $\tau_1(r = 0, C = 6)$, $T_2(r = 0, C = 3)$, $\tau_3(r = 0, C = 3)$, $\tau_4(r = 0, C = 2)$, $\tau_5(r = 3, C = 5)$, $\tau_6(r = 3, C = 3)$. At time $t = 0$, the algorithm builds the schedule on the time interval $[0, 6]$ shown in Figure 5.8. Since $C_+$ is equal to 6, $C_S/3$ is equal to 4.66 (14/3) and thus the

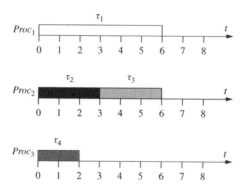

**Figure 5.8**  Schedule of independent tasks with the same deadline on three processors according to the algorithm given in McNaughtan (1959) (schedule built at time $t = 0$)

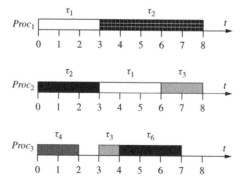

**Figure 5.9**  Schedule of independent tasks with the same deadline on three processors according to the algorithm given in McNaughtan (1959) (schedule built at time $t = 3$)

maximum bound of the interval is equal to 6. At time $t = 3$, $C_+$ is equal to 6, $C_S/3$ is equal to 7.3 (22/3) and thus the maximum bound of the interval is equal to 8. The schedule modified from time $t = 3$ is shown in Figure 5.9.

## 5.6  Conclusion

In this presentation of multiprocessor scheduling, we restricted the field of analysis: on the one hand to underline the difficulties of this problem (complexity and anomalies) and on the other hand to analyse centralized on-line preemptive scheduling on identical processors, which seems more adapted to real-time applications. In the field of multiprocessor scheduling, a lot of problems remain to be solved (Buttazzo, 1997; Ramamritham et al., 1990; Stankovic et al., 1995, 1998). New works that utilize techniques applied in other fields will perhaps bring solutions: fuzzy logic (Ishii et al., 1992), neural networks (Cardeira and Mammeri, 1994), and so on.

# 6

# Joint Scheduling of Tasks and Messages in Distributed Systems

This chapter and the next one discuss mechanisms to support real-time communications between remote tasks. This chapter deals with some techniques used in multiple access local area networks and Chapter 7 deals with packet scheduling when the communications are supported by packet-switching networks such as ATM or IP-based networks.

## 6.1  Overview of Distributed Real-Time Systems

The complexity of control and supervision of physical processes, the high number of data and events dealt with, the geographical dispersion of the processes and the need for robustness of systems on one hand, and the advent, for several years, on the market of industrial local area networks on the other, have all been factors which resulted in reconsidering real-time applications (Stankovic, 1992). Thus, an information processing system intended to control or supervise operations (for example, in a vehicle assembly factory, in a rolling mill, or in an aircraft) is generally composed of several nodes, which may be central processing units (computers or programmable automata), sensors, actuators, or peripherals of visualization and dialogue with operators. The whole of these nodes is interconnected by a network or by a set of interconnected networks (industrial local area networks, fieldbuses, etc.) (Pimentel, 1990). These systems are called distributed real-time systems (Kopetz, 1997; Stankovic, 1992).

Several aspects have to be distinguished when we speak about distributed systems. First of all, it is necessary to differentiate the physical (or hardware) allocation from the software allocation. The hardware allocation is obtained by using several central processing units which are interconnected by a communication subsystem. The taxonomy is more complex when it is about the software. Indeed, it is necessary to distinguish:

- data allocation (i.e. the assignment of data to appropriate nodes);

- processing allocation (i.e. the assignment of tasks to appropriate nodes);

- control allocation (i.e. the assignment of control roles to nodes for starting tasks; synchronizing tasks, controlling access to data, etc.).

Distributed real-time systems introduce new problems, in particular:

- computations based on timing constraints which refer to periods of time or to an absolute instant are likely to comprise too significant computational errors, and are therefore not credible, because of too large drifts between the clocks of the various nodes;

- the evolution of the various components of the physical process is observed with delays that differ from one node to another because of variable delays of communication;

- distributed real-time scheduling requires schedulability analysis (computations to guarantee time constraints of communicating tasks), and this analysis has to cope with clock drifts and communication delays;

- fault-tolerance is much more complex, which makes the problem of tolerating faults while respecting time constraints even more difficult.

In this book, we are only interested in the scheduling problem.

## 6.2  Task Allocation in Real-Time Distributed Systems

Task scheduling in distributed systems is dealt with at two levels: on the level of each processor (local scheduling), and on the level of the allocation of tasks to processors (global scheduling).

Local scheduling consists of assigning the processor to tasks, by taking into account their urgency and their importance. The mission of global scheduling is to guarantee the constraints of tasks by exploiting the processing capabilities of the various processors composing the distributed system (while possibly carrying out migrations of tasks). Thus, a local scheduling aims to answer the question of 'when to execute a task on the local processor, so as to guarantee the constraints imposed on this task?'. A global scheduling seeks to answer the question 'which is the node best adapted to execute a given task, so as to guarantee its constraints?'.

In distributed real-time applications, task allocation and scheduling are closely related: it is necessary to allocate the tasks to the set of processors so that local scheduling leads imperatively to the guarantee of the time constraints of the critical tasks. Local scheduling uses algorithms like those presented in the preceding chapters (i.e. rate monotonic, earliest deadline first, and so on). We are interested here in global scheduling, i.e. with allocation and migration of tasks, and with support for real-time communications.

The problem of allocating $n$ tasks to $p$ processors often consists in initially seeking a solution which respects the initial constraints as much as possible, and then to choose the best solution, if several solutions are found. The search for a task allocation must take into account the initial constraints of the tasks, and the support environment, as well as the criteria (such as maximum lateness, scheduling length, number of processors used) to optimize.

The tasks composing a distributed application can be allocated in a static or dynamic way to the nodes. In the first case, one speaks about static allocation; in the second, of dynamic allocation. In the first case, there cannot be any additional allocations of the tasks during the execution of the application; the allocation of the tasks is thus fixed at system initialization. In the second case, the scheduling algorithm chooses to place each task on the node capable of guaranteeing its time constraints, at the release time of the task.

Dynamic allocation algorithms make it possible to find a node where a new task will be executed. If a task allocated to a node must be executed entirely on the node which was chosen for it, one speaks about a distributed system 'without migration'; if a task can change node during its execution, one speaks about a distributed system 'with migration'. The migration of a task during its execution consists of transferring its context (i.e. its data, its processor registers, and so on), which continuously changes as the task is executed, and, if required, its code (i.e. the instructions composing the task program), which is invariable. To minimize the migration time of a task, the code of the tasks likely to migrate is duplicated on the nodes on which these tasks can be executed. Thus, in the case of migration, only the context of the task is transferred. Task migration is an important function in a global scheduling algorithm. It enables the evolution of the system to be taken into account by assigning, in a dynamic way, the load of execution of the tasks to the set of processors. In addition, dynamically changing the nodes executing tasks is a means of increasing the fault-tolerance of the system.

Many syntheses on task allocation techniques, in the case of non-real-time parallel or distributed systems, have been proposed in the literature. The reader can refer in particular to Eager et al. (1986) and Stankovic (1992). On the other hand, few works have studied task allocation in the case of real-time and distributed systems. The reader can find examples of analysis and experimentation of some task allocation methods in (Chu and Lan, 1987; Hou and Shin, 1992; Kopetz, 1997; Shih et al., 1989; Storch and Liu, 1993; Tia and Liu, 1995; Tindell et al., 1992). In the following, we assume that tasks are allocated to nodes, and we focus on techniques used to support real-time communications between tasks.

# 6.3   Real-Time Traffic

## 6.3.1   Real-time traffic types

In real-time distributed systems, two attributes are usually used to specify messages: end-to-end transfer delay and delay jitter:

- *End-to-end transfer delay* (or simply end-to-end delay) is the time between the emission of the first bit of a message by the transmitting end-system (source) and its reception by the receiving end-system (destination).

- *Delay jitter* (or simply jitter) is the variation of end-to-end transfer delay (i.e. the difference between the maximum and minimum values of transfer delay). It is a distortion of the inter-message arrival times compared to the inter-message times of the original transmission. This distortion is particularly damaging to multimedia traffic. For example, the playback of audio or video data may have a jittery or shaky quality.

In a way similar to tasks, one can distinguish three types of messages:

- Periodic (also called synchronous) messages are generated and consumed by periodic tasks, and their characteristics are similar to the characteristics of their respective source tasks. Adopting the notation used for periodic tasks, a periodic message $M_i$ is usually denoted by a 3-tuple $(T_i, L_i, D_i)$. This means that the instances of message $M_i$ are generated periodically with a period equal to $T_i$, the maximum length of $M_i$'s instances is $L_i$ bits, and each message instance must be delivered to its destination within $D_i$ time units. $D_i$ is also called end-to-end transfer delay bound (or deadline). Some applications (such as audio and video) require that jitter should be bounded. Thus a fourth parameter $J_i$ may be used to specify the jitter that should be guaranteed by the underlying network.

- Sporadic messages are generated by sporadic tasks. In general, a sporadic message $M_s$ may be characterized by a 5-tuple $(T_s, AT_s, I_s, L_s, D_s)$. The parameters $T_s$, $L_s$ and $D_s$ are the minimum inter-arrival time between instances of $M_s$, maximum length and end-to-end deadline of instances of $M_s$. $AT_s$ is the average inter-arrival time, where the average is taken over a time interval of length $I_s$.

- Aperiodic messages are generally generated by aperiodic tasks and they are characterized by their maximum length and end-to-end delay.

In addition to the previous parameters, which are similar to the ones associated with tasks, other parameters inherent to communication networks, such as message loss rate, may be specified in the case of real-time traffic.

## 6.3.2  End-to-end communication delay

Communication delay between two tasks placed on the same machine is often considered to be negligible. It is evaluated according to the machine instructions necessary to access a data structure shared by the communicating tasks (shared variables, queue, etc.). The communication delay between distant tasks (i.e. tasks placed on different nodes) is much more complex and more difficult to evaluate with precision. The methods of computation of the communication delay differ according to whether the nodes on which the communicating tasks are placed are directly connected — as is the case when the application uses a local area network with a bus, loop or star topology — or indirectly connected — as is the case when the application uses a meshed network. When the communicating nodes are directly connected, the communication delay between distant tasks can be split into several intermediate delays, as shown in Figure 6.1:

- A delay of crossing the upper layers within the node where the sending task is located ($d_1$). The upper layers include the application, presentation and transport layers of the OSI model when they are implemented.

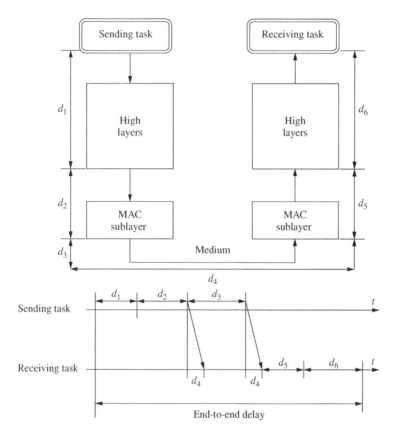

**Figure 6.1**  Components of end-to-end delay of communication between two tasks when tasks are allocated to nodes directly connected by a local area network

- A queuing delay in the medium access control (MAC) sublayer of the sending node ($d_2$). This queuing delay is the most difficult to evaluate.

- A delay of physical transmission of the message on the medium ($d_3$).

- A delay of propagation of a bit on the medium up to the receiving node ($d_4$).

- A delay of reception and waiting time in the MAC sublayer of the receiving node ($d_5$).

- A delay of crossing the upper layers in the node where the receiving task is located ($d_6$).

In order for a task to receive a message in time, it is necessary that the various intermediate delays ($d_1, \ldots, d_6$) are determined and guaranteed. The delays $d_1$ and $d_6$ do not depend on the network (or more exactly do not depend on the medium access protocol). The delay $d_5$ is often regarded as fixed and/or negligible, if the assumption is made that any received message is immediately passed to the upper layers. The delays $d_3$ and $d_4$ are easily computable. Transmission delay $d_3$ depends on the network bit rate and the length of the message. Delay $d_4$ depends on the length of the network. Delay

$d_2$ is directly related to the medium access control of the network. The upper bound of this delay is guaranteed by reserving the medium at the right time for messages. There is no single solution for this problem. The technique of medium reservation depends on the MAC protocol of the network used. We will reconsider this problem by taking examples of networks (see Section 6.4.3).

When the communicating tasks are allocated to nodes that are not directly connected, in a network such as ATM or the Internet, the end-to-end transfer delay is determined by considering the various communication delays along the path going from the sending node to the receiving node. The techniques of bandwidth reservation and scheduling of real-time messages are much more complex in this case. The next chapter will focus on these techniques in the case of packet-switching networks.

# 6.4  Message Scheduling

## 6.4.1  Problems of message scheduling

Distributed real-time applications impose time constraints on task execution, and these constraints are directly reflected on the messages exchanged between the tasks when they are placed on different nodes. The guarantee (or non-guarantee) of the time constraints of messages is directly reflected on those of tasks, because waiting for a message is equivalent to waiting for the acquisition of a resource by a task; if the message is not delivered in time, the time constraints of the task cannot be guaranteed.

In real-time applications, certain tasks can have hard time constraints and others not. Similarly, the messages exchanged between these tasks can have hard time constraints or not. For example, a message indicating an alarm must be transmitted and received with hard time constraints in order to be able to treat the cause of the alarm before it leads to a failure, whereas a file transfer does not generally require hard time constraints.

Communication in real-time systems has to be predictable, because unpredictable delays in the delivery of messages can adversely affect the execution of tasks dependent on these messages. If a message arrives at its destination after its deadline has expired, its value to the end application may be greatly reduced. In some circumstances messages are considered 'perishable', that is, are useless to the application if delayed beyond their deadline. These messages are discarded and considered lost. A message must be correct from the content point of view (i.e. it must contain a valid value), but also from the time point of view (i.e. it must be delivered in time). For example, a temperature measurement which is taken by a correct sensor, but which arrives two seconds later at a programmable logic controller (PLC) of regulation having a one-second cycle, is regarded as obsolete and therefore incorrect.

The support of distributed real-time applications requires communication protocols which guarantee that the communicating tasks will receive, within the deadlines, the messages which are intended to them. For messages with hard deadlines, the protocols must guarantee maximal transfer delays. For non-time-critical messages, the strategy of the protocols is 'best effort' (i.e. to minimize the transfer delay of messages and the number of late messages). However, the concept of 'best effort' must be used with some care in the case of real-time systems. For example, the loss of one image out of ten in the case of a video animation in a control room is often without consequence; on the other hand, the loss of nine images out of ten makes the supervision system useless for the human operators.

Guarantee of message time constraints requires an adequate scheduling of the messages according to the communication protocols used by the support network. Various works have been devoted to the consideration of the time constraints of messages in packet-switching networks and in multiple access local area networks. In the first category of networks, studies have primarily targeted multimedia applications (Kweon and Shin, 1996; Zheng et al., 1994). In the second category of networks, work has primarily concerned CSMA/CA (the access method used in particular by CAN networks; see Section 6.4.3) based networks, token bus, token ring, FDDI and FIP (Agrawal et al., 1993; Malcolm and Zhao, 1995; Sathaye and Strosnider, 1994; Yao, 1994; Zhao and Ramamritham, 1987).

As far as scheduling of real-time messages is considered, these two categories of networks present significant differences.

*1. Packet-switched networks*:

- Each node of task location connected to the network is regarded as a subscriber (or client) and does not know the protocols used inside the switching network.

- To transmit its data, each subscriber node establishes a connection according to a traffic contract specifying a certain quality of service (loss rate, maximum transfer delay, etc.). Subscriber nodes can neither enter into competition with each other, nor consult each other, to know which node can transmit data. A subscriber node addresses its requests to the network switch (an ATM switch or an IP router, for example) to which it is directly connected, and this switch (or router) takes care of the message transfer according to the negotiated traffic contract.

- The time constraints are entirely handled by the network switches (or routers), provided that each subscriber node negotiates a sufficient quality of service to take into account the characteristics of messages it wishes to transmit. Consequently, the resource reservation mechanisms used are implemented in the network switches (or routers) and not in the subscriber nodes.

*2. Multiple access local area networks (LAN)*

- The nodes connected to the network control the access to the medium via a MAC technique implemented on each node. Generally, a node obtains the right to access the shared medium either by competition, or by consultation (by using a token, for example) according to the type of MAC technique used by the LAN.

- Once a node has sent a frame on the medium, this frame is directly received by its recipient (obviously excepting the case of collision with other frames or the use of a network with interconnection equipment such as bridges).

- The nodes must be set up (in particular, by setting message or node priorities, token holding times, and so on) to guarantee message time constraints. Consequently, resource reservation mechanisms are implemented in the nodes supporting the tasks.

Techniques to take into account time constraints are similar, whether they are integrated above the MAC sublayer, in the case of LANs, or in the network switches, in the case of packet-switching networks. They rely on the adaptation of task scheduling algorithms (for instance EDF or RM algorithms). In this chapter we consider LANs and in the next, packet-switching networks.

## 6.4.2 Principles and policies of message scheduling

The scheduling of real-time messages aims to allocate the medium shared between several nodes in such a way that the time constraints of messages are respected. Message scheduling thus constitutes a basic function of any distributed real-time system. As we underlined previously, not all of the messages generated in a distributed real-time application are critical from the point of view of time. Thus, according to time constraints associated with the messages, three scheduling strategies can be employed:

- *Guarantee strategy* (or *deterministic strategy*): if messages are scheduled according to this strategy, any message accepted for transmission is sent by respecting its time constraints (except obviously in the event of failure of the communication system). This strategy is generally reserved for messages with critical time constraints whose non-observance can have serious consequences (as is the case, for example, in the applications controlling industrial installations or aircraft).

- *Probabilistic and statistical strategies*: in a probabilistic strategy, the time constraints of messages are guaranteed at a probability known in advance. Statistical strategy promises that no more than a specified fraction of messages will see performance below a certain specified value. With both strategies, the messages can miss their deadlines. These strategies are used for messages with hard time constraints whose non-observance does not have serious consequences (as is the case, for example, in multimedia applications such as teleconferencing).

- *Best-effort strategy*: no guarantee is provided for the delivery of messages. The communication system will try to do its best to guarantee the time constraints of the messages. This strategy is employed to treat messages with soft time constraints or without time constraints.

In a distributed real-time system, the three strategies can cohabit, to be able to meet various communication requirements, according to the constraints and the nature of the communicating tasks.

With the emergence of distributed real-time systems, new needs for scheduling appeared: it is necessary, at the same time, to guarantee the time constraints of the tasks and those of the messages. As messages have similar constraints (mainly deadlines) as tasks, the scheduling of real-time messages uses techniques similar to those used in the scheduling of tasks.

Whereas tasks can, in general, accept preemption without corrupting the consistency of the results that they elaborate, the transmission of a message does not admit preemption. If the transmission of a message starts, all the bits of the message must be transmitted, otherwise the transmission fails. Thus, some care must be taken to apply task scheduling algorithms to messages:

- one has to consider only non-preemptive algorithms;

- one has to use preemptive algorithms with the proviso that transmission delays of messages are lower than or equal to the basic time unit of allocation of the medium to nodes;

- one has to use preemptive algorithms with the proviso that long messages are segmented (by the sending node) in small packets and reassembled (by the receiving node). The segmentation and reassembly functions must be carried out by a layer above the MAC sublayer; traditionally, these functions concern the transport layer.

Some communication protocols provide powerful mechanisms to take into account time constraints. This is the case, in particular, of FDDI and token bus protocols, which make it possible to easily treat periodic messages. Other, more general, protocols like CSMA/CD require additional mechanisms to deal with time constraints. Consequently, scheduling, and therefore the adaptation of task scheduling algorithms to messages, are closely related to the type of time constraints (in particular, whether messages are periodic or aperiodic) and the type of protocol (in particular, whether the protocol guarantees a bounded waiting time or not). The reader eager to look further into the techniques of message scheduling can refer to the synthesis presented in Malcolm and Zhao (1995). In the following section, we treat the scheduling of a set of messages, and consider three basically different types of protocols (token bus, FIP and CAN). The protocols selected here are the basis of many industrial LANs.

## 6.4.3 Example of message scheduling

We consider a set of periodic messages with hard time constraints where each message must be transmitted once each interval of time equal to its period. We want to study the scheduling of these messages in the case of three networks: token bus, FIP and CAN. Let us first briefly present the networks we use in this example and in Exercise 6.1. Our network presentation focuses only on the network mechanisms used for message scheduling.

### Overview of token bus, FDDI, CAN and FIP networks

*Token bus*    In the medium access control of the token bus, the set of active nodes is organized in a logical ring (or virtual ring). The configuration of a logical ring consists of determining, for each active node, the address of the successor node on the logical ring. Figure 6.2 shows an example of a logical ring composed of nodes 2, 4, 7 and 6. Once the logical ring is set up, the right of access to the bus (i.e. to transmit data) is reserved, at a given moment, for only one node: it is said that this node has the right to transmit. This right is symbolized by the possession of a special frame called a *token*. The token is transmitted from node to node as long as there are at least two nodes in the logical ring. When a node receives the token, it transmits its frames

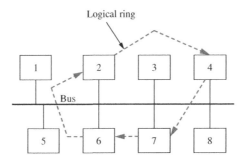

**Figure 6.2**   Example of a logical ring

without exceeding a certain fixed amount of time (called *token holding time*) and then transmits the token to its successor on the logical ring. If a node has no more data to transmit and its token holding time is not yet exceeded, it releases the token (ISO, 1990; Stallings, 1987, 2000).

The token bus can function with priorities (denoted 6, 4, 2 and 0; 6 being the highest priority and 0 the lowest) or without priorities. The principle of access control of the bus, with priorities, is the following:

- at network initialization, the following parameters are set:

  - a token holding time (THT), which indicates the amount of time each node can transmit its frames each time it receives the token for transmitting its data of priority 6 (this time is sometimes called synchronous allocation),

  - three counters $TRT_4$, $TRT_2$ and $TRT_0$. Counter $TRT_4$ (token rotation time for priority 4) limits the transmission time of frames with priority 4, according to the effective time taken by the current token rotation time. Counters $TRT_2$ and $TRT_0$ have the same significance as $TRT_4$ for priorities 2 and 0.

- Each node uses a counter (TRT) to measure the token rotation time. When any node receives the token:

  - It stores the current value of TRT in a variable (let us call it $V$), resets TRT and starts it.

  - It transmits its data of priority 6, for an amount of time no longer than the value of its THT.

  - Then, the node can transmit data of lower priorities (respecting the order of the priorities) if the token is received in advance compared to the expected time. It can transmit data of priority $p$ ($p = 4, 2, 0$) as long as the following condition is satisfied: $V + \sum_{i>p} t_i < TRT_p \cdot t_i$ indicates the time taken by the data transmission of priority $i$.

  - It transmits the token to its successor on the logical ring.

- When the token bus is used without priorities, only parameter THT is used to control access to the bus.

| 1 or $m$ bytes | 1 byte | 1 byte | 2 or 6 bytes | 2 or 6 bytes | $n \geq 0$ bytes | 4 bytes | 1 byte |
|---|---|---|---|---|---|---|---|
| Preamble | Start delimiter | Frame control | Destination address | Source address | Data | CRC | End sequence |

**Figure 6.3**   Format of token bus frame

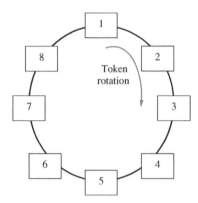

**Figure 6.4**   Simplified architecture of FDDI network

Figure 6.3 shows the format of the token bus frame.

It is worth noting that the token bus protocol is the basis of some industrial local area networks like MAP (Manufacturing Automation Protocol) (MAP, 1987) and Profibus (PROcess FIeldBUS) (Deutsche Institut für Normung, 1991).

***FDDI network***    FDDI (Fibre Distributed Data Interface) is a network with a ring topology (Figure 6.4). The access to the medium is controlled by a token. The token is passed from node to node in the order of the physical ring. In FDDI, the logical successor of a node is also its physical successor. No specific procedure is required to create and maintain the ring in the case of FDDI. The configuration of FDDI is similar to that of token bus:

- A common value of a parameter called TTRT (Target Token Rotation Time) is used by all the nodes.

- Each node has a fixed amount of time to transmit data at each round of the token (these data are called synchronous data and correspond to the data of priority 6 in the case of the token bus).

- A node can transmit asynchronous data (these data have priorities ranging between 0 and 7 and they correspond to the data of priorities 4 to 0 in the case of the token bus), if the current token rotation time is less than the value of the TTRT.

***CAN***    CAN (Controller Area Network) was originally designed to support communications in vehicles (ISO, 1994a). In CAN, the nodes do not have addresses and they reach the bus via the CSMA/CA (Carrier Sense Multiple Access with Collision Avoidance) access technique. Any object (e.g. a temperature or a speed) exchanged on the

CAN medium has a unique identifier. The identifier contained in a frame defines the level of priority of the frame: the smaller the identifier is, the higher the frame priority is. The objects can be exchanged between nodes in a periodic or aperiodic way, or according to the consumer's request.

The arbitration of access to the medium is made bit by bit. A bit value of 0 is dominant and a bit value of 1 is recessive. In the event of simultaneous transmissions, the bus conveys a 0 whenever there is at least one node which transmits a bit 0. Two or several nodes can start to transmit simultaneously. As long as nodes transmit bits with the same value, they continue transmitting (no node loses access to the medium). Whenever a node transmits a bit 1 and receives at the same time a bit 0, it stops transmitting and the nodes transmitting bit 0 continue transmitting. Consequently, in the event of simultaneous transmissions, the node which emits the object whose identifier is the smallest obtains the right to transmit its entire frame. For this reason it is said that CAN is based on access to the medium with priority and non-destructive resolution of collisions. Figure 6.5 gives an example of bus arbitration.

Listening on the bus to detect collisions imposes a transmission delay of a bit that is higher than or equal to twice the round trip propagation delay over the entire medium. As a consequence, the bit rate of a CAN network depends on the length of the medium: the shorter the network, the higher the bit rate.

Figure 6.6 shows the format of a CAN frame.

***FIP network*** FIP (Factory Instrumentation Protocol), also called WorldFIP, is a network for the interconnection of sensors, actuators and automata (Afnor, 1990; Cenelec, 1997; Pedro and Burns, 1997). A FIP network is based on a centralized structure in

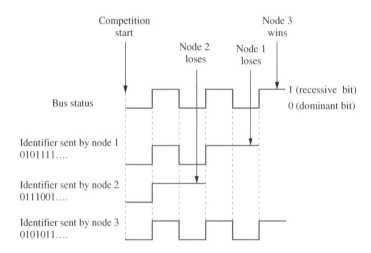

**Figure 6.5** Example of bus arbitration in a CAN network

| 1 bit | 12 bits | 6 bits | 0–8 bytes | 15 + 1 bits | 2 bits | 7 bits | ≥ 3 bits |
|---|---|---|---|---|---|---|---|
| Start of frame | Arbitration field (Identifier + 1 bit) | Control | Data | CRC and CRC delimiter | ACK | End of frame | Interframe |

**Figure 6.6** CAN frame format

which a node, called the *bus arbitrator*, gives the medium access right to the other nodes. FIP is based on the producer/distributor/consumer model in which the objects (variables or messages) exchanged on the network are produced by nodes called *producers* and consumed by other nodes called *consumers*.

Each object has a unique identifier. The objects can be exchanged, between producers and consumers, in a periodic or aperiodic way, under the control of the bus arbitrator. FIP allows the exchange of aperiodic objects only when there remains spare time after the periodic objects have been exchanged. According to the periods of consumption of the objects, the application designer defines a static table known as the *bus arbitrator table*, which indicates the order in which the objects must be exchanged on the bus.

In a FIP network, each identified object is assigned a buffer in the object producer node. This buffer (called the production buffer) contains the last produced value of the object. A buffer (called the consumption buffer) is also associated with each object, with each node consuming this object. This buffer contains the last value of the object conveyed by the network. By using its table, the bus arbitrator broadcasts a frame containing an object identifier, then the node of production recognizes the identifier and broadcasts the contents of the production buffer associated with the identifier. Then the broadcast value is stored in all the consumption buffers of the various consumers of the broadcast identifier. Figure 6.7 summarizes the exchange principle of a FIP network, Figure 6.8 shows the format of FIP frames, and Figure 6.9 gives an example of the bus arbitrator table.

The principle of communication of FIP differs from the other networks especially in the following ways, which are significant for guaranteeing upper bounds on the communication delays:

- The sender (i.e. the producer) does not ask for the transmission of an object (as in the case of CAN or token bus), it waits until it is requested by the bus arbitrator

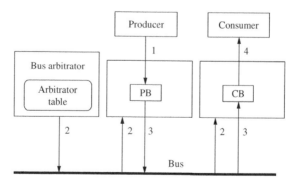

1  Production of an object value.
2  Transmission of an identifier frame called ID-Dat frame.
3  Transmission of an object value frame called RP-Dat frame. The object value is then copied by consumer nodes.
4  Consumer reads the object value.

PB: Production buffer   CB: Consumption buffer

**Figure 6.7**  Basic exchanges on FIP network

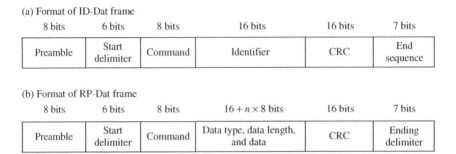

Figure 6.8 FIP frame formats

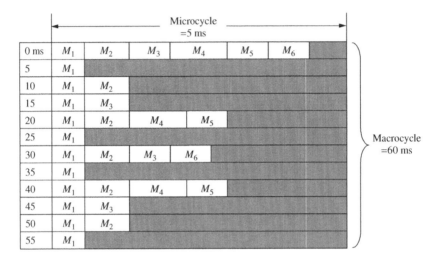

**Figure 6.9** Bus arbitrator table for the set of messages defined in Table 6.1

to transmit a value of an object. The delay between the time when a new value is written in the production buffer (this moment corresponds to the time when a message arrives in the MAC sublayer of the other two networks) and the time when the value of this object is received by the consumer depends on the table of the bus arbitrator.

• In CAN and token bus networks, a message submitted by the sender to the MAC sublayer is removed from the queue and transmitted on the medium. When the queue is empty, the MAC sublayer cannot transmit any more. In FIP, the principle is completely different. The interface (where the production buffers are located) always answers the request of the bus arbitrator by sending the value that is present in the production buffer. Consequently, the same value can be received several times by a consumer, if the broadcasting request period is smaller than the production

**Table 6.1** Example of a set of periodic messages

| Message | Period (ms) | Length (bytes) |
|---------|-------------|----------------|
| $M_1$ | 5 | 2 |
| $M_2$ | 10 | 4 |
| $M_3$ | 15 | 4 |
| $M_4$ | 20 | 8 |
| $M_5$ | 20 | 4 |
| $M_6$ | 30 | 4 |

period. Moreover, the value contained in the production buffer can be invalid (i.e. non-fresh) if the producer does not deposit the values in the buffer during the production period which was fixed to it.

### Solution for message scheduling

Let us consider the set of messages described in Table 6.1. We chose messages of small sizes in order to avoid message segmentation. Eight bytes is to the maximum size of message authorized by CAN; the other networks make it possible to convey longer messages. To simplify computations, we suppose that the three selected networks have the same bit rate, equal to 1 Mb/s, and that the propagation delay on the physical medium is negligible.

*Transmission delay computation*    To schedule tasks, it is necessary to know their execution times. To schedule messages, it is necessary to know their transmission delays. The transmission delay of a message depends on its size, the network bit rate, the length of the network, the format of the frames of the network, and the protocol of the network. We note $d_N(m)$ the transmission delay of message $m$ on network $N$ (where $N$ = token bus, FIP or CAN).

For token bus, the transmission delay of a message of $n$ bytes is equal to $96 + 8n$ μs, by considering that the node addresses are coded on two bytes and that only one byte is used as frame preamble (see Figure 6.3). It is considered that the inter-frame time is null. The transmission delay of a token is equal to $96$ μs.

For CAN, the transmission delay of a message of $n$ bytes is equal to $47 + 8n + \lfloor (34 + 8n)/4 \rfloor$ μs. $\lfloor x \rfloor$ ($x \geq 0$) denotes the largest integer less than or equal to $x$. This value is explained in the following way: the length of a frame at MAC level is equal to $47 + 8n$ bits (see Figure 6.6). Whenever a transmitter detects five consecutive bits (including stuffing bits) of identical value in the bitstream to be transmitted, it automatically inserts a complementary bit which is deleted by the receiver; this is the concept of bit stuffing. The stuffing mechanism does not take account of the fields: CRC (cyclic redundancy check) delimiter, ACK (acknowledgement) and frame end. Consequently, the maximum number of bits inserted by this mechanism is equal to $\lfloor (34 + 8n)/4 \rfloor$.

In FIP, one distinguishes the identified objects and the messages. The term *message* used in this example does not indicate a message within the meaning of FIP. A message transmitted by a task corresponds to an identified object of FIP. For FIP, the

**Table 6.2**   Message transmission delay according to network

| Message | Transmission delay ($\mu$s) | | |
|---------|-------------------|-------------|------------|
|         | $d_{\text{token bus}}$ | $d_{\text{FIP}}$ | $d_{\text{CAN}}$ |
| $M_1$   | 112 | 178 | 75  |
| $M_2$   | 128 | 194 | 95  |
| $M_3$   | 128 | 194 | 95  |
| $M_4$   | 160 | 226 | 135 |
| $M_5$   | 128 | 194 | 95  |
| $M_6$   | 128 | 194 | 95  |

transmission delay of a message of $n$ bytes is equal to $122 + 2\text{TR} + 8n$ $\mu$s, which is obtained by adding a transmission delay of a ID-Dat frame (61 bits) which conveys the identifier of the object to be sent, the transmission delay of a response frame RP-Dat ($61 + 8n$ bits) which contains the value of the object, and twice the turnaround time (TR). TR is the time which separates the end of reception of a frame and the beginning of transmission of the subsequent frame. Its value lies between $10\,\mu$s and $70\,\mu$s for a bit rate of 1 Mb/s. We fix here TR to $20\,\mu$s. In an ID-Dat frame, the identifier is represented by two bytes (see Figure 6.8a). In an RP-Dat frame, $n$ payload bytes plus two bytes are added by the application layer; these bytes contain the length and the type of the data (see Figure 6.8b).

The transmission delays of the messages of Table 6.1 are given in Table 6.2.

### Solution for message scheduling using token bus network

When a technique of medium access is based on the timed token (like the technique of the token bus or FDDI), the guarantee of time constraints of messages depends on the manner of fixing the parameters of operation of the network (particularly the amounts of time allocated to the nodes and the maximum token rotation time). A lot of work was devoted to FDDI and significant results were proved, in particular concerning the maximum queuing time of messages and the condition of guarantee of time constraints according to message periods and to the parameters of operation of the network (Agrawal et al., 1993; Chen et al., 1992; Johnson, 1987; Sevcik and Johnson, 1987; Zhang and Burns, 1995). The token bus was not the subject of thorough works, which is why the results obtained for FDDI are adapted to the token bus.

To be able to use correctly the results obtained for FDDI, one must fix a maximum value, TRTmax, for the three counters $\text{TRT}_4$, $\text{TRT}_2$ and $\text{TRT}_0$ of all the nodes of a logical ring. The TRTmax value thus fixed plays the same role as the TTRT in FDDI. No node can transmit frames of priority 4, 2 or 0 if counter TRT has reached TRTmax. Thus TTRT is replaced by TRTmax in the formulas suggested for FDDI. In addition, priority 6 is associated with the periodic messages and the other priorities with the aperiodic messages.

*1. Medium allocation techniques*   The main techniques of medium allocation to periodic messages, in the case of FDDI, are presented in Agrawal et al. (1993) and Zhang and Burns (1995). We study here two of the suggested techniques:

- Full length allocation scheme:

$$Q_i = C_i \qquad\qquad (6.1)$$

$Q_i$ indicates the synchronous allocation time for node $i$, and $C_i$ the transmission delay of its message. With this strategy, each node uses, at each token round, an amount of time which enables it to transmit completely its message (i.e. without segmentation). In general, this technique is usable for short messages (like those treated in this example). The existence of messages requiring significant transmission delays can lead to the non-guarantee of the time constraints of messages having small periods, even under low global load.

- Normalized proportional allocation scheme:

$$Q_i = \left(\frac{\text{TTRT} - \alpha}{U}\right) \cdot \left(\frac{C_i}{T_i}\right) \qquad U = \sum_{i=1}^{n} \frac{C_i}{T_i} \qquad (6.2)$$

$T_i$ indicates the period of the message of node $N_i$, $\alpha$ indicates the time that the nodes cannot use to transmit their periodic messages (this time includes, in particular, the time taken by the token to make a full rotation of the ring, and the time reserved explicitly for the transfer of aperiodic messages).

***2. Solution based on the full length allocation scheme***    Let us suppose that the message $M_i$ $(i = 1, \ldots, 6)$ is transmitted by node number $i$. The synchronous allocation time of FDDI corresponds to the token holding time in the token bus protocol. Consequently, the token holding time of node $N_i$ ($\text{THT}_i$) is defined in the following way: $\text{THT}_i = d_{\text{token bus}}(M_i)_{(i=1,\ldots,6)}$.

One can easily show that the set of considered messages (whose transmission delays are given in Table 6.2) is feasible if one takes $1360\,\mu\text{s}$ as the value of TRTmax (this value corresponds to the sum of allocation times required by the six nodes plus six times the transmission token time). As the minimal period is 5 ms, the selected TRTmax makes it possible for each node to receive the token at least once during each interval of time equal to its period. The maximum value of TRTmax which makes it possible to guarantee the time constraints of the six messages is given by applying the theorem shown in Johnson (1987), which stipulates that the maximum bound of the token rotation time on an FDDI ring is equal to twice the value of the TTRT. By applying this theorem to our example, it is necessary that TRTmax be lower than half of the minimal period of the set of the considered messages. Thus all the values of TRTmax ranging between $1360\,\mu\text{s}$ and $2500\,\mu\text{s}$ make it possible to guarantee the message time constraints under the condition that no node other than those that transmit the six considered messages can have a value of THT higher than 0.

***3. Solution based on the normalized proportional allocation scheme***    We suppose here that one does not explicitly allocate time for aperiodic messages and that only the nodes which transmit the messages $M_1$ to $M_6$ have non-null token holding time. The application of formula (6.2) to the case of the token bus results in replacing $\alpha$ by $n \cdot \Im$ (where $n$ is the maximum number of nodes being able to form part of the logical ring and $\Im$, the transmission delay of the token between a node and its successor) and TTRT by TRTmax. Thus, token holding times assigned to the six nodes are computed in the following way:

$$\text{THT}_i = \left(\frac{\text{TRTmax} - n \cdot \Im}{U}\right) \cdot \left(\frac{d_{\text{token bus}}(M_i)}{T_i}\right), \qquad (i = 1, \ldots, 6) \qquad (6.3)$$

If we consider that the logical ring is made up of only the six nodes which transmit the six messages considered in this example, and there is no segmentation of messages, it is necessary to choose the amounts of times assigned to the nodes such that $\text{THT}_i \geq d_{\text{token bus}}(M_i)$, $i = 1, \ldots, 6$. That leads to fix TRTmax such as:

$$\left(\frac{\text{TRTmax} - 576}{U}\right) \cdot \left(\frac{d_{\text{token bus}}(M_i)}{T_i}\right) \geq d_{\text{token bus}}(M_i), \qquad (i = 1, \ldots, 6) \qquad (6.4)$$

As $U$ is equal to 6.24%, a value of TRTmax equal to $2448\,\mu s$ is sufficient to satisfy inequality (6.4). Thus, the token holding times of the nodes are fixed as follows:

$$\begin{aligned}
\text{THT}_1 &= 672\,\mu s & \text{THT}_2 &= 384\,\mu s & \text{THT}_3 &= 256\,\mu s \\
\text{THT}_4 &= 240\,\mu s & \text{THT}_5 &= 192\,\mu s & \text{THT}_6 &= 128\,\mu s
\end{aligned}$$

In consequence TRTmax should be fixed at $2448\,\mu s$ ($2448 = 576 + \sum \text{THT}_i$) when the network is used only by the six nodes. If other nodes can use the network, the value of TRTmax should be fixed according to Johnson's (1987) theorem previously mentioned (i.e. TRTmax must be lower than or equal to half of the minimal period). Consequently, all the values of TRTmax ranging between $2448\,\mu s$ and $2500\,\mu s$ make it possible to guarantee the time constraints of messages without segmentation.

### Solution for message scheduling using CAN

One of the techniques of scheduling periodic messages used in the case of networks having global priorities (as is the case of CAN) derives from the rate monotonic algorithm described in Chapter 2. As the priority of a message is deduced from its identifier, the application of the RM algorithm to the scheduling of periodic messages consists of fixing the identifiers of the messages according to their periods. For the sake of simplicity, the messages considered here are short and thus do not require segmentation and reassembly to take into account preemption, an aspect that is inherent in RM. When two messages have the same period, the choice of the identifiers results in privileging one of the messages (this choice can be made in a random way, as we do it here, or on the basis of information specific to the application). The assignment of the identifiers, $Id()$, to the messages can be done, for example, as follows:

$$Id(M_1) = 1, Id(M_2) = 2, Id(M_3) = 3, Id(M_4) = 5, Id(M_5) = 4, Id(M_6) = 6$$

In an informal way, one can show the feasibility of the set of the considered messages in the following way: as the sum of transmission delays of the six messages ($M_1$ to $M_6$) is equal to $590\,\mu s$, even if all the messages appeared with the minimal period (which is equal to $5\,ms$), they are transmitted by respecting their deadlines. Indeed, when a message $M_1$ arrives, it waits, at most, $\Delta t_1$ before being transmitted. $\Delta t_1 \leq 135\,\mu s$, because the transmission delay of the longest message which can block $M_1$ is $135\,\mu s$ (which corresponds to $M_4$ transmission delay). Thus, message $M_1$ is always transmitted before the end of its arrival period. When a message $M_2$ arrives, it waits, at most, $\Delta t_2$. $\Delta t_2 \leq 135 + 75\,\mu s$, which corresponds to the situation where a message $M_4$ is being transmitted when $M_2$ arrives. Then a message $M_1$ arrives while $M_4$ is still being transmitted and therefore $M_1$ is transmitted before $M_2$ because it has higher priority. One can then apply the same argument for messages $M_3$, $M_4$ and $M_5$. Message $M_6$, which has the lowest priority waits, at most, $495\,\mu s$. In consequence, all the messages are transmitted respecting their periods.

*Solution for message scheduling using FIP network*

The solution consists in building a bus arbitrator table which acts as a scheduling table of messages computed off-line. The bus arbitrator table is built by taking into account the minimal period of the messages — called the microcycle — which is equal to 5 ms for this example, and the least common multiple of the periods — called the macrocycle — which is equal to 60 ms for this example. The bus arbitrator table is a sufficient condition to guarantee the schedulability of the set of considered messages. Figure 6.9 shows a bus arbitrator table which makes it possible to guarantee the time constraints of the considered example. In the chosen bus arbitrator, during the first macrocycle the six messages are exchanged, during the second microcycle only message $M_1$ is exchanged, and so on. When the twelfth microcycle is finished, the bus arbitrator starts a new cycle and proceeds according to the first microcycle.

# 6.5 Conclusion

Real-time applications are becoming increasingly large and complex, thus requiring the use of distributed systems to guarantee time constraints and to reinforce dependability. However, the use of distributed systems leads to new problems that should be solved. Among these problems is real-time message scheduling. This problem is complex because of the diversity of the communication protocols to consider and it is in full evolution. The existing communication protocols undergo extensions and modifications to integrate real-time scheduling and guarantee timely delivery of messages.

This chapter has studied the scheduling problem when multiple-access local area networks are used to support communications. Only the medium access control (MAC) level has been considered. Thus, other aspects have to be considered to take into account the time constraints of messages at all levels of communication (from the physical up to the application layer). We have limited our study to the MAC level, because handling message time constraints at higher layers is complex and is achieved by considering multiple factors: operating system kernel, multitasking, the number of layers under consideration, the protocols used at each layer, etc. In the next chapter, we will see the techniques used to guarantee time constraints when packet-switching networks are used.

Finally, let us note the development of some prototypes of distributed real-time systems such as: MARS (Damm et al., 1989), SPRING (Stankovic and Ramamriham, 1989; Stankovic et al., 1999), MARUTI (Levi et al., 1989), DELTA-4 XPA (Verissimo et al., 1991), ARTS (Tokuda and Mercer, 1989), CHAOS (Schwan et al., 1987) and DARK (Scoy et al., 1992). These systems integrate the real-time scheduling of tasks and messages.

# 6.6 Exercise 6.1: Joint Scheduling of Tasks and Messages

## 6.6.1 Informal specification of problem

In this exercise, we are interested in joint scheduling of tasks and messages in a distributed real-time application. Let us take again the example of the application composed of five tasks which have precedence constraints, as presented in Chapter 3 (see Section 3.1.3, Figure 3.5, Table 3.2). The tasks are supposed to be scheduled by the earliest deadline first algorithm. The initial values of the parameters of the tasks are the same as those presented in Section 3.1.3, except that they are declared in microseconds and not in unspecified time units, as previously (see Table 6.3).

The tasks are assigned to three nodes, $N_1$, $N_2$ and $N_3$ (see Figure 6.10) interconnected by a network, which can be a token bus, a CAN or a FIP network. At each execution end, task $\tau_1$ transmits a message $M_1$ of two bytes to task $\tau_4$, task $\tau_3$ transmits a message $M_2$ of eight bytes to task $\tau_5$ and task $\tau_4$ transmits a message $M_3$ of four bytes to task $\tau_5$.

We suppose that:

- The propagation delay on the medium is negligible (i.e. the delay $d_4$ presented in Figure 6.1 is null).

- The network used is reliable (there are no transmission errors) and has a bit rate of 1 Mb/s.

- The delay of crossing (i.e. message processing and queuing) upper layers at the transmitter or the receiver and the waiting delay in the receiver MAC sublayer are negligible (i.e. the delays $d_1$, $d_5$ and $d_6$ presented in Figure 6.1 are null). In other

**Table 6.3**  Example of a task set with precedence constraints

| | Initial task parameters | | |
|---|---|---|---|
| **Task** | $r_i$ ($\mu$s) | $C_i$ ($\mu$s) | $d_i$ ($\mu$s) |
| $\tau_1$ | 0 | 1000 | 5000 |
| $\tau_2$ | 5000 | 2000 | 7000 |
| $\tau_3$ | 0 | 2000 | 5000 |
| $\tau_4$ | 0 | 1000 | 10 000 |
| $\tau_5$ | 0 | 3000 | 12 000 |

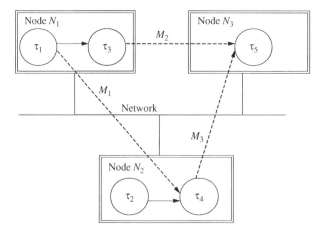

**Figure 6.10**  Example of allocation of tasks of a real-time application

words, all the local processing delays related to messages are negligible. Only the transmission and transmitter MAC queuing delays are significant here.

- A task can begin its execution only when all the messages it uses are received and it can transmit messages only at the end of its execution.

- The clocks used by the three nodes are perfectly synchronized.

**Q1**   Taking as a starting point the preceding example (see Section 6.4.3), compute the transmission delay of the messages $M_1$, $M_2$ and $M_3$, for the three networks presented previously (token bus, CAN and FIP).

**Q2**   Task parameters ($r_i^*$ and $d_i^*$), obtained after the modification of the initial task parameters ($r_i$ and $d_i$) in order to take into account local precedence constraints, must be modified to take into account the delays of communication between tasks assigned to remote nodes. What are the new values of the task parameters?

**Q3**   What is the maximum communication delay acceptable for each message ($M_1$, $M_2$ and $M_3$), so that all the task deadlines are met?

**Q4**   Suppose that the five tasks are periodic and have the same period, equal to 12 ms, and that the values of the release times and deadlines of the $k$th period are deduced from the values of Table 6.3 by adding $(k - 1) \times 12$ ms. The communication delays are assumed to be guaranteed by the network. Verify the feasibility of the task set.

**Q5**   Give a solution guaranteeing the timing constraints of the messages when the token bus is used with full allocation scheme, assuming that the logical ring is composed only of the three nodes $N_1$, $N_2$ and $N_3$.

**Q6**   Give a solution guaranteeing the timing constraints of the messages when CAN is used.

**Q7**   Give a solution guaranteeing the timing constraints of the messages when a FIP network is used.

## 6.6.2   Answers

**Q1**   The transmission delays (Table 6.4) are computed using the same assumptions as in the preceding example (see Section 6.4.3): turnaround time equal to 20 μs for FIP and null inter-frame delay for the token bus, etc.

**Q2**   Task parameters: when the earliest deadline first algorithm is used to schedule a set of tasks on a single processor, the initial parameters of the tasks are modified in the following way (Chetto et al., 1990) (see Section 3.1.2):

$$r_i^* = \text{Max}\{r_i, (r_j^* + C_j)\}, \qquad \tau_j \rightarrow \tau_i \tag{6.5}$$

$$d_i^* = \text{Min}\{d_i, (d_j^* - C_j)\}, \qquad \tau_i \rightarrow \tau_j \tag{6.6}$$

When a task $\tau_i$ precedes a task $\tau_j$ ($\tau_i \rightarrow \tau_j$) and, moreover, task $\tau_i$ sends, at the end of its execution, a message to task $\tau_j$, then the parameter $r_j$ must take

**Table 6.4**   Message transmission delay according to network used

| Message | Length | Transmission delay ($\mu$s) | | |
|---------|--------|-----------------------------|---|---|
|         | (bytes) | $d_{\text{token bus}}$ | $d_{\text{CAN}}$ | $d_{\text{FIP}}$ |
| $M_1$ | 2 | 112 | 75 | 178 |
| $M_2$ | 8 | 160 | 135 | 226 |
| $M_3$ | 4 | 128 | 95 | 194 |

into account the communication delay between $\tau_i$ and $\tau_j$ (because, with the assumption of this exercise, a task can begin its execution only if it has received all messages). To take into account, at the same time, precedence constraints between tasks allocated to the same node or to different nodes and exchanges of messages, we modify the rule of computation of $r_i^*$ proposed by Chetto et al. (1990) by the following rule:

$$r_i^* = \text{Max}\{r_i, (r_j^* + C_j + \Delta_j^i)\}, \qquad \tau_j \to \tau_i \qquad (6.7)$$

$\Delta_j^i$ represents the maximum delay of communication between tasks $\tau_j$ and $\tau_i$. If tasks $\tau_i$ and $\tau_j$ are allocated to the same node, $\Delta_j^i$ is equal to zero (it is supposed that the local communication delay is negligible). Under the previous assumptions, $\Delta_j^i$ corresponds to the sum of the delays $d_2$ and $d_3$ (Figure 6.1). It should be noted that the transformation of the parameter $r_i^*$ by rule (6.7) is deduced from the one given by rule (6.5), by adding the communication delay to the execution time of the tasks which precede task $\tau_i$. Then, after application of equations (6.6) and (6.7), we obtain the new task parameters presented in Table 6.5.

It should be noted that the parameter transformation rules (6.6) and (6.7) suppose that there is one task precedence graph and that all the tasks are in this graph. If this is not the case, i.e. when there are several graphs of precedence or independent tasks, one needs other rules for adapting the task parameters.

**Q3**   Upper bounds of communication delays. By taking again the computed values in Table 6.5, we can determine the upper bounds of the communication delays for the three messages. The tasks that depend on the network are $\tau_4$ and $\tau_5$. Thus a timing fault (i.e. a missing deadline) of the task $\tau_5$ (respectively $\tau_4$)

**Table 6.5**   Task parameters taking into account task allocation to nodes, and precedence constraints

| Task | $C_1$ ($\mu$s) | $r_i^*$ ($\mu$s) | $d_i^*$ ($\mu$s) |
|------|----------------|------------------|------------------|
| $\tau_1$ | 1000 | 0 | 3000 |
| $\tau_2$ | 2000 | 5000 | 7000 |
| $\tau_3$ | 2000 | 1000 | 5000 |
| $\tau_4$ | 1000 | $\text{Max}\{7000, 1000 + \Delta_4^1\}$ | 9000 |
| $\tau_5$ | 3000 | $\text{Max}\{3000 + \Delta_5^3, \text{Max}\{8000, 2000 + \Delta_4^1\} + \Delta_5^4\}$ | 12 000 |

would occur, if the condition $r_5^* > d_5^* - C_5$ (respectively $r_4^* > d_4^* - C_4$) holds. By using Table 6.5 we have:

$$\text{Max}\{3000 + \Delta_5^3, \text{Max}\{8000 + \Delta_5^4, 2000 + \Delta_4^1 + \Delta_5^4\}\} > 9000 \tag{6.8}$$

$$\text{Max}\{7000, 1000 + \Delta_4^1\} > 8000 \tag{6.9}$$

To verify the inequality (6.8), one of the following conditions should be satisfied:

$$\Delta_5^3 > 6000 \tag{6.10}$$

$$\Delta_5^4 > 1000 \tag{6.11}$$

$$\Delta_4^1 + \Delta_5^4 > 7000 \tag{6.12}$$

To verify the inequality (6.9), the following condition should be satisfied:

$$\Delta_4^1 > 7000 \tag{6.13}$$

From inequalities (6.10)–(6.13), we deduce the maximum bounds of the three communication delays that guarantee the feasibility of the tasks of the application:

$$\text{Max } \Delta_4^1 = 6000\,\mu\text{s}, \quad \text{Max } \Delta_5^3 = 6000\,\mu\text{s}, \quad \text{Max } \Delta_5^4 = 1000\,\mu\text{s} \tag{6.14}$$

These values represent maximum bounds which should not be exceeded whatever the network used. However, as we will see in the case of the token bus, the maximum values of communication delays which guarantee the time constraints of the tasks can be smaller than these bounds for some networks.

**Q4** Schedulability analysis for periodic tasks. Given the small number of tasks of the considered application, we can easily check that EDF scheduling guarantees the deadlines of tasks $\tau_1$ and $\tau_3$ on node $N_1$, and tasks $\tau_2$ and $\tau_4$ on node $N_2$. To check the feasibility of the tasks with earliest deadline first algorithm, during the first interval of 12 ms, one can also use the following lemma proved in Chetto and Chetto (1987):

**Lemma:**
A set n tasks is feasible by the earliest deadline first algorithm, if and only if

$$\forall i = 1, \ldots, n, \forall j = 1, \ldots, n, r_i \leq r_j, d_i \leq d_j, \sum_{\substack{r_k \leq r_i \\ d_k \leq d_j}} C_k \leq d_j - r_i$$

We apply the preceding lemma three times, since the initial set of tasks of the considered application is allocated to three nodes. We take $d_i^*$ instead of $d_i$ and $r^*$ instead of $r_i$ (this change of terms in the lemma does not affect its validity). For node $N_1$, there is a set of two tasks $\tau_1$ and $\tau_3$. The preceding lemma is checked because we have:

$$r_1^* \leq r_3^*, d_1^* \leq d_3^* \text{ and } C_1 + C_3 \leq d_3^* - r_1^* \tag{6.15}$$

For node $N_2$, we have a set of two tasks $\tau_2$ and $\tau_4$. The preceding lemma is verified because we have:

$$r_2^* \le r_4^*, d_2^* \le d_4^* \text{ and } C_2 + C_4 \le d_4^* - r_2^* \tag{6.16}$$

The feasibility check of task $\tau_5$ is obvious, because task $\tau_5$ alone uses the processor of node $N_3$. Indeed, $C_5 \le d_5^* - r_5^*$. The five tasks are thus feasible for the first period. It is enough to show that the five tasks remain feasible for any period $k$ $(k > 1)$. We note $r_{i,k}^*$, the modified release time of task $\tau_i$ for the $k$th period, and $d_{i,k}^*$ its modified deadline. By using the rules of modification of the values of the task parameters and the assumption fixed in question Q4, according to which the values of the task parameters of the $k$th period are obtained from those of the first period by adding $(k - 1) \times 12$ ms, and by considering that the network guarantees the maximum bounds of the communication delays, we obtain:

$$r_{i,k}^* = r_i^* + (k - 1) \times 12\,000 \text{ and}$$

$$d_{i,k}^* = d_i^* + (k - 1) \times 12\,000 \ (i = 1, \dots, 5) \tag{6.17}$$

By using the lemma again, one deduces, as previously, that tasks $\tau_1$ and $\tau_3$ are feasible at the $k$th period on the node $N_1$, and tasks $\tau_2$ and $\tau_4$ are feasible on node $N_2$. The feasibility check of task $\tau_5$ is commonplace, because it alone uses the processor of node $N_3$. Indeed, $C_5 \le d_{5,k}^* - r_{5,k}^*$.

**Q5**  Scheduling using token bus network. We develop here a solution based on the full length allocation scheme (i.e. without segmentation of messages). As mentioned in Section 6.4.3, the token holding time, $THT_i$, assigned to a node $N_i$ is equal to the transmission delay of its message. Nevertheless, in this exercise, node $N_1$ is the source of two messages ($M_1$ and $M_2$). $M_1$ is transmitted at the end of task $\tau_1$, and $M_2$ at the end of task $\tau_3$. As task $\tau_3$ requires $2000\,\mu s$ to complete execution, node $N_1$ cannot transmit both messages in the same token round. To enable node $N_1$ to transmit its longest message, the token holding times are set as follows:

- $THT_1 = Max(d_{\text{token bus}}(M_1), d_{\text{token bus}}(M_2)) = 160\,\mu s$

- $THT_2 = d_{\text{token bus}}(M_3) = 128\,\mu s$

- $THT_3 = 0$ (node $N_3$ does not transmit messages)

Following the principle of the token bus, each node receives the token at each token round and can transmit its data during a time at most equal to its token holding time, before passing the token to its successor. According to assumptions fixed for this exercise, only the queuing delay at the sender MAC sublayer and the transmission delay are significant. The other deadlines (propagation delay and delays of crossing upper layers) are supposed to be negligible. Consequently, $\Delta_j^i$ (transfer delay of message from node $N_j$ to node $N_i$) is equal to the queuing delay at sender MAC sublayer plus the transmission delay of the message. If we assume that the logical ring is made up only of the nodes $N_1$, $N_2$ and $N_3$, the maximum waiting time to transmit a message is equal to TRTmax (maximum token rotation time). In other words, the worst case for the waiting time of a periodic message is when the message arrives at the MAC sublayer right at the time when the first bit of the token has just left this node, and hence the node must wait for the next token round (i.e. to wait at most for TRTmax) to transmit its message. Thus, we must have:

$$\text{Max } \Delta_4^1 \geq \text{TRTmax} + 112\,\mu\text{s} \tag{6.18}$$

$$\text{Max } \Delta_5^3 \geq \text{TRTmax} + 160\,\mu\text{s} \tag{6.19}$$

$$\text{Max } \Delta_5^4 \geq \text{TRTmax} + 128\,\mu\text{s} \tag{6.20}$$

As we assumed that the logical ring is made up only of the nodes $N_1$, $N_2$ and $N_3$, the value of TRTmax must satisfy the following inequality:

$$\text{TRTmax} \geq 3\Im + \sum_{1 \leq i \leq 3} \text{THT}_i \tag{6.21}$$

where $\Im$ indicates the token transmission delay, which is equal to $96\,\mu\text{s}$ according to the assumptions of Section 6.4.3. From (6.14) and (6.18)–(6.21), we can deduce the value of TRTmax:

$$576\,\mu\text{s} \leq \text{TRTmax} \leq 872\,\mu\text{s} \tag{6.22}$$

By fixing TRTmax, one fixes the values of the three communication delays. By making substitutions in Table 6.5, all the values of TRTmax defined by the double inequality (6.22) make it possible to guarantee the time constraints of the task set.

**Q6** Scheduling using CAN. Communication delay $\Delta_j^i$ includes the waiting time in node $i$ and the transmission delay of the message on the CAN network. In the case of CAN, the waiting time of a message before transmission depends, at the same time, on the identifier of this message and the identifiers of other messages sharing the medium. To know the maximum waiting time of a message, it is necessary to know its identifier as well as the identifiers and the times of emission or the transmission periods of the other messages.

If we assume that the traffic network is generated only by the tasks $\tau_1$, $\tau_3$ and $\tau_4$, then the upper bounds of communication delays are never reached, however the identifiers are assigned to the three messages $M_1$, $M_2$ and $M_3$. In the worst case, a message can be blocked while waiting for the transmission of both others. The maximum time of blocking is $230\,\mu\text{s}$ (see Table 6.4). With such a waiting time, the upper bounds of transfer delays (see equation (6.14)) are never reached.

If the three messages $M_1$, $M_2$ and $M_3$ are not alone in using the network, the choice of identifiers is much more complex; it depends on the other messages. The reader can refer to the work of Tindell et al. (1995) to see how to compute the transfer delay of messages in the general case.

**Q7** Scheduling using FIP network. According to whether the three messages are alone in using the FIP network or not, there are two possible solutions to define the table of the bus arbitrator.

*Case 1: Messages $M_1$, $M_2$ and $M_3$ alone use the network*    In this case, we use a bus arbitrator table which contains only the identifiers of messages $M_1$, $M_2$ and $M_3$ (see Figure 6.11). The duration of a macrocycle is equal to the sum of the transmission

**Figure 6.11**   Bus arbitrator table when the three messages alone use the network

delays of the three messages, i.e. 598 µs (see Table 6.4). Even if the same message is conveyed several times by the network (because the duration of the macrocycle is small compared to the period of the tasks), the consuming task reads only the value present in the consumption buffer at its release time. With a macrocycle of 598 µs, the upper bounds of the communication delays of the three messages are always guaranteed (the waiting time of a value in a production buffer is lower than or equal to the sum of the transmission delays of the two longest messages, i.e. 420 µs).

*Case 2: Messages $M_1$, $M_2$ and $M_3$ share the network with other messages*    In order not to transmit the same message several times in a period of 12 ms (as in the preceding solution), the broadcasting message request (i.e. ID-Dat frame) must be posterior to the deadline of the task which produces this message. This means that when the bus arbitrator asks for the broadcasting of a message one is sure that the task which produces it has already finished. The request for broadcasting a message $M_p(p = 1, 2, 3)$ produced by task $\tau_i$ and issued by a task $\tau_j$ must be made at the earliest at time $r_j^* - \Delta_j^i$ and at the latest at time $r_j^* - d_{\mathrm{FIP}}(M_p)$.

Given the maximum values of $\Delta_j^i$ (see equations (6.14) and the values of transmission delays in FIP (see Table 6.4), one can build a bus arbitrator table. As there are several possibilities for fixing the moment of request for broadcasting of a message sent by task $\tau_i$ to task $\tau_j$ in the interval $[r_j^* - \Delta_j^i, r_j^* - d_{\mathrm{FIP}}(M_p)]$, several tables of bus arbitrator can be used to guarantee the upper bounds of communication delays of the three messages.

# 7
# Packet Scheduling in Networks

The networks under consideration in this chapter have a point-to-point interconnection structure; they are also called multi-hop networks and they use packet-switching techniques. In this case, guaranteeing time constraints is more complicated than for multiple access LANs, seen in the previous chapter, because we have to consider message delivery time constraints across multiple stages (or hops) in the network. In this type of network, there is only one source node for any network link, so the issue to be addressed is not only that of access to the medium but also that of packet scheduling.

## 7.1 Introduction

The advent of high-speed networks has introduced opportunities for new distributed applications, such as video conferencing, medical imaging, remote command and control systems, telephony, distributed interactive simulation, audio and video broadcasts, games, and so on. These applications have stringent performance requirements in terms of throughput, delay, jitter and loss rate (Aras et al., 1994). Whereas the guaranteed bandwidth must be large enough to accommodate motion video and audio streams at acceptable resolution, the end-to-end delay must be small enough for interactive communication. In order to avoid breaks in continuity of audio and video playback, delay jitter and loss must be sufficiently small.

Current packet-switching networks (such as the Internet) offer only a best effort service, where the performance of each user can degrade significantly when the network is overloaded. Thus, there is a need to provide network services with performance guarantees and develop scheduling algorithms supporting these services. In this chapter, we will be concentrating on issues related to packet scheduling to guarantee time constraints of messages (particularly end-to-end deadlines and jitter constraints) in connection-oriented packet-switching networks.

In order to receive a service from the network with guaranteed performance, a connection between a source and a destination of data must first go through an admission control process in which the network determines whether it has the needed resources to meet the requirements of the connection. The combination of a connection admission control (test and protocol for resource reservation) and a packet scheduling algorithm is called a *service discipline*. Packet scheduling algorithms are used to control rate (bandwidth) or delay and jitter. When the connection admission control function is not significant for the discussion, the terms 'service discipline' and 'scheduling algorithm' are interchangeable. In the sequel, when 'discipline' is used alone, it implicitly means 'service discipline'.

In the past decade, a number of service disciplines that aimed to provide performance guarantees have been proposed. These disciplines may be categorized as work-conserving or non-work-conserving disciplines. In the former, the packet server is never idle when there are packets to serve (i.e. to transmit). In the latter, the packet server may be idle even when there are packets waiting for transmission. Non-work-conserving disciplines have the advantage of guaranteeing transfer delay jitter for packets. The most well known and used disciplines in both categories are presented in Sections 7.4 and 7.5.

Before presenting the service disciplines, we start by briefly presenting the concept of a 'switch', which is a fundamental device in packet-switching networks. In order for the network to meet the requirements of a message source, this source must specify (according to a suitable model) the characteristics of its messages and its performance requirements (in particular, the end-to-end transfer delay and transfer delay jitter). These aspects will be presented in Section 7.2.2. In Section 7.3, some criteria allowing the comparison and analysis of disciplines are presented.

## 7.2  Network and Traffic Models

### 7.2.1  Message, packet, flow and connection

Tasks running on source hosts generate *messages* and submit them to the network. These messages may be periodic, sporadic or aperiodic, and form a *flow* from a source to a destination. Generally, all the messages of the same flow require the same quality of service (QoS). The unit of data transmission at the network level is commonly called a *packet*. The packets transmitted by a source also form a flow. As the buffers used by switches for packet management have a maximum size, messages exceeding this maximum size are segmented into multiple packets. Some networks accept a high value for maximum packet length, thus leading to exceptional message fragmentation, and others (such as ATM) have a small value, leading to frequent message fragmentation. Note that in some networks such as ATM, the unit of data transmission is called a *cell* (a maximum of 48 data bytes may be sent in a cell). The service disciplines presented in this chapter may be used for cell or packet scheduling. Therefore, the term packet is used below to denote any type of transmission data unit.

Networks are generally classified as connection-oriented or connectionless. In a connection-oriented network, a connection must be established between the source and the destination of a flow before any transfer of data. The source of a connection negotiates some requirements with the network and the destination, and the connection is accepted only if these requirements can be met. In connectionless networks, a source submits its data packets without any establishment of connection.

A connection is defined by means of a host source, a *path* composed of one or multiple switches and a host destination. For example, Figure 7.1 shows a connection between hosts 1 and 100 on a path composed of switches A, C, E and F.

Another important aspect in networks is the routing. Routing is a mechanism by which a network device (usually a router or a switch) collects, maintains and disseminates information about paths (or routes) to various destinations on a network. There exist multiple routing algorithms that enable determination of the best, or shortest,

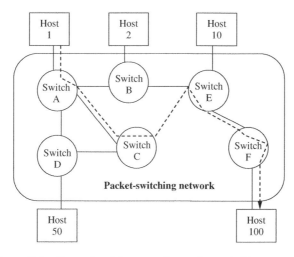

**Figure 7.1**  General architecture of a packet-switching network

path to a particular destination. In connectionless networks, such as IP, routing is generally dynamic (i.e. the path is selected for each packet considered individually) and in connection-oriented networks, such as ATM, routing is generally fixed (i.e. all the packets on the same connection follow the same path, except in the event of failure of a switch or a link). In the remainder of this chapter, we assume that prior to the establishment of a connection, a routing algorithm is run to determine a path from a source to a destination, and that this algorithm is rerun whenever required to recompute a new path, after a failure of a switch or a link on the current path. Thus, routing is not developed further in this book.

The service disciplines presented in this chapter are based on an explicit reservation of resources before any transfer of data, and the resource allocation is based on the identification of source–destination pairs. In the literature, multiple terms (particularly connections, virtual circuits, virtual channels and sessions) are used interchangeably to identify source–destination pairs. In this chapter we use the term 'connection'. Thus, the disciplines we will study are called connection-oriented disciplines.

## 7.2.2  Packet-switching network issues

### Input and output links

A packet-switching network is any communication network that accepts and delivers individual packets of information. Most modern networks are packet-switching. As shown in Figure 7.1, a packet-switching network is composed of a set of nodes (called *switches* in networks like ATM, or *routers* in Internet environments) to which a set of hosts (or user end-systems) is connected. In the following, we use the term 'switch' to designate packet-switching nodes; thus, the terms 'switch' and 'router' are interchangeable in the context of this chapter. Hosts, which represent the sources of data, submit packets to the network to deliver them to their destination. The packets are routed hop-by-hop, across switches, before reaching their destinations (host destinations).

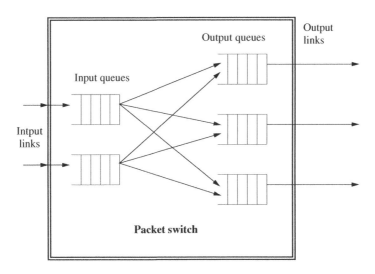

**Figure 7.2**   Simplified architecture of a packet switch

A simple packet switch has input and output links (see Figure 7.2). Each link has a fixed rate (not all the links need to have the same rate). Packets arrive on input links and are assigned an output link by some routing/switching mechanism. Each output link has a queue (or multiple queues). Packets are removed from the queue(s) and sent on the appropriate output link at the rate of the link. Links between switches and between switches and hosts are assumed to have bounded delays. By link delay we mean the time a packet takes to go from one switch (or from the source host) to the next switch (or to the destination host). When the switches are connected directly, the link delay depends mainly on the propagation delay. However, in an interconnecting environment, two switches may be interconnected via a local area network (such as a token bus or Ethernet); in this case, the link delay is more difficult to bound.

A plethora of proposals for identifying suitable architectures for high-speed switches has appeared in the literature. The design proposals are based on various queuing strategies, mainly output queuing and input queuing. In output queuing, when a packet arrives at a switch, it is immediately put in the queue associated with the corresponding output link. In input queuing, each input link maintains a first-come-first-served (FCFS) queue of packets and only the first packet in the queue is eligible for transmission during a given time slot. Such a strategy, which is simple to implement, suffers from a performance bottleneck, namely head-of-line blocking (i.e. when the packet at the head of the queue is blocked, all the packets behind it in the queue are prevented from being transmitted, even when the output link they need is idle). Few works have dealt with input queuing strategies, and the packet scheduling algorithms that are most well known and most commonly used in practice, by operational switches, are based on output queuing. This is the reason why, in this book, we are interested only in the algorithms that belong to the output queuing category.

In general, a switch can have more than one output link. When this is the case, the various output links are managed independently of each other. To simplify the notations, we assume, without loss of generality, that there is one output link per switch, so we do not use specific notations to distinguish the output links.

### *End-to-end delay of packet in a switched network*

The end-to-end delay of each packet through a switched network is the sum of the delays it experiences passing through all the switches en route. More precisely, to determine the end-to-end delay a packet experiences in the network, four delay components must be considered for each switch:

- *Queuing delay* is the time spent by the packet in the server queue while waiting for transmission. Note that this delay is the most difficult to bound.

- *Transmission delay* is the time interval between the beginning of transmission of the first bit and the end of transmission of the last bit of the packet on the output link. This time depends on the packet length and the rate of the output link.

- *Propagation delay* is the time required for a bit to go from the sending switch to the receiving switch (or host). This time depends on the distance between the sending switch and the next switch (or the destination host). It is also independent of the scheduling discipline.

- *Processing delay* is any packet delay resulting from processing overhead that is not concurrent with an interval of time when the server is transmitting packets.

On one hand, some service disciplines consider the propagation delay and others do not. On the other hand, some authors ignore the propagation delay and others do not, when they analyse the performances of disciplines. Therefore, we shall slightly modify certain original algorithms and results of performance analysis to consider the propagation delay, which makes it easier to compare algorithm performances. Any modification of the original algorithms or performance analysis results is pointed out in the text.

### *High-speed networks requirements*

High-speed networks call for simplicity of traffic management algorithms in terms of the processing cost required for packet management (determining deadlines or finish times, insertion in queues, etc.), because a significant number (several thousands) of packets can traverse a switch in a short time interval, while requiring very short times of traversing. In order not to slow down the functioning of a high-speed network, the processing required for any control function should be kept to a minimum. In consequence, packet scheduling algorithms should have a low overhead. It is worth noting that almost all switches on the market are based on hardware implementation of some packet management functions.

## 7.2.3 Traffic models and quality of service

### *Traffic models*

The efficiency and the capabilities of QoS guarantees provided by packet scheduling algorithms are widely influenced by the characteristics of the data flows transmitted by sources. In general, it is difficult (even impossible) to determine a bound on packet delay and jitter if there is no constraint on packet arrival patterns when the bandwidth allocated to connections is finite. As a consequence, the source should specify the characteristics of its traffic.

A wide range of traffic specifications has been proposed in the literature. However, most techniques for guaranteeing QoS have investigated only specific combinations of traffic specifications and scheduling algorithms. The models commonly used for characterizing real-time traffic are: the periodic model, the $(Xmin, Xave, I)$ model, the $(\sigma, \rho)$ model and the leaky bucket model.

- *Periodic model.* Periodic traffic travelling on a connection $c$ is generated by a periodic task and may be specified by a couple $(Lmax^c, T^c)$ where $Lmax^c$ is the maximum length of packets, and $T^c$ is the minimum length of the interval between the arrivals of any two consecutive packets (it is simply called the *period*).

- $(Xmin, Xave, I)$ *model.* Three parameters are used to characterize the traffic: $Xmin$ is the minimum packet inter-arrival time, $Xave$ is the average packet inter-arrival time, and $I$ is the time interval over which $Xave$ is computed. The parameters $Xave$ and $I$ are used to characterize bursty traffic.

- $(\sigma, \rho)$ *model* (Cruz, 1991a, b). This model describes traffic in terms of a rate parameter $\rho$ and a burst parameter $\sigma$ such that the total number of packets from a connection in any time interval is no more than $\sigma + \rho t$.

- *Leaky bucket model.* Various definitions and interpretations of the leaky bucket have been proposed. Here we give the definition of Turner, who was the first to introduce the concept of the leaky bucket (1986): a counter associated with each user transmitting on a connection is incremented whenever the user sends packets and is decremented periodically. If the counter exceeds a threshold, the network discards the packets. The user specifies a rate at which the counter is decremented (this determines the average rate) and a value of the threshold (a measure of burstiness). Thus, a leaky bucket is characterized by two parameters, rate $\rho$ and depth $\sigma$. It is worth noting that the $(\sigma, \rho)$ model and the leaky bucket model are similar.

## *Quality of service requirements*

Quality of service (QoS) is a term commonly used to mean a collection of parameters such as reliability, loss rate, security, timeliness, and fault tolerance. In this book, we are only concerned with timeliness QoS parameters (i.e. transfer delay of packets and jitter).

Several different ways of categorizing QoS may be identified. One commonly used categorization is the distinction between deterministic and statistical guarantees. In the deterministic case, guarantees provide a bound on performance parameters (for example a bound on transfer delay of packets on a connection). Statistical guarantees promise that no more than a specified fraction of packets will see performance below a certain specified value (for example, no more than 5% of the packets would experience transfer delay greater than 10 ms). When there is no assurance that the QoS will in fact be provided, the service is called best effort service. The Internet today is a good example of best effort service. In this book we are only concerned with deterministic approaches for QoS guarantee.

For distributed real-time applications in which messages arriving later than their deadlines lose their value either partially or completely, delay bounds must be guaranteed. For communications such as distributed control messages, which require absolute delay bounds, the guarantee must be deterministic. In addition to delay bounds, delay jitter (or delay variation) is also an important factor for applications that require smooth delivery (e.g. video conferencing or telephone services). Smooth delivery can be provided either by rate control at the switch level or buffering at the destination.

Some applications, such as teleconferencing, are not seriously affected by delay experienced by packets in each video stream, but jitter and throughput are important for these applications. A packet that arrives too early to be processed by the destination is buffered. Hence, a larger jitter of a stream means that more buffers must be provided. For this reason, many packet scheduling algorithms are designed to keep jitter small. From the point of view of a client requiring bounded jitter, the ideal network would look like a link with a constant delay, where all the packets passed to the network experience the same end-to-end transfer delay.

Note that in the communication literature, the term 'transfer delay' (or simply 'delay') is used instead of the term 'response time', which is currently used in the task scheduling literature.

## *Quality of service management functions*

Numerous functions are used inside networks to manage the QoS provided in order to meet the needs of users and applications. These functions include:

- *QoS establishment*: during the (connection) establishment phase it is necessary for the parties concerned to agree upon the QoS requirements that are to be met in the subsequent systems activity. This function may be based on QoS negotiation and renegotiation procedures.

- *Admission control*: this is the process of deciding whether or not a new flow (or connection) should be admitted into the network. This process is essential for QoS control, since it regulates the amount of incoming traffic into the network.

- *QoS signalling protocols*: they are used by end-systems to signal to the network the desired QoS. A corresponding protocol example is the Resource ReSerVation Protocol (RSVP).

- *Resource management*: in order to achieve the desired system performance, QoS mechanisms have to guarantee the availability of the shared resources (such as buffers, circuits, channel capacity and so on) needed to perform the services requested by users. Resource reservation provides the predictable system behaviour necessary for applications with QoS constraints.

- *QoS maintenance*: its goal is to maintain the agreed/contracted QoS; it includes QoS monitoring (the use of QoS measures to estimate the values of a set of QoS parameters actually achieved) and QoS control (the use of QoS mechanisms to modify conditions so that a desired set of QoS characteristics is attained for some systems activity, while that activity is in progress).

- *QoS degradation and alert*: this issues a QoS indication to the user when the lower layers fail to maintain the QoS of the flow and nothing further can be done by QoS maintenance mechanisms.

- *Traffic control*: this includes traffic shaping/conditioning (to ensure that traffic entering the network adheres to the profile specified by the end-user), traffic scheduling (to manage the resources at the switch in a reasonable way to achieve particular QoS), congestion control (for QoS-aware networks to operate in a stable and efficient fashion, it is essential that they have viable and robust congestion control capabilities), and flow synchronization (to control the event ordering and precise timings of multimedia interactions).

- *Routing*: this is in charge of determining the 'optimal' path for packets.

In this book devoted to scheduling, we are only interested in the function related to packet scheduling.

# 7.3   Service Disciplines

There are two distinct phases in handling real-time communication: connection establishment and packet scheduling. The combination of a connection admission control (CAC) and a packet scheduling algorithm is called a *service discipline*. While CAC algorithms control acceptation, during connection establishment, of new connections and reserve resources (bandwidth and buffer space) to accepted connections, packet scheduling algorithms allocate, during data transfer, resources according to the reservation. As previously mentioned, when the connection admission control function is not significant for the discussion, the terms 'service discipline' and 'scheduling algorithm' are interchangeable.

## 7.3.1   Connection admission control

The connection establishment selects a path (route) from the source to the destination along which the timing constraints can be guaranteed. During connection establishment, the client specifies its traffic characteristics (i.e. minimum inter-arrival of packets, maximum packet length, etc.) and desired performance requirements (delay bound, delay jitter bound, and so on). The network then translates these parameters into local parameters, and performs a set of *connection admission control* tests at all the switches along the path of each accepted connection. A new connection is accepted only if there are enough resources (bandwidth and buffer space) to guarantee its performance requirements at all the switches on the connection path. The network may reject a connection request due to lacks of resources or administrative constraints.

     Note that a switch can provide local guarantees to a connection only when the traffic on this connection behaves according to its specified traffic characteristics. However, load fluctuations at previous switches may distort the traffic pattern of a connection and cause an instantaneous higher rate at some switch even when the connection satisfied the specified rate constraint at the entrance of the network.

## 7.3.2 Taxonomy of service disciplines

In the past decade, a number of service disciplines that aimed to provide performance guarantees have been proposed. These disciplines may be classified according to various criteria. The main classifications used to understand the differences between disciplines are the following:

- *Work-conserving versus non-work-conserving disciplines.* Work-conserving algorithms schedule a packet whenever a packet is present in the switch. Non-work-conserving algorithms reduce buffer requirements in the network by keeping the link idle even when a packet is waiting to be served. Whereas non-work-conserving disciplines can waste network bandwidth, they simplify network resource control by strictly limiting the output traffic at each switch.

- *Rate-allocating versus rate-controlled disciplines.* Rate-allocating disciplines allow packets on each connection to be transmitted at higher rates than the minimum guaranteed rate, provided the switch can still meet guarantees for all connections. In a rate-controlled discipline, a rate is guaranteed for each connection, but the packets from a connection are never allowed to be sent above the guaranteed rate.

- *Priority-based versus frame-based disciplines.* In priority-based schemes, packets have priorities assigned according to the reserved bandwidth or the required delay bound for the connection. The packet transmission (service) is priority driven. This approach provides lower delay bounds and more flexibility, but basically requires more complicated control logic at the switch. Frame-based schemes use fixed-size frames, each of which is divided into multiple packet slots. By reserving a certain number of packet slots per frame, connections are guaranteed with bandwidth and delay bounds. While these approaches permit simpler control at the switch level, they can sometimes provide only limited controllability (in particular, the number of sources is fixed and cannot be adapted dynamically).

- *Rate-based versus scheduler-based disciplines.* A rate-based discipline is one that provides a connection with a minimum service rate independent of the traffic characteristics of other connections (though it may serve a connection at a rate higher than this minimum). The QoS requested by a connection is translated into a transmission rate or bandwidth. There are predefined allowable rates, which are assigned static priorities. The allocated bandwidth guarantees an upper delay bound for packets. The scheduler-based disciplines instead analyse the potential interactions between packets of different connections, and determine if there is any possibility of a deadline being missed. Priorities are assigned dynamically based on deadlines. Rate-based methods are simpler to implement than scheduler-based ones. Note that scheduler-based methods allow bandwidth, delay and jitter to be allocated independently.

## 7.3.3  Analogies and differences with task scheduling

In the next sections, we describe several well-known service disciplines for real-time packet scheduling. These disciplines strongly resemble the ones used for task scheduling seen in previous chapters. Compared to scheduling of tasks, the transmission link plays the same role as the processor as a central resource, while the packets are the units of work requiring this resource, just as tasks require the use of a processor. With this analogy, task scheduling methods may be applicable to the scheduling of packets on a link. The scheduler allocates the link according to some predefined discipline.

Many of the packet scheduling algorithms assign a priority to a packet on its arrival and then schedule the packets in the priority order. In these scheduling algorithms, a packet with higher priority may arrive after a packet with lower priority has been scheduled. On one hand, in non-preemptive scheduling algorithms, the transmission of a lower priority is not preempted even after a higher priority packet arrives. Consequently, such algorithms elect the highest priority packet known at the time of the transmission completion of every packet. On the other hand, preemptive scheduling algorithms always ensure that the packet in service (i.e. the packet being transmitted) is the packet with the highest priority by possibly preempting the transmission of a packet with lower priority.

Preemptive scheduling, as used in task scheduling, cannot be used in the context of message scheduling, because if the transmission of a message is interrupted, the message is lost and has to be retransmitted. To achieve the preemptive scheduling, the message has to be split into fragments (called packets or cells) so that message transmission can be interrupted at the end of a fragment transmission without loss (this is analogous to allowing an interrupt of a task at the end of an instruction execution). Therefore, a message is considered as a set of packets, where the packet size is bounded. Packet transmission is non-preemptive, but message transmission can be considered to be preemptive. As we shall see in this chapter, packet scheduling algorithms are non-preemptive and the packet size bound has some effects on the performance of the scheduling algorithms.

## 7.3.4  Properties of packet scheduling algorithms

A packet scheduling algorithm should possess several desirable features to be useful for high-speed switching networks:

- Isolation (or protection) of flows: the algorithm must isolate a connection from undesirable effects of other (possibly misbehaving) connections.

- Low end-to-end delays: real-time applications require from the network low end-to-end delay guarantees.

- Utilization (or efficiency): the scheduling algorithm must utilize the output link bandwidth efficiently by accepting a high number of connections.

- Fairness: the available bandwidth of the output link must be shared among connections sharing the link in a fair manner.

- Low overhead: the scheduling algorithm must have a low overhead to be used online.

- Scalability (or flexibility): the scheduling algorithm must perform well in switches with a large number of connections, as well as over a wide range of output link speeds.

## 7.4 Work-Conserving Service Disciplines

In this section, we present the most representative and most commonly used work-conserving service disciplines, namely the weighted fair queuing, virtual clock, and delay earliest-due-date disciplines. These disciplines have different delay and fairness properties as well as implementation complexity. The priority index, used by the scheduler to serve packets, is called 'auxiliary virtual clock' for virtual clock, 'virtual finish time' for weighted fair queuing, and 'expected deadline' for delay earliest-due-date. The computation of priority index is based on just the rate parameter or on both the rate and delay parameters; it may be dependent on the system load.

### 7.4.1 Weighted fair queuing discipline

*Fair queuing discipline*

Nagle (1987) proposed a scheduling algorithm, called *fair queuing*, based on the use of separate queues for packets from each individual connection (Figure 7.3). The objective

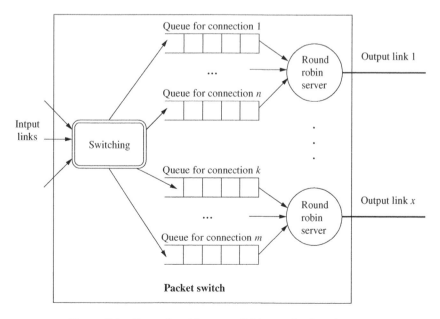

**Figure 7.3** General architecture of fair queuing based server

of this algorithm is to protect the network from hosts that are misbehaving: in the presence of well-behaved and misbehaving hosts, this strategy ensures that well-behaved hosts are not affected by misbehaving hosts. With fair queuing discipline, connections share equally the output link of the switch. The multiple queues of a switch, associated with the same output link, are served in a round-robin fashion, taking one packet from each nonempty queue in turn; empty queues are skipped over and lose their turn.

### Weighted fair queuing discipline

Demers et al. (1989) proposed a modification of Nagle's fair queuing discipline to take into account some aspects ignored in Nagle's discipline, mainly the lengths of packets (i.e. a source sending long packets should get more bandwidth than one sending short packets), delay of packets, and importance of flows. This scheme is known as the *weighted fair queuing* (WFQ) discipline even though it was simply called fair queuing by its authors (Demers et al.) in the original paper. The same discipline has also been proposed by Parekh and Gallager (1993) under the name *packet-by-packet generalized processor sharing system* (PGPS). WFQ and PGPS are interchangeable.

To define the WFQ discipline, Demers et al. introduced a hypothetical service discipline where the transmission occurs in a bit-by-bit round-robin (BR) fashion. Indeed, 'ideal fairness' would have as a consequence that each connection transmits a bit in each turn of the round-robin service. The bit-by-bit round-robin algorithm is also called *Processor Sharing* (PS) *service discipline*.

*Bit-by-bit round-robin discipline* (*or processor sharing discipline*)     Let $R_s(t)$ denote the number of rounds made in the Round-Robin discipline up to time $t$ at a switch $s$; $R_s(t)$ is a continuous function, with the fractional part indicating partially completed rounds. $R_s(t)$ is also called *virtual system time*. Let $Nac_s(t)$ be the number of active connections at switch $s$ (a connection is active if it has bits waiting in its queue at time $t$). Then:

$$\frac{dR_s}{dt} = \frac{r_s}{Nac_s(t)}$$

where $r_s$ is the bit rate of the output link of switch $s$.

A packet of length $L$ whose first bit gets serviced at time $t_0$ will have its last bit serviced $L$ rounds later, at time $t$ such that $R_s(t) = R_s(t_0) + L$. Let $AT_s^{c,p}$ be the time that packet $p$ on connection $c$ arrives at the switch $s$, and define the numbers $S_s^{c,p}$ and $F_s^{c,p}$ as the values of $R_s(t)$ when the packet $p$ starts service and finishes service. $F_s^{c,p}$ is called the *finish number* of packet $p$. The finish number associated with a packet, at time $t$, represents the time at which this packet would complete service in the corresponding BR service if no additional packets were to arrive after time $t$. $L^{c,p}$ denotes the size of the packet $p$. Then,

$$S_s^{c,p} = \max\{F_s^{c,p-1}, R_s(AT_s^{c,p})\} \qquad \text{for } p > 1 \tag{7.1}$$

$$F_s^{c,p} = S_s^{c,p} + L^{c,p} \qquad \text{for } p \geq 1 \tag{7.2}$$

Equation (7.1) means that the $p$th packet from connection $c$ starts service when it arrives if the queue associated with $c$ is empty on packet $p$'s arrival, or when packet $p - 1$ finishes otherwise. Packets are numbered $1, 2, \ldots$ and $S_s^{c,1} = AT_s^{c,1}$ (for all connections). Only one packet per queue can start service.

*Weighted bit-by-bit round-robin discipline*    To take into account the requirements (mainly in terms of bandwidth) and the importance of each connection, a weight $\phi_s^c$ is assigned to each connection $c$ in each switch $s$. This number represents how many queue slots that the connection gets in the bit-by-bit round-robin discipline. In other words, it represents the fraction of output link bandwidth allocated to connection $c$. The new relationships for determining $R_s(t)$ and $F_s^{c,p}$ are:

$$Nac_s(t) = \sum_{x \in CnAct_s(t)} \phi_s^x \qquad (7.3)$$

$$F_s^{c,p} = S_s^{c,p} + \frac{L^{c,p}}{\phi_s^c} \qquad \text{for } p \geq 1 \qquad (7.4)$$

where $CnAct_s(t)$ is the set of active connections at switch $s$ at time $t$. Note that the combination of weights and BR discipline is called *weighted bit-by-bit round-robin* (WBR), and is also called the *generalized processor sharing* (GPS) discipline, which is the term most often used in the literature.

*Practical implementation of WBR (or GPS) discipline*    The GPS discipline is an idealized definition of fairness as it assumes that packets can be served in infinitesimally divisible units. In other words, GPS is based on a fluid model where the packets are assumed to be indefinitely divisible and multiple connections may transmit traffic through the output link simultaneously at different rates. Thus, sending packets in a bit-by-bit round-robin fashion is unrealistic (i.e. impractical), and the WFQ scheduling algorithm can be thought of as a way to emulate the hypothetical GPS discipline by a practical packet-by-packet transmission scheme. With the packet-by-packet round-robin scheme, a connection $c$ is active whenever condition (7.5) holds (i.e. whenever the round number is less than the largest finish number of all packets queued for connection $c$).

$$R_s(t) \leq F_s^{c,p} \qquad \text{for } p = \max\{j \mid AT_s^{c,j} \leq t\} \qquad (7.5)$$

The quantities $F_s^{c,p}$, computed according to equality (7.4), define the sending order of the packets. Whenever a packet finishes transmission, the next packet transmitted (serviced) is the one with the smallest $F_s^{c,p}$ value. In Parekh and Gallager (1993), it is shown that over sufficiently long connections, this packetized algorithm asymptotically approaches the fair bandwidth allocation of the GPS scheme.

*Round-number computation*    The round number $R_s(t)$ is defined to be the number of rounds that a GPS server would have completed at time $t$. To compute the round number, the WFQ server keeps track of the number of active connections, $Nac_s(t)$, defined according to equality (7.3), since the round number grows at a rate that is inversely proportional to $Nac_s(t)$. However, this computation is complicated by the fact that determining whether or not a connection is active is itself a function of the round number. Many algorithms have been proposed to ease the computation of $R_s(t)$. The interested reader can refer to solutions suggested by Greenberg and Madras (1992), Keshav (1991) and Liu (2000). Note that $R_s(t)$, as previously defined, cannot be computed whenever there is no connection active (i.e. if $Nac_s(t) = 0$). This problem may be simply solved by setting $R_s(t)$ to 0 at the beginning of the busy period of each switch (i.e. when the switch begins servicing packets), and by computing $R_s(t)$ only during busy periods of the switch.

***Example 7.1: Computation of the round number***    Consider two connections, 1 and 2, sharing the same output link of a switch $s$ using a WFQ discipline. Suppose that the speed of the output link is 1. Each connection utilizes 50% of the output link bandwidth (i.e. $\phi_s^1 = \phi_s^2 = 0.5$). At time $t = 0$, a packet $P^{1,1}$ of size 100 bits arrives on connection 1 and a packet $P^{2,1}$ of size 150 bits arrives on connection 2 at time $t = 50$. Let us compute the values of $R_s(t)$ at times 50 and 100.

At time $t = 0$, packet $P^{1,1}$ arrives, and it is assigned a finish number $F_s^{1,1} = 200$. Packet $P^{1,1}$ starts immediately service. During the interval [0, 50], only connection 1 is active, thus $N_{ac}(t) = 0.5$ and $dR(t)/dt = 1/0.5$. In consequence, $R(50) = 100$. At time $t = 50$, packet $P^{2,1}$ arrives, and it is assigned a finish number $F_s^{2,1} = 100 + 150/0.5 = 400$. At time $t = 100$, packet $P^{1,1}$ completes service. In the interval [50, 100], $N_{ac}(t) = 0.5 + 0.5 = 1$. Then, $R(100) = R(50) + 50 = 150$.

*Bandwidth and end-to-end delay bounds provided by WFQ*    Parekh and Gallager (1993) proved that each connection $c$ is guaranteed a rate $r_s^c$, at each switch $s$, defined by equation (7.6):

$$r_s^c = \frac{\phi_s^c}{\displaystyle\sum_{j \in C_s} \phi_s^j} r_s \qquad (7.6)$$

where $C_s$ is the set of connections serviced by switch $s$, and $r_s$ is the rate of the output link of the switch. Thus, with a GPS scheme, a connection $c$ can be guaranteed a minimum throughput independent of the demands of the other connections. Another consequence, is that the delay of a packet arriving on connection $c$ can be bounded as a function of the connection $c$ queue length independent of the queues associated with the other connections. By varying the weight values, one can treat the connections in a variety of different ways. When a connection $c$ operates under leaky bucket constraint, Parekh and Gallager (1994) proved that the maximum end-to-end delay of a packet along this connection is bounded by the following value:

$$\frac{\sigma^c + (K^c - 1)L^c}{\rho^c} + \sum_{s=1}^{K^c} \frac{Lmax_s}{r_s} + \pi \qquad (7.7)$$

where $\sigma^c$ and $\rho^c$ are the maximum buffer size and the rate of the leaky bucket modelling the traffic of connection $c$, $K^c$ is the total number of switches in the path taken by connection $c$, $L^c$ is the maximum packet size from connection $c$, $Lmax_s$ is the maximum packet size of the connections served by switch $s$, $r_s$ is the rate of the output link associated with server $s$ in $c$'s path, and $\pi$ is the propagation delay from the source to destination. ($\pi$ is considered negligible in Parekh and Gallager (1994).)

Note that the WFQ discipline does not integrate any mechanism to control jitter.

## Hierarchical generalized processor sharing

The hierarchical generalized processor sharing (H-GPS) system provides a general flexible framework to support hierarchical link sharing and traffic management for different service classes (for example, three classes of service may be considered: hard real-time, soft real-time and best effort). H-GPS can be viewed as a hierarchical integration of one-level GPS servers. With one-level GPS, there are multiple packet queues, each associated with a service share. During any interval when there are backlogged connections, the server services all backlogged connections simultaneously in proportion to their corresponding service shares. With H-GPS, the queue at each internal node is a logical one, and the service that this queue receives is distributed instantaneously to its child nodes in proportion to their relative service shares until the H-GPS server reaches the leaf nodes where there are physical queues (Bennett and Zhang, 1996b). Figure 7.4 gives an example of an H-GPS system with two levels.

### Other fair queuing disciplines

Although the WFQ discipline offers advantages in delay bounds and fairness, its implementation is complex because of the cost of updating the finish numbers. Its computation complexity is asymptotically linear in the number of connections serviced by the switch. To overcome this drawback, various disciplines have been proposed to approximate the GPS with a lower complexity: worst-case fair weighted fair queuing (Bennett and Zhang, 1996a), frame-based fair queuing (Stiliadis and Varma, 1996), start-time fair queuing (Goyal et al., 1996), self-clocked fair queuing (Golestani, 1994), and deficit round-robin (Shreedhar and Varghese, 1995).

## 7.4.2 Virtual clock discipline

The virtual Clock discipline, proposed by Zhang (1990), aims to emulate time division multiplexing (TDM) in the same way as fair queuing emulates the bit-by-bit round-robin discipline. TDM is a type of multiplexing that combines data streams by assigning each connection a different time slot in a set. TDM repeatedly transmits a

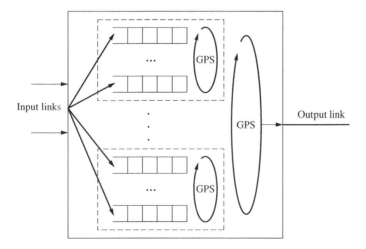

**Figure 7.4** Hierarchical GPS server with two levels

fixed sequence of time slots over the medium. A TDM server guarantees each user a prescribed transmission rate. It also eliminates interference among users, as if there were firewalls protecting individually reserved bandwidth. However, users are limited to transmission at a constant bit rate. Each user is allocated a slot to transmit. Capacities are wasted when a slot is reserved for a user that has no data to transmit at that moment. The number of users in a TDM server is fixed rather than dynamically adjustable.

The goal of the virtual clock (VC) discipline is to achieve both the guaranteed throughput for users and the firewall of a TDM server, while at the same time preserving the statistical multiplexing advantages of packet switching.

Each connection $c$ reserves its average required bandwidth $r^c$ at connection establishment time. The reserved rates for connections, at switch $s$, are constrained by:

$$\sum_{x \in C_s} r^x \leq r_s \tag{7.8}$$

where $C_s$ is the set of connections multiplexed at server $s$ (i.e. the set of connections that traverse the switch $s$) and $r_s$ is the rate of switch $s$ for the output link shared by the multiplexed connections. Each connection $c$ also specifies an average time interval, $A^c$. That is, over each $A^c$ time period, dividing the total amount of data transmitted by $A^c$ should result in $r^c$. This means that a connection may vary its transmission rate, but with respect to specified parameters $r^c$ and $A^c$.

### *Packet scheduling*

Each switch $s$ along the path of a connection $c$ uses two variables $VC_s^c$ (virtual clock) and $auxVC_s^c$ (auxiliary virtual clock) to control and monitor the flow of connection $c$. The virtual clock $VC_s^c$ is advanced according to the specified average bit rate ($r^c$) of connection $c$; the difference between this virtual clock and the real-time indicates how closely a running connection is following its specified bit rate. The auxiliary virtual clock $auxVC_s^c$ is used to compute virtual deadlines of packets. $VC_s^c$ and $auxVC_s^c$ will contain the same value most of the time — as long as packets from a connection arrive at the expected time or earlier. $auxVC_s^c$ may have a larger value temporarily, when a burst of packets arrives very late in an average interval, until being synchronized with $VC_s^c$ again.

Upon receiving the first packet on a connection $c$, those two virtual clocks are set to the arrival (real) time of this packet. When a packet $p$, whose length is $L^{c,p}$ bits, arrives, at time $AT_s^{c,p}$, on connection $c$, at the switch $s$, the virtual clocks are updated as follows:

$$auxVC_s^c \longleftarrow \max\{AT_s^{c,p}, auxVC_s^c\} + L^{c,p}/r^c \tag{7.9}$$

$$VC_s^c \longleftarrow VC_s^c + L^{c,p}/r^c \tag{7.10}$$

Then, the packet $p$ is stamped with the $auxVC_s^c$ value and inserted in the output link queue of the switch $s$. Packets are queued and served in order of increasing stamp *auxVC* values (ties are ordered arbitrarily). The *auxVC* value associated with a packet is also called *finish time* (or *virtual transmission deadline*).

### Flow monitoring

Since connections specify statistical parameters ($r^c$ and $A^c$), a mechanism must be used to control the data submitted by these connections according to their reservations. Upon receiving each set of $A^c \cdot r^c$ bits (or the equivalent of this bit-length expressed in packets) from connection $c$, the switch $s$ checks the connection in the following way:

- If $VC_s^c -$ *'Current Real-time'* $>$ *Threshold*, a warning message is sent to the source of connection $c$. Depending on how the source reacts, further control actions may be necessary (depending on resource availability, connection $c$ may be punished by longer queuing delay, or even packet discard).

- If $VC_s^c <$ *'Current Real-time'*, $VC_s^c$ is assigned *'Current Real-time'*.

The $auxVC_s^c$ variable is needed to take the arrival time of packets into account. When a burst of packets arrives very late in an average interval, although the $VC_s^c$ value may be behind real-time at that moment, the use of $auxVC_s^c$ will ensure the first packet to bear a stamp value with an increment of $L^{c,p}/r^c$ to the previous one. These stamp values will then cause this burst of packets to be interleaved, in the waiting queue, with packets that have arrived from other connections, if there are any. If a connection transmits at a rate lower than its specified rate, the difference between the virtual clock $VC$ and real-time may be considered as a 'credit' that the connection has built up. By replacing $VC_s^c$ by $auxVC_s^c$ in the packet stamping, a connection can no longer increase the priority of its packets by saving credits, even within an average interval. $VC_s^c$ retains its role as a connection meter that measures the progress of a statistical packet flow; its value may fall behind the real-time clock between checking (or monitoring) points in order to tolerate packet burstiness within each average interval. If a connection were allowed to save up an arbitrary amount of credit, it could remain idle during most of the time and then send all its data in burst; such behaviour may cause temporary congestion in the network.

In cases where some connections violate their reservation (i.e. they transmit at a rate higher than that agreed during connection establishment) well-behaved connections will not be affected, while the offending connections will receive the worst service (because their virtual clocks advance too far beyond real-time, their packets will be placed at the end of the service queue or even discarded).

### Some properties of the virtual clock discipline

Figueira and Pasquale (1995) proved that the upper bound of the packet delay for the VC discipline is the same as that obtained for the WFQ discipline (see (7.7)) when the connections are leaky bucket constrained.

Note that the VC algorithm is more efficient than the WFQ one, as it has a lower overhead: computing virtual clocks is simpler than computing finish times as required by WFQ.

## 7.4.3 Delay earliest-due-date discipline

A well-known dynamic priority-based service discipline is delay earliest-due-date (also called delay EDD), introduced by Ferrari and Verma (1990), and refined by Kandlur et al. (1991). The delay EDD discipline is based on the classic EDF scheduling algorithm presented in Chapter 2.

### *Connection establishment procedure*

In order to provide real-time service, each user must declare its traffic characteristics and performance requirements at the time of establishment of each connection $c$ by means of three parameters: $Xmin^c$ (the minimum packet inter-arrival time), $Lmax^c$ (the maximum length of packets), and $D^c$ (the end-to-end delay bound). To establish a connection, a client sends a connection request message containing the previous parameters. Each switch along the connection path performs a test to accept (or reject) the new connection. The test consists of verifying that enough bandwidth is available, under worst case, in the switch to accommodate the additional connection without impairing the guarantees given to the other accepted connections. Thus, inequality (7.11) should be satisfied:

$$\sum_{x \in C_s} ST_s^x / Xmin^x < 1 \qquad (7.11)$$

where $ST_s^x$ is the maximum service time in the switch $s$ for any packet from connection $c$. It is the maximum time to transmit a packet from connection $c$ and mainly depends on the speed of the output link of switch $s$ and the maximum packet size on connection $c$, $Lmax^c$. $C_s$ is the set of the connections traversing the switch $s$ including the connection $c$ to be established.

If inequality (7.11) is satisfied, the switch $s$ determines the local delay $OD_s^c$ that it can offer (and guarantee) for connection $c$. Determining the local deadline value depends on the utilization policy of resources at each switch. The delay EDD algorithm may be used with multiple resource allocation strategies. For example, assignment of local deadline may be based on $Xmin^c$ and $D^c$. If the switch $s$ accepts the connection $c$, it adds its offered local delay to the connection request message and passes this message to the next switch (or to the destination host) on the path. The destination host is the last point where the acceptance/rejection decision of a connection can be made. If all the switches on the path accept the connection, the destination host checks if the sum of the local delays plus the end-to-end propagation delay $\pi$ (in the original version of delay EDD, $\pi$ is considered negligible) is less than the end-to-end delay, and then balances the end-to-end delay $D^c$ among all the traversed switches. Thus, the destination host assigns to each switch $s$ a local delay $D_s^c$ as follows:

$$D_s^c = \frac{D^c - \pi - \sum_{j=1}^{N} OD_j^c}{N} + OD_s^c \qquad (7.12)$$

where $N$ is the number of switches traversed by the connection $c$. Note that the local delay $D_s^c$ assigned to switch $s$ by the destination host is never less than the local delay $OD_s^c$ previously accepted by this switch. The destination host builds a connection response message containing the assigned local delays and sends it along the reverse of the path taken by the connection request message. When a switch receives a connection response message, the resources previously reserved must be committed or released. In particular, in each switch $s$ on the connection path, the offered local delay $OD_s^c$ is replaced by the assigned local delay $D_s^c$, if connection $c$ is accepted. If any acceptance test fails at a switch or at destination host, the connection cannot be established along the considered path. When a connection is rejected, the source is notified and may try another path or relax some traffic and performance parameters, before trying once again to establish the connection.

## *Scheduling*

Scheduling in the switches is deadline-based. In each switch, the scheduler maintains one queue for deterministic packets, and one or multiple queues for the other types of packets. As we are only concerned with deterministic packets (i.e. packets requiring guarantee of delay bound), only the first queue is considered here. A packet $p$ travelling on a connection $c$ and arriving at switch $s$ at time $AT_s^{c,p}$ is assigned a deadline (also called *expected deadline*) $ExD_s^{c,p}$ defined as follows:

$$ExD_s^{c,1} = AT_s^{c,1} + D_s^c \tag{7.13}$$

$$ExD_s^{c,p} = \max\{ExD_s^{c,p-1} + Xmin^c, AT_s^{c,p} + D_s^c\} \qquad \text{for } p > 1 \tag{7.14}$$

The ordering of the packet queue is by increasing deadlines. Deadlines are considered as dynamic priorities of packets.

Malicious or faulty users could send packets into the network at a higher rate than the parameters declared during connection establishment. If no appropriate counter-measures are taken, such behaviour can prevent the guarantee of the deadlines of the other well-behaved users. The solution to this problem consists of providing distributed rate control by increasing the deadlines of the offending packets (see equality (7.14)), so that they will be delayed in heavily loaded switches. When buffer space is limited, some of them might even be dropped because of buffer overflow.

*Example 7.2: Scheduling with delay EDD discipline*    Let us consider a connection $c$ passing by two switches 1 and 2 (Figure 7.5). Both switches use the delay EDD discipline. The parameters declared during connection establishment are: $Xmin^c = 4$, $D^c = 8$, and $Lmax^c = L$. All the packets have the same size. The transmission time of a packet is equal to 1 for the source and both switches, and propagation delay is taken to be 0, for all links. Let us assume that during connection establishment, the local deadlines assigned to connection $c$ are: $D_1^c = 5$, and $D_2^c = 3$. Figure 7.5 shows the arrivals of four packets on connection $c$ at switch 1. Using equations (7.13) and (7.14), the expected deadlines of the four packets are: $ExD_1^{c,1} = 6$, $ExD_1^{c,2} = 10$, $ExD_1^{c,3} = 14$, and $ExD_1^{c,4} = 19$.

The actual delay (i.e. waiting time plus transmission time) experienced by each packet at switch 1 depends on the load of this switch, but never exceeds the local deadline assigned to connection $c$ (i.e. $D_1^c = 5$). For example, the actual delays of packets 1 to 4 are 5, 5, 3 and 2, respectively. In consequence, the arrival times of packets at switch 2 are 6, 8, 11, and 16, respectively. Using equations (7.13) and

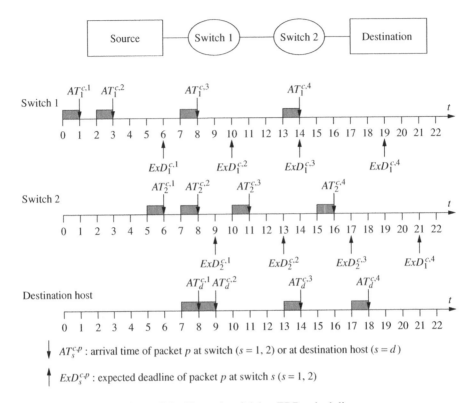

$AT_s^{c,p}$ : arrival time of packet $p$ at switch ($s = 1, 2$) or at destination host ($s = d$)

$ExD_s^{c,p}$ : expected deadline of packet $p$ at switch $s$ ($s = 1, 2$)

**Figure 7.5**   Example of delay EDD scheduling

(7.14), the expected deadlines of the packets at switch 2 are: $ExD_2^{c,1} = 9$, $ExD_2^{c,2} = 13$, $ExD_2^{c,3} = 17$, and $ExD_2^{c,4} = 21$.

The actual delays of packets at switch 2 depend on the load of this switch, but never exceed the local deadline assigned to connection $c$ (i.e. $D_2^c = 3$). For example, the actual delays of packets 1 to 4 are 2, 1, 3 and 2, respectively. In consequence, the arrival times of packets, at the destination host, are 8, 9, 14 and 18, respectively. Thus, the end-to-end delay of any packet is less than the delay bound (i.e. 8) declared during connection establishment.

### End-to-end delay and jitter bounds provided by delay EDD

As the local deadlines are guaranteed by the switches, the end-to-end delay of a packet from a connection $c$, traversing $N$ switches, is bounded by $\sum_{s=1}^{N} D_s^c + \pi$. ($\pi$ is the end-to-end propagation delay.) Since no jitter control is achieved, the jitter bound provided by delay EDD is the same order of magnitude as the end-to-end delay bound.

## 7.5 Non-Work-Conserving Service Disciplines

With work-conserving disciplines, the traffic pattern from a source is distorted inside the network due to load fluctuation of switches. A way of avoiding traffic pattern distortion is by using non-work-conserving disciplines. Several non-working disciplines have been proposed. The most important and most commonly used of these disciplines are: hierarchical round-robin (HRR), stop-and-go (S&G), jitter earliest-due-date (jitter EDD) and rate-controlled static-priority (RCSP). In each case, it has been shown that end-to-end deterministic delay bounds can be guaranteed. For jitter EDD, S&G and RCSP, it has also been shown that end-to-end jitter can be guaranteed.

## 7.5.1 Hierarchical round-robin discipline

Hierarchical round-robin (HRR) discipline is a time-framing and non-work-conserving discipline (Kalmanek et al., 1990). It is also called *framed round-robin* discipline. It has many interesting properties, such as implementation simplicity and service guarantee. HRR also provides protection for well-behaved connections since each connection is allowed to use only its own fixed slots. The HRR discipline is an extension of the round-robin discipline suitable for networks with fixed packet size, such as ATM. Since the HRR discipline is based on the round-robin discipline, we start by describing the latter for fixed-size packets.

### *Weighted round-robin discipline*

With round-robin discipline, packets from each connection are stored in a queue associated with this connection, so that each connection is served separately (Figure 7.6). When a packet arrives on a connection $c$, it is stored in the appropriate queue and its connection identifier, $c$, is added to the tail of a service list that indicates the packets eligible for transmission. (Note that a packet may have to wait for an entire round even when there is no other packet on the connection waiting at the switch when the packet arrives.) In order to ensure that each connection identifier is entered on the service list only once, there is a flag bit (called the round-robin flag bit) per connection, which is set to indicate that the connection identifier is on the service list. Each connection

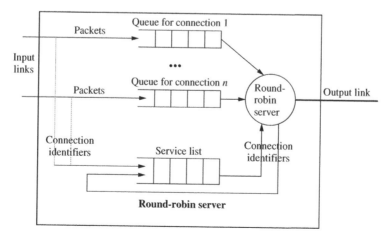

**Figure 7.6** General architecture of round-robin server

$c$ is assigned a number $\omega^c$ of slots it can use in each round of the server to transmit data. This number is also called the connection *weight*. The number of service slots can be different from one connection to another and in this case the discipline is called *weighted round-robin* (WRR). The service time of a packet is equal to one slot.

The (weighted) round-robin server periodically takes a connection identifier from the head of the service list and serves it according to its number of service slots. If the packet queue of a connection goes empty, the flag bit of this connection is cleared and the server takes another connection identifier from the head of the service list. If the packet queue is not empty, when all the slots assigned to this connection have been spent, the server returns the connection identifier to the tail of the service list before going on.

An important parameter of this discipline is the round length, denoted $RL$. The upper limit of the round length $RL$ is imposed by the delay guarantee that the switch provides to each connection. With the WRR algorithm, the actual length of a round varies with the amounts of traffic on the connections, but it never exceeds $RL$. It is important to notice that WRR is work-conserving while its extension, HRR, is non-work-conserving and that WRR controls delay bound, but not jitter bound.

### Hierarchical round-robin discipline

To cope with various requirements of connections (i.e. various end-to-end delay and jitter bounds), the HRR discipline uses different round lengths for different levels of service: the higher the service level, the shorter the round length. The service levels are numbered $1, 2, \ldots, n$ and organized hierarchically. The topmost server is the one associated with service level 1. The server associated with level $L$ is called server $L$.

Each level $L$ is assigned a round length $RL_L$. The round length is also called *frame*. The server of level 1 has the shortest round length, and it serves connections that are allocated the highest service rate.

An HRR server has a hierarchy of service lists associated with the hierarchy of levels. The topmost list is the one associated with service level 1. A server may serve multiple connections, but each connection is served by only one server.

When server $L$ is scheduled, it transmits packets on the connections serviced by it in the round-robin manner. Once a connection is served, it is returned to the end of the service list, and it is not served again until the beginning of the next round associated with this connection. To do this, server $L$ has two lists: *CurrentList*$_L$ (from which connections are being served in the current round) and *NextList*$_L$ (containing the identifiers of connections to serve in the next round). Each incoming packet on a connection serviced at level $L$ is placed in the input queue associated with this connection, and the identifier of this connection is added at the tail of *NextList*$_L$ if the queue associated with this connection was empty at the arrival of the packet. (Recall that each connection has a bit flag that indicates if the connection has packets waiting for transmission.) At the beginning of each round, server $L$ swaps *CurrentList*$_L$ and *NextList*$_L$.

The bandwidth of the output link is divided between the servers by allocating some fraction of the slots assigned to each server to servers that are lower in the hierarchy. In other words, in each round of length $RL_L$, the server $L$ has $ns_L$ slots ($ns_L \leq RL_L$) used as follows: $ns_L - b_L$ slots are used to serve connections of level $L$ and $b_L$ ($b_L \leq ns_L$)

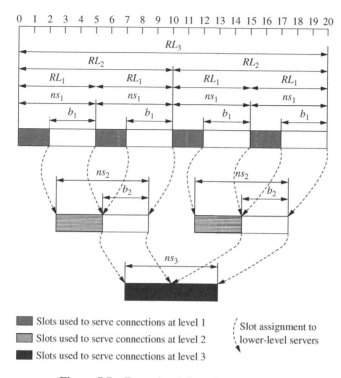

Figure 7.7   Example of time slot assignment

are used by the servers at lower levels. At the bottom of the hierarchy, there is a server associated with best effort traffic. Figure 7.7 shows an example of time slot assignment to servers.

A server $L$ is either active or inactive. It is active if all the servers at levels lower than $L$ are active and have completed service of their own service lists (i.e. each server $k = 1, \ldots, L - 1$ is active and has used $ns_k - b_k$ slots to serve the packets attached to its service list). Server 1 is always active.

As for the WRR discipline, to allow multiple service quanta, a service quantum $\omega^c$ is associated with each connection $c$, and it indicates the number of slots the connection can use in each round of the server to which it is assigned: if $\omega^c$ or fewer packets are waiting, all the packets of the connection are transmitted; if more than $\omega^c$ packets are waiting, only $\omega^c$ packets are transmitted and the remaining packets will be scheduled in the next round(s). $\omega^c$ is also called the weight associated with connection $c$ at connection establishment.

Note that the values of the counters $RL_L$, $ns_L$ and $b_L$ associated with each server $L$, and the weight $\omega^c$ associated with connection $c$ depend on the traffic characteristics of all the connections traversing a switch. Example 7.3 below shows how these values can be computed.

The complete HRR algorithm proposed by Kalmanek et al. (1990) is given below. Note that the algorithm is composed of two parts: the first part is in charge of periodic initialization of the rounds of the $n$ servers, and the second is in charge of serving connection queues. These two parts may be implemented as two parallel tasks.

Each server $L$ ($L = 1, 2, ..., n$) has three counters:

- $NB_L$ determines how many slots are used for connections associated with level $L$;

- $B_L$ determines how many slots are used for connections associated with levels lower than $L$;

- $G_L$ keeps track of service quanta larger than one slot.

$Q^c(t)$ denotes the number of packets queued at connection $c$ at time $t$.

1. /* *Initialization of round of any server L:* */
Periodically, every $RL_L$ slots, a new round of server $L$ starts. At the beginning of each round at level $L$, the counters and service lists associated with server $L$ are initialized:
$$NB_L \leftarrow ns_L - b_L; \ B_L \leftarrow b_L; \ swap(NextList_L, \ CurrentList_L).$$

----------------------------------------------------------------

2. **Loop**
    2.1. /* *Server and connection selection:* */
      Let $S$ be the index of the lowest rate active server at current time $t$.
    **If** $CurrentList_S$ is empty and $NB_S \neq 0$
      **Then** Activate Best effort server for one slot.
    **Else** Server $S$ picks a connection $c$ from the head of $CurrentList_S$
      **If** $G_S = 0$ **Then** $G_S \leftarrow \min(\omega^c, \ Q^c(t))$
      **EndIf**
      Serve connection $c$ for one slot;
      Decrement $G_S$
    **EndIf**
      Decrement $NB_S$ and $B_{S-1}, ..., B_1$

    2.2. /* *Adjust service list:* */
    **If** packet queue of connection $c$ is empty
      **Then** $G_S \leftarrow 0$;
        Clear the round-robin flag bit of connection $c$;
    **Else If** $G_S = 0$
        **Then** server $S$ places connection $c$ at the tail of $NextList_S$
      **Else** server $S$ places connection $c$ at the head of $CurrentList_S$
      **EndIf**
    **EndIf**

```
2.3.      /*  Check for change of active server: */
If any of B_{S-1}, ... B_1 is 0
   Then server S becomes inactive
Else If   NB_S  =  0 and B_S ≠ 0
      Then server S activates server S+1
   EndIf
EndIf
End loop
```

**Example 7.3: Determining counter values for the HRR discipline**    Consider a set of five periodic connections numbered 1, 2, 3, 4 and 5, transmitting packets with the same fixed length, and served by an HRR switch. Assume that the service time of one packet is equal to one time slot. The period $T^c$ of each connection $c$ and the number of packets ($NP^c$) it issues per period are given in Table 7.1.

As the packets have a fixed size and the time required to serve a packet is equal to one slot, the weight $\omega^c$ associated with connection $c$ is equal to $NP^c$. In consequence, we have:

$$\omega^1 = 1; \omega^2 = 1; \omega^3 = 2; \omega^4 = 1; \omega^5 = 3$$

As there are three types of periods, three levels of service can be used: level 1 is used by connections 1 and 2, level 2 is used by connection 3, and level 3 is used by connections 4 and 5. The lengths of the rounds are derived from the periods of the served connections. In consequence, we have $RL_1 = 5$, $RL_2 = 10$ and $RL_3 = 20$. Server 1 must use at least 2 slots to serve connections associated with level 1 in each round. Server 2 must use at least 2 slots to serve connections associated with level 2 in each round. Server 3 must use at least 4 slots to serve connections associated with level 3 in each round. There are multiple combinations of values of the server counters that enable serving the five connections correctly. We choose the values given in Table 7.2 (in this choice, servers 2 and 3 may activate the best effort server, or the

**Table 7.1**  Example of characteristics of connections

| Connection | $T^c$ | $NP^c$ |
|---|---|---|
| 1 | 5 | 1 |
| 2 | 5 | 1 |
| 3 | 10 | 2 |
| 4 | 20 | 1 |
| 5 | 20 | 3 |

**Table 7.2**  Values of the server counters

| Service level | $RL_L$ | $ns_L$ | $b_L$ |
|---|---|---|---|
| 1 | 5 | 5 | 3 |
| 2 | 10 | 6 | 3 |
| 3 | 20 | 6 | 0 |

output link may be idle during time intervals where these two servers are active). Figure 7.7 shows the assignment of time slots to the three servers.

### End-to-end delay and jitter bounds provided by HRR discipline

In Kalmanek et al. (1990), it is proven that the end-to-end delay bound and the jitter bound of a connection served at level $L$ are equal to $2N \cdot RL_L + \pi$ and $2N \cdot RL_L$ respectively, if this connection obeys its traffic specification (i.e. it transmits a maximum of $\omega^c$ packets per $RL_L$ slots). $N$ is the number of traversed switches, $RL_L$ is the round length of service $L$, and $\pi$ is the end-to-end propagation delay. $\pi$ is considered negligible in Kalmanek et al. (1990).

## 7.5.2 Stop-and-go discipline

### Single-frame stop-and-go discipline

The stop-and-go (S&G) discipline is a non-work-conserving discipline based on time-framing (Golestani, 1990). In the S&G discipline, the start is given from a reference point in time, common to all the switches of the network (thus the S&G discipline requires clock synchronization of all the switches), and the time axis is divided into periods of the same constant length $T$, called frames. In general, it is possible to have different reference points for different switches. For simplicity, we present the S&G discipline based on a single common reference point.

The S&G discipline defines *departing* and *arriving* frames for each link between two switches. Over each link, one can view the time frames as travelling with the packets from one end of the link (i.e. from one switch) to the other end (i.e. to another switch). Therefore, if $\pi_l$ denotes the sum of propagation delay plus the processing delay at the receiving end of a link $l$, the frames at the receiving end (arriving frames) will be $\pi_l$ time units behind the corresponding frames at the transmitting end (departing frames). At each switch, to synchronize arriving frames on a link $l'$ and departing frames on a link $l$, a constant $\theta_{l',l}(0 \leq \theta_{l',l} < T)$ is introduced so that $\theta_{l',l} + \pi_{l'}$ is a multiple of $T$. Figure 7.8 shows an example of frame synchronization.

At each switch, the arriving frame of each input link is mapped to the departing frame of the output link. All packets from one arriving frame of an input link $l'$ and going to output $l$ are delayed by $\theta_{l',l}$ and put into the corresponding departure frame of $l$. Thus, a packet which has arrived at a switch during a frame $f$ should always be postponed until the beginning of the next frame (Figure 7.8). Since the packets arriving during a frame $f$ are not eligible for transmission in frame $f$, the output link may be idle even when there are packets waiting for transmission.

Each connection $c$ is defined by means of a rate $r^c$ and the connection must transmit no more than $r^c \cdot T$ bits during each frame of length $T$. Thus a fraction of each frame is allocated to each connection.

### Multiframe stop-and-go discipline

Framing introduces a coupling between delay bound and bandwidth allocation granularity. The delay of any packet at a single switch is bounded by a multiple of frame

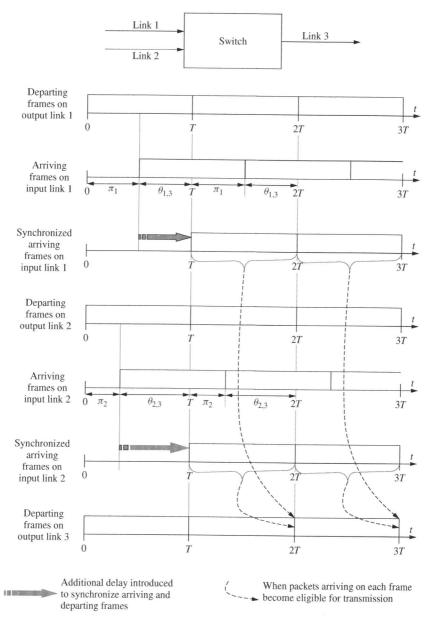

**Figure 7.8**  Relationships between arriving frames, departing frames, $\pi_l$ and $\theta_{l',l}$ (case where $\pi_l < T$)

length. To reduce the delay, a smaller value of $T$ (the frame length) is required. However, since $T$ is also used to specify traffic, it is tied to bandwidth allocation. Assuming a fixed packet length $L$, the minimum granularity of bandwidth allocation is $L/T$. To have more flexibility in bandwidth allocation, or a smaller bandwidth allocation granularity, a larger $T$ is preferred. In consequence, low delay bound and fine granularity of bandwidth allocation cannot be provided simultaneously in a framing discipline. To overcome this coupling problem, a generalized version of S&G with multiple frame lengths, called multiframe stop-and-go, has been proposed (Golestani 1990). In this generalized S&G discipline, the time axis is divided into a hierarchical framing structure. For $G$ levels of framing, $G$ frame lengths are considered, $T_1 \ldots, T_G$. The time axis is divided into frames of size $T_1$, each frame of length $T_1$ is divided into $K_1$ frames of length $T_2, \ldots$, until frames with length $T_G$ are obtained. Every connection is set up as a type $p$ connection ($1 \le p \le G$), in which case it is associated with the frame length $T_p$. Figure 7.9 shows an example with three levels of framing, where $k_1 = 2$, and $k_2 = 3$.

The packets from a type $p$ connection are referred to as type $p$ packets. The value of $p$ is indicated in the header of each packet. Packets on a level $p$ connection need to observe the S&G rule with $T_p$. That is, packets which have arrived during a $T_p$ frame will not be eligible until the beginning of the next $T_p$ frame. Any eligible type $p$ packet has non-preemptive priority over packets of type $p' < p$.

### Delay and jitter bounds provided by stop-and-go discipline

Golestani (1991) proved that the end-to-end delay and delay jitter of a connection $c$ that traverses $N$ S&G switches connected in cascade are bounded by $(2N + 1) \cdot T_p + \pi$ and $2 \cdot T_p$ respectively, if the connection $c$ is assigned to frame length $T_p$ and obeys its traffic specification. $\pi$ is the end-to-end propagation and processing delay. Note that when a single-frame S&G discipline is used, $T_p$ replaces $T$ in the previous two bounds.

### Difference between S&G and HRR

The S&G and HRR disciplines are both time-framing and are similar. The most important difference between S&G and HRR is that S&G synchronizes the arriving frames of the input links and the departing frames of the output link at each switch. There are two implications:

- by this synchronization, tight delay jitter can be provided by S&G,

- the synchronization also means that in multiframe S&G, the frame times of connection should be non-decreasing. The HRR does not have this restriction, thus

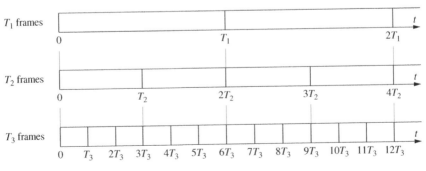

**Figure 7.9**   Example of multiframing with $T_1 = 2T_2 = 6T_3$

HRR gives more flexibility in assigning connections with different frame length at different switches.

Another difference is the ability to control the effects of misbehaving connections. In HRR, the packets of each connection are queued in a separate queue; thus if a connection is misbehaving, it can only cause its own packets to be dropped. On the other hand, an S&G server has no way to prevent itself from being flooded, and misbehaving connections could cause packets of the other connections to be discarded.

## 7.5.3   Jitter earliest-due-date discipline

Jitter earliest-due-date (also called jitter EDD) is an extension of the delay EDD discipline to guarantee jitter bounds (Verma et al., 1991). In order to provide a delay jitter guarantee, the original arrival pattern of the packets on the connection needs to be sufficiently faithfully preserved. Thus, each switch reconstructs and preserves the original arrival pattern of packets, and ensures that this pattern is not distorted too much, so that it is also possible for the next switch on the path to reconstruct the original pattern.

### *Connection establishment procedure*

As for the delay EDD discipline, the client must declare its traffic characteristics and performance requirements at the establishment time of each connection $c$ by means of three parameters: $Xmin^c$ (the minimum packet inter-arrival time), $Lmax^c$ (the maximum length of packets), and $D^c$ (the end-to-end delay bound). In addition, the client must specify the delay jitter $J^c$ required for the connection $c$.

In addition to the procedure used by the delay EDD discipline to determine local delay $D_s^c$ for each switch $s$ traversed by the connection $c$ being established, the jitter EDD discipline must determine local jitter $J_s^c$. A switch $s$ must guarantee that every packet $p$ on the connection $c$ must experience a delay $D_s^{c,p}$ in switch $s$ such that: $D_s^c - J_s^c \leq D_s^{c,p} \leq D_s^c$. The paradigm followed is similar to that of delay EDD: each switch $s$ offers a value for the local deadline, $OD_s^c$, and the local jitter, $OJ_s^c$, it can guarantee. For simplicity, local jitter is equal to local deadline (i.e. $OD_s^c = OJ_s^c$). If the switch $s$ accepts the connection $c$, it adds its offered local jitter — note that only one value is added to the connection request message, since the offered local jitter and offered local delay are equal — to the connection request message and passes this message to the next switch (or to the destination host) on the path. The destination host is the last point where the acceptance/rejection decision of a connection can be made. If all the switches on the path accept the connection, the destination host performs the following test to assure that the end-to-end delay and jitter bounds are met:

$$OJ_N^c \leq J^c \text{ and } D^c \geq \pi + \sum_{s=1}^{N} OJ_s^c \qquad (7.15)$$

where $N$ is the number of switches traversed by the connection $c$, and $\pi$ is the end-to-end propagation delay (in the original version of jitter EDD, $\pi$ is considered negligible).

If condition (7.15) is satisfied, the destination host divides the surplus of end-to-end deadline and end-to-end jitter among all the traversed switches and assigns the local deadline and local jitter for each switch $s$ as follows:

$$D_s^c = \frac{D^c - \pi - \sum_{j=1}^N OJ_j^c}{N} + OJ_s^c, \qquad \text{for } s = 1, \ldots, N-1 \qquad (7.16)$$

$$J_s^c = D_s^c, \qquad \text{for } s = 1, \ldots, N-1 \qquad (7.17)$$

$$J_N^c = J^c \qquad (7.18)$$

The destination host builds a connection response message containing the assigned local delay and jitter bounds and sends it along the reverse of the path taken by the connection request message. When a switch receives a connection response message, the resources previously reserved must be committed or released. Particularly, in each switch $s$, the offered local delay and jitter, $OD_s^c$ and $OJ_s^c$, are replaced by the assigned local delay and local jitter, $D_s^c$ and $J_s^c$, if the connection $c$ is accepted.

### *Rate control and scheduling*

Two functions are performed to guarantee delay and jitter bounds: rate control and scheduling. Scheduling is based on the deadlines assigned to packets. The rate control is used to restore the arrival pattern of packets that is distorted in the previous switch. After a packet is served in a switch, a field in its header is stamped with the difference between its deadline and the actual finish time. A regulator at the next switch holds the packet for this period before it is made eligible to be scheduled. One important consequence of this rate control is that the arrival pattern of packets entering the scheduler queue at any intermediate switch is identical to the arrival pattern at the entry point of the network, provided that the client obeyed the $Xmin^c$-constraint (i.e. the minimum interval between two consecutive packets).

A packet $p$ arriving, at time $AT_s^{c,p}$, at switch $s$, on connection $c$, is assigned an eligibility time $ET_s^{c,p}$ and a deadline $ExD_s^{c,p}$ defined as follows:

$$ET_1^{c,p} \quad = AT_1^{c,p} \qquad (7.19)$$

$$ET_s^{c,p} \quad = AT_s^{c,p} + Ahead_{s-1}^{c,p} \text{ for } s > 1 \qquad (7.20)$$

$$ExD_s^{c,1} \quad = ET_s^{c,1} + D_s^c \qquad (7.21)$$

$$ExD_s^{c,p} \quad = \max\{ET_s^{c,p} + D_s^c, ExD_s^{c,p-1} + Xmin^c\} \text{ for } p > 1 \qquad (7.22)$$

where $Ahead_{s-1}^{c,p}$ is the amount of time the packet $p$ is ahead of schedule at the switch $s - 1$; it is equal to the difference between the local deadline $D_{s-1}^c$ and the actual delay at switch $s - 1$; server $s - 1$ puts this difference in the header of packet $p$ before transmitting it to the next switch.

The packet $p$ is ineligible for transmission until its eligibility time $ET_s^{c,p}$. Ineligible packets are kept in a queue from which they are transferred to the scheduler queue as they become eligible. The ordering and servicing of the packet queue is by increasing deadlines. Deadlines are considered as dynamic priorities of packets. Note that the local delay assigned to a connection does not take into account the time a packet is held before being eligible; it only considers the delay at scheduler level and transmission delay.

### End-to-end delay and jitter bounds provided by jitter EDD

Verma et al. (1991) proved that if a connection does not violate its traffic specification, then its end-to-end delay and jitter requirements are guaranteed by the jitter EDD discipline. In consequence, packets from a connection $c$ experience an end-to-end delay ranging between $D^c - J^c$ and $D^c$. Recall that performance parameters $D^c$ and $J^c$ are specified by the client in its connection request.

## 7.5.4 Rate-controlled static-priority discipline

The disciplines presented in the previous sections are either frame-based (i.e. they use time-framing) or priority-based (i.e. they use a sorted priority queue mechanism). Time-framing introduces dependencies between scheduling priority and bandwidth allocation granularity, so that connections with both low delay and low bandwidth requirements cannot be supported efficiently. A sorted priority queue has an insertion operation with a high overhead: the insertion operation is $O(\log(M))$, where $M$ is the number of packets in the queue. This may not be acceptable in a high-speed network where the number of packets may be high. Moreover, in order to decouple scheduling priority and bandwidth allocation, a scheme based on sorted priority queue requires a complicated schedulability test at connection establishment time. The rate-controlled static-priority (RCSP) discipline, proposed by Zhang and Ferrari (1993), overcomes the previous limitations.

### Functional architecture of an RCSP server

An RCSP server consists of two components: a *rate controller* and a *static-priority scheduler* (Figure 7.10). The rate controller shapes the input traffic from each connection into the desired traffic pattern by assigning an eligibility time to each packet. The scheduler orders the transmission of eligible packets.

The rate controller consists of a set of regulators associated with the connections traversing the switch. Regulators control interactions between switches and eliminate jitter. Two types of jitter may be guaranteed: *rate jitter* and *delay jitter*. Rate jitter is used to capture burstiness of the traffic, and is defined as the maximum number of packets in a jitter averaging interval. Delay jitter is used to capture the magnitude of the distortion of the traffic caused by the network, and is defined as the maximum difference between the delays experienced by any two consecutive packets on the same connection. Consequently, there are two types of regulators: rate-jitter controlling regulators and delay-jitter controlling regulators. According to the requirements of each connection, one type of regulator is associated with the connection in an RCSP server. Both types of regulators assign each packet an *eligibility time* upon its arrival and hold the packet until that time before handing it to the scheduler. Note that the conceptual

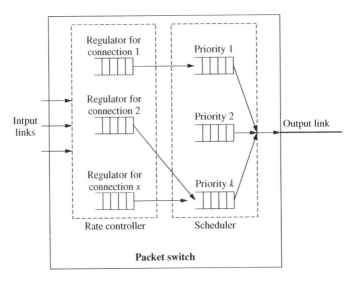

**Figure 7.10**   General architecture of an RCSP server

decomposition of the rate controller into a set of regulators does not imply that there must be multiple physical regulators in an implementation of the RCSP discipline; a common mechanism can be shared by all the logical regulators.

### Connection establishment phase

In the RCSP discipline, each connection $c$ specifies its requirements with four parameters: $Xmin^c$, $Xave^c$, $I^c$ and $Lmax^c$. $Xmin^c$ is the minimum packet inter-arrival time, $Xave^c$ is the average packet inter-arrival time over an averaging interval of length $I^c$, and $Lmax^c$ is the maximum packet size. During the connection establishment, each switch $s$ on the connection $c$ path assigns a local delay bound $D_s^c$ (a bound it can guarantee) and a priority level to connection $c$. Such an assignment is based on a mechanism that depends on the policy of resource reservation in each switch (this mechanism is out of the scope of the RCSP discipline). For example, the local delay bound may be assigned using the same procedure as the one proposed for delay EDD (see Section 7.4.3) and the priority level may be assigned using the following optimal procedure called _D_Order procedure_ (Kandlur et al., 1991):

Let $s$ be the index of the switch executing the D_Order procedure and $x$ the index of the connection to establish.

1. Arrange the connections already accepted by switch $s$ in ascending order of their associated local delay $D_s^c$.

2. Assign the highest priority to the new connection $x$. Assign priorities to the other connections based on this order, with high priority assigned to connections with small local delays.

3. Compute the new worst-case response times $r^c$ (i.e. the maximum waiting time of a packet on connection $c$ at switch $s$) for the existing connections based on the priority assignment.

4. In the priority order, find the smallest position $q$ such that $r^c \le D_s^c$ for all connections with position greater than $q$ (i.e. with priority lower than $q$).

5. Assign priority $q$ to the new connection and compute the response time $r^x$. Then, the local delay $D_s^x$ assigned to the connection $x$ has to be such that $D_s^x \ge r^x$.

### *RCSP algorithm*

Consider a packet $p$ from connection $c$ that arrives, at switch $s$, at time $AT_s^{c,p}$. Let $ET_s^{c,p}$ be the eligibility time assigned by switch $s$ to this packet. When a rate-jitter controlling regulator is associated with the connection $c$ in the switch $s$, the eligibility time of packet $p$ is defined as follows:

$$ET_s^{c,p} = -I^c, \text{ for } p < 0 \tag{7.23}$$

$$ET_s^{c,p} = AT_s^{c,p}, \text{ for } p = 1 \tag{7.24}$$

$$ET_s^{c,p} = \max \left\{ ET_s^{c,p-1} + Xmin^c, ET_s^{c,p-\left\lfloor \frac{1}{Xave^c} \right\rfloor + 1} + I^c, AT_s^{c,p} \right\}, p > 1 \tag{7.25}$$

When a delay-jitter controlling regulator is associated with a connection $c$ in a switch $s$, the eligibility time of packet $p$ is defined, with reference to the eligibility time of the same packet at the previous switch, as follows:

$$ET_s^{c,p} = AT_s^{c,p}, \text{ for } s = 0 \tag{7.26}$$

$$ET_s^{c,p} = ET_{s-1}^{c,p} + D_{s-1}^c + \pi_{s-1,s}, \text{ for } s > 0 \tag{7.27}$$

where switch 0 is the source of the connection, $D_{s-1}^c$ is the delay bound of packets on the connection $c$ at the scheduler of switch $s - 1$, and $\pi_{s-1,s}$ is the propagation delay between switches $s$ and $s - 1$.

The assignment of eligibility times achieved using equalities (7.26) and (7.27), by a delay-jitter controlling regulator, satisfies equality (7.28), which means that the traffic pattern on a connection at the output of the regulator of every server traversed by the connection is exactly the same as the traffic pattern of the connection at the entrance of the network:

$$ET_s^{c,p} - ET_s^{c,p-1} = AT_0^{c,p} - AT_0^{c,p-1}, p > 1 \tag{7.28}$$

The scheduler in an RCSP switch consists of prioritized real-time packet queues and a non-real-time queue (we will not discuss further the non-real-time queue management). A packet on a connection is inserted in the scheduler queue associated with the priority level assigned to this connection when its eligibility time is reached. The scheduler services packets using a non-preemptive static-priority discipline which chooses packets in FCFS order from the highest-priority non-empty queue.

Equality (7.28) means that a switch absorbs jitter that may be introduced in the previous switch by holding a packet transmitted early by the previous switch. In the first switch on the path, the packet is directly eligible and is inserted in the scheduler queue; the scheduler of this switch transmits the packet within the delay assigned to the considered connection. The second switch may delay the packet only if the packet is ahead of schedule of the first switch, and so on until the last switch, which delivers the packet to the destination host. In consequence, when a delay-jitter controlling regulator is used, the amount of holding time is exactly the amount of time the packet was ahead when it left the previous switch. In the same way, the analysis of equality (7.25) leads to the following observation: when a rate-jitter controlling regulator is used, the amount of time a packet is to be held is computed according to the packet spacing requirement, which may be less than the amount of time it was ahead of the schedule in the previous switch.

### *Delay and jitter bounds provided by RCSP discipline*

Zhang (1995) and Zhang and Ferrari (1993) proved the following results:

- The end-to-end delay for any packet on a connection $c$ is bounded by $\sum_{s=1}^{N} D_s^c + \pi + B$, if rate-jitter controlling regulators are used.

- The end-to-end delay and delay jitter for any packet on a connection $c$ are bounded by $\sum_{s=1}^{N} D_s^c + \pi + B$ and $D_N^c + B$, respectively, if delay-jitter controlling regulators are used.

where $N$ is the number of switches connected in cascade traversed by the connection $c$, $\pi$ is the end-to-end propagation delay, $D_1^c, D_2^c, \ldots, D_N^c$ are the local deadlines assigned to connection $c$ in the $N$ switches. $B$ is equal to 0 if the traffic on connection $c$ obeys the $[Xmin^c, Xave^c, I^c, Lmax^c]$ specification at the entrance of the first switch, and $B$ is equal to $\sigma^c/\rho^c$ if the traffic on connection $c$ conforms to a leaky bucket with size $\sigma^c$ and rate $\rho^c$.

## 7.6   Summary and Conclusion

We have presented a variety of service disciplines to provide QoS guarantees for hard real-time communications. The emphasis has been on examining their mechanisms and the specific properties that can provide delay and jitter guarantees. Some disciplines are work-conserving and some others are not. While work-conserving disciplines are dominant in conventional networks, non-work-conserving disciplines exhibit features that are suitable for providing guaranteed performance, particularly jitter bounds.

In general, frame-based algorithms have advantages over priority-based algorithms in that the delay bounds as well as bandwidth are guaranteed deterministically by reserving a fixed amount of traffic in a certain time interval. Moreover, in frame-based algorithms, delays at switches can be analysed independently and simply added together to determine the end-to-end delay bounds. These properties make QoS analysis, service prediction, and even the connection establishment process dramatically simpler compared to priority-based approaches. Unfortunately, frame-based algorithms have the drawback of coupling the delay and granularity of bandwidth allocation. Delay bounds and unit of bandwidth allocation are dependent on the frame size. With larger frame sizes, connections are supported with a wider range of bandwidth requirements, but delay bounds increase proportionally.

The delay EDD, jitter EDD and RCSP disciplines are scheduler-based disciplines and require the use of procedures to determine the local delay accepted by each switch during connection establishment. Jitter EDD also requires a procedure for determining local jitter, and RCSP requires a procedure for determining static priorities assigned to connections. All these procedures depend on the policy of resource reservation in each switch.

It is worth noticing that in modern packet-switching networks, the flow rates are very high and the number of connections traversing a switch can reach several thousands. It is consequently necessary to have algorithms whose overhead is reduced to its minimum. A significant aspect which can be a brake for the use of disciplines such as WFQ is their implementation cost (i.e. costs associated with computation of the system virtual time and with the management of priority queues to order the transmission of packets). The interested reader can find some guidelines for implementing packet scheduling algorithms in high-speed networks in Stephens et al. (1999). Tables 7.3–7.5 summarize

**Table 7.3**   Classification of service disciplines (1)

| Type | Rate allocation | Delay allocation |
|---|---|---|
| Work-conserving | Packet-by-packet GPS (PGPS) | Delay earliest-due-date (D-EDD) |
| | Weighted fair queuing (WFQ) Virtual clock (VC) Weighted round-robin (WRR) | |
| Non-work-conserving | Hierarchical round-robin (HRR) Stop-and-go (S&G) | Jitter earliest-due-date (J-EDD) Rate-controlled static-priority (RCSP) |

**Table 7.4**   Classification of service disciplines (2)

| Type | Scheduler-based | Rate-based |
|---|---|---|
| Priority-based | Delay EDD Jitter EDD RCSP | WFQ PGPS VC |
| Frame-based | | S&G HRR WRR |

**Table 7.5**   Properties of service disciplines

| Property | WFQ PGPS | VC | D-EDD | HRR | S&G | J-EDD | RCSP |
|---|---|---|---|---|---|---|---|
| Delay guarantee* | Yes | Yes | Yes | Yes | Yes | Yes | Yes |
| Jitter guarantee* | No | No | No | No | Yes | Yes | Yes |
| Decoupled delay and bandwidth allocation | No | No | Yes | No | No | Yes | Yes |
| Protection of well-behaved connections | Yes | Yes | Yes | Yes | No | Yes | Yes |

* To guarantee delay and jitter, the connection must obey user traffic specification.

the main features of the presented disciplines. A good synthesis and comparison of the scheduling disciplines presented in this chapter is given in Zhang (1995).

Finally, it is worth noting that most disciplines presented in this chapter have been integrated in experimental or commercial ATM switches, and for a, few years, they have been used experimentally in the context of the next generation of the Internet, which will be deployed using *Integrated Services* (called *IntServ*) and *Differentiated Services* (called *DiffServ*) architectures that provide QoS guarantees.

# 7.7  Exercises

## 7.7.1  Questions

---

***Exercise 7.1:   Scheduling with the WFQ discipline family***

Consider 6 connections (1, ..., 6) sharing the same output link of a switch $s$. For simplicity, assume that all packets have the same size, which is equal to $S$ bits. The output link speed is 10 $S/6$ *bits/s*. Also, assume that the total bandwidth of the output link is allocated as follows: 50% for connection 1 and 10% for each of the other five connections. Connection 1 sends 6 back-to-back packets starting at time 0 while all the other connections send only one packet at time 0.

**Q1**  Build the schedule of the packets when the server utilizes the GPS discipline.

**Q2**  Build the schedule of the packets when the server utilizes the WFQ discipline.

**Q3**  Bennett and Zhang (1996a) proposed a discipline, called $WF^2Q$ (worst-case fair weighted fair queuing), that emulates GPS service better than WFQ. $WF^2Q$ increases fairness. In a $WF^2Q$ server, when the next packet is chosen for service at time $t$, rather than selecting it from among all the packets at the server as in WFQ, the server only considers the set of packets that have started (and possibly finished) receiving service in the corresponding GPS server at time $t$, and selects the packet among them that would complete service first in the corresponding GPS server. Build the schedule of the packets of the six connections when the server utilizes the $WF^2Q$ discipline.

---

***Exercise 7.2:   Computation of round number for WFQ***

Consider again Example 7.1, presented in Section 7.4.1, where two connections share the same output link of a switch $s$. Each connection utilizes 50% of the output link bandwidth. At time $t = 0$, a packet $P^{1,1}$ of size 100 bits arrives on

_____ *Continued on page 165* _____

_Continued from page 164_

connection 1, and a packet $P^{2,1}$ of size 150 bits arrives on connection 2 at time $t = 50$.

**Q1**  What is the value of $R_s(t)$, the round number, at time 250?

---

**Exercise 7.3:  _Scheduling with the virtual clock discipline_**

Consider three connections (1, 2 and 3) sharing the same output link of a switch $s$ using the virtual clock discipline. For simplicity, we assume that packets from all the connections have the same size, $L$ bits, and that the output link has a speed of $L$ bits/s. Thus, the transmission of one packet takes one time unit. Each connection $c$ is specified by a couple of parameters $r^c$ and $A^c : r^1 = 0.5L$, $r^2 = 0.2L$, $r^3 = 0.2L$, $A^1 = 2$, $A^2 = 5$, $A^3 = 5$. The arrival patterns of the three connections are as follows:

- Packets on connection 1 arrive at times $t = 2$ and $t = 4$;

- Packets on connection 2 arrive at times $t = 0, t = 1, t = 2$ and $t = 3$;

- Packets on connection 3 arrive at times $t = 0, t = 1, t = 2$ and $t = 3$.

**Q1**  Build the schedule of the packets when the switch utilizes the virtual clock discipline.

---

**Exercise 7.4:  _Scheduling with the HRR discipline_**

Example 7.3, presented in Section 7.5.1, considered a set of five periodic connections transmitting packets with the same fixed length, and served by an HRR switch. The service time of a packet is assumed equal to one time slot. The period $T^c$ of each connection $c$ and the number of packets ($NP^c$) it issues per period are given in Table 7.1. We have chosen three levels of service, and determined the weights associated with connections and the counter values ($RL_L$, $ns_L$ and $b_L$) associated with service levels (see Table 7.2).

**Q1**  Assume that all the connections start at the same time 0, and that each connection issues its packet(s) at the beginning of its period. The five traffics enter an HRR switch specified by the values given in Table 7.2. Assume that the propagation delay is negligible. Give a schedule of packets during the time interval [0, 20].

*Exercise 7.5:    Determining end-to-end delay and jitter bounds*
                  *for the stop-and-go discipline*

Let $c$ be a connection passing by $N$ switches that use the stop-and-go discipline with a frame of length $T$. We denote the links by $0, 1, \ldots, N$. A packet $p$ travels in the network in a sequence of arriving and departing frames denoted by $AF_0^p, DF_1^p, AF_1^p, DF_2^p, AF_2^p, \ldots, DF_N^p, AF_N^p$. ($AF_l^p$ and $DF_l^p$ denote the arriving frame and departing frame, on link $l$, respectively.) As shown in Figure 7.11a, a packet $p$ arrives on the access link (link 0), at

(a) Frames conveying a packet $p$

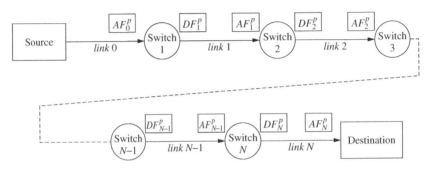

(b) Frame sequencing

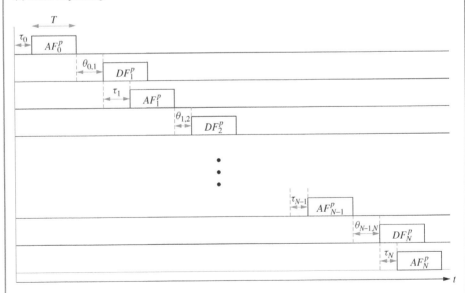

**Figure 7.11**   Stop-and-go frames

*Continued on page 167*

*Continued from page 166*

the first switch, in frame $AF_0^p$, it leaves the first switch in the departing frame $DF_1^p$, it arrives on link 1, at the second switch, in frame $AF_1^p$, and so on.

The sum of propagation delay plus the processing delay of a link $l$ is denoted by $\tau_l$. Assume that the delay $\tau_l$ is less than the frame length for all the links. An additional delay (denoted by $\theta_{l,l+1}$) is introduced in each switch to synchronize arriving frames on link $l$ and departing frames on link $l+1$. This delay is fixed such that: $\tau_l + \theta_{l,l+1} = T (l = 0, \ldots, N-1)$. Figure 7.11b shows the sequencing of the frames conveying the packet $p$.

**Q1**  Find the time difference between frames $AF_l^p$ and $DF_{l+1}^p (l = 0, \ldots, N-1)$.

**Q2**  Find the time difference between frames $DF_l^p$ and $AF_l^p (l = 1, \ldots, N)$.

**Q3**  Find the time difference between frames $AF_N^p$ and $AF_0^p$.

**Q4**  Determine the minimum and maximum end-to-end delay on connection $c$ using the answers of the previous questions.

**Q5**  Prove the end-to-end delay and jitter bounds proved by Golestani given in Section 7.5.2, using the answers of the previous questions.

---

### Exercise 7.6:  *Scheduling with the jitter EDD discipline*

Consider a connection $c$ traversing two switches 1 and 2 (there are only two switches). Both switches use the jitter EDD discipline. The parameters declared during connection establishment are: $Xmin^c = 5$, $D^c = 6$, $J^c = 2$, and $Lmax^c = L$. All the packets have the same size. The transmission time of a packet is equal to 1 for the source and both switches, and the propagation delay is taken to be 0, for all links. Assume that during connection establishment, the local deadlines and jitter assigned to connection $c$ are: $D_1^c = 4$, $D_2^c = 2$, $J_1^c = 4$, $J_2^c = 2$. Note that the local deadline values ($D_1^c$ and $D_2^c$) and jitter values ($J_1^c$ and $J_2^c$) assigned to connection $c$ satisfy the equalities (7.15)–(7.18).

**Q1**  Give a packet schedule, for both switches, for five packets that arrive at switch 1 at times 1, 6, 11, 16 and 21, from a periodic source. Give the packet arrival times at destination for the chosen schedules.

**Q2**  Verify that end-to-end delay and jitter are guaranteed by the packet schedules given for the previous question.

## 7.7.2 Answers

---

*Exercise 7.1: Scheduling with the WFQ discipline family*

**Q1** *GPS server.* To simplify, we assume that a round-robin turn duration is 1 second. In each round of the round-robin algorithm, connection 1 utilizes *0.5* of the bandwidth (i.e. it transmits a fragment with $5S/6$ bits of the packet in the head of queue associated with it) and each of the other connections utilizes 0.1 of the bandwidth (i.e. each connection transmits a fragment of $S/6$ bits of its packet). The schedule obtained with the GPS algorithm is shown in Figure 7.12.

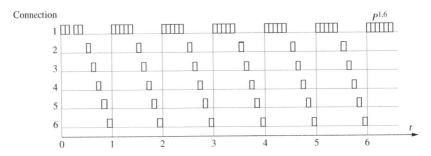

$\square$ : Packet fragment ($S/6$ bits)

**Figure 7.12**    Scheduling with GPS

**Q2** *WFQ server.* Let $S_s^{c,p}$ and $F_s^{c,p}$ be the start time and the finish time of packet $p$ $(p = 1, \ldots, 6)$ on connection $c$ $(c = 1, \ldots, 6)$, respectively. The 6 packets of connection 1 are sent back-to-back; this means that during the time interval between the arrival of the first packet and the 6th one the increase of number of rounds of the round-robin server is negligible. For simplicity, we consider that the packets of connection 1 arrive at the server at the same time $t = 0$. $R_s(0)$, the number of rounds at time $t = 0$, is 0. Using equations (7.1) and (7.4), we have:

$$S_s^{1,1} = 0; \quad F_s^{1,1} = 0 + S/(0.5 \times 10S/6) = 6/5$$
$$S_s^{1,2} = 6/5; \quad F_s^{1,2} = S_s^{1,2} + S/(0.5 \times 10S/6) = 12/5$$

$$\ldots$$

$$S_s^{1,6} = 6; \quad F_s^{1,6} = S_s^{1,6} + S/(0.5 \times 10S/6) = 36/5$$
$$S_s^{2,1} = 0; \quad F_s^{2,1} = 0 + S/(0.1 \times 10S/6) = 6$$

$$\ldots$$

$$S_s^{6,1} = 0; \quad F_s^{6,1} = 0 + S/(0.1 \times 10S/6) = 6$$

*Continued on page 169*

*Continued from page 168*

WFQ disciplines schedules the packets according to their finish numbers, thus the packets of the 6 connections are transmitted as shown in Figure 7.13. $P^{c,j}$ means the $j$th packet on connection $c$.

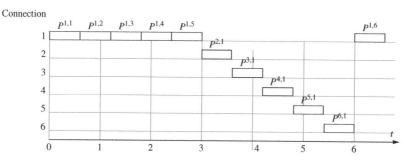

**Figure 7.13**   Scheduling with WFQ

**Q3**   *WF$^2$Q server.* At time $t = 0$, there is one packet at the head of each queue. The finish and start numbers are computed in the same way as for Q2. At time $t = 0$, the first packets, $P^{c,1}$, of connections $c = 1, \ldots, 6$ start their service in the GPS server. Among them, $P^{1,1}$ has the smallest finish time in GPS, so it will be served first in WF$^2$Q. At time 6/10, $P^{1,1}$ is completely transmitted and there are still 10 packets. Although $P^{1,2}$ has the smallest finish time, it will not start service in the GPS server until time 6/5 (because its start number is 6/5), therefore it will be not eligible for transmission at time 6/10. The packets of the other 5 connections have all started service at time $t = 0$ at the GPS server, and thus are eligible. Since they all have the same finish number in the GPS server, the tie-breaking rule of giving the highest priority to the connection with the smallest number will yield $P^{2,1}$. At time 12/10, $P^{2,1}$ finishes transmission and $P^{1,2}$ becomes eligible and has the smallest finish number, thus it will start service next. The rest of the *WF$^2$Q* schedule is shown in Figure 7.14.

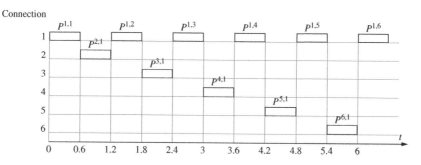

**Figure 7.14**   Scheduling with WF$^2$Q

---

*Exercise 7.2:    Computation of round number for WFQ*

**Q1**  At time $t = 0$, the packet $P^{1,1}$ arrives, it is assigned a finish number $F_s^{1,1} = 200$, and it starts service. During the interval $[0, 50]$, only connection 1 is active, thus $N_{ac}(t) = 0.5$ and $dR(t)/dt = 1/0.5$. In consequence, $R(50) = 100$.

At time $t = 50$, the packet $P^{2,1}$ arrives, it is assigned a finish number $F_s^{2,1} = 100 + 150/0.5 = 400$. At time $t = 100$, $P^{1,1}$ completes service. In the interval $[50, 100]$, $N_{ac}(t) = 0.5 + 0.5 = 1$. Then $R(100) = R(50) + 50 = 150$. Since $F_s^{1,1} = 200$, connection 1 is still active, and $N_{ac}(t)$ stays at 1.

At $t = 100$, packet $P^{2,1}$ starts service. At $t = 250$, packet $P^{2,1}$ completes service. The number $N_{ac}(t)$ went down to 0.5 when $R(t) = 200$ (i.e. when connection 1 became inactive). $R(200) = R(100) + 100 = 250$. During the interval $[200, 250]$, $N_{ac}(t) = 0.5$, thus $R(250) = R(200) + 50 \times 1/0.5 = 350$.

---

*Exercise 7.3:    Scheduling with the virtual clock discipline*

**Q1**  Let $P^{c,j}$ be the $j$th packet from connection $c$. The auxiliary virtual clocks of the packets are computed, on packet arrival times, according to equality (7.9):

- At time $t = 0$, packets $P^{2,1}$ and $P^{3,1}$ arrive simultaneously. $auxVC_s^2 = auxVC_s^3 = 5$. Thus packets $P^{2,1}$ and $P^{3,1}$ are stamped with a virtual clock value equal to 5.

- At time $t = 1$, packets $P^{2,2}$ and $P^{3,2}$ arrive simultaneously. $auxVC_s^2 = auxVC_s^3 = 10$. Thus packets $P^{2,2}$ and $P^{3,2}$ are stamped with a virtual clock value equal to 10.

- At time $t = 2$, packets $P^{1,1}$, $P^{2,3}$ and $P^{3,3}$ arrive simultaneously. $auxVC_s^1 = 4$, and $auxVC_s^2 = auxVC_s^3 = 15$. Thus packet $P^{1,1}$ is stamped with a virtual clock value equal to 4, and $P^{2,3}$ and $P^{3,3}$ are stamped with a virtual clock value equal to 15.

- At time $t = 3$, packets $P^{2,4}$ and $P^{3,4}$ arrive simultaneously. $auxVC_s^2 = auxVC_s^3 = 20$. Thus packets $P_4^2$ and $P_4^3$ are stamped with a virtual clock value equal to 20.

- At time $t = 4$, packet $P^{1,2}$ arrives. $auxVC_s^1 = 6$. Thus packet $P^{1,2}$ is stamped with a virtual clock value equal to 6.

As virtual clock scheduling is based on the values of $auxVC$, the schedule of packets obtained is given by Figure 7.15. Note that although connections 2 and 3 are sending packets at higher rates (both connections do not comply

*Continued on page 171*

___ *Continued from page 170* ___

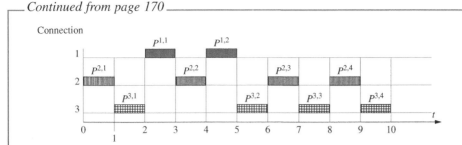

**Figure 7.15** Scheduling with virtual clock

with their $A^c$ parameter), the virtual clock algorithm ensures that each well-behaved connection (in this case connection 1) gets good performance.

---

*Exercise 7.4:* **Scheduling with the HRR discipline**

**Q1** Following the algorithm of the HRR discipline with three service levels, the packets issued from the five connections during the interval $[0, 20]$ are scheduled on the output link of the switch as shown by Figure 7.16. For simplicity, we assume that the arrivals of packets at the switch are synchronized with the beginning of the rounds, i.e. the packets from

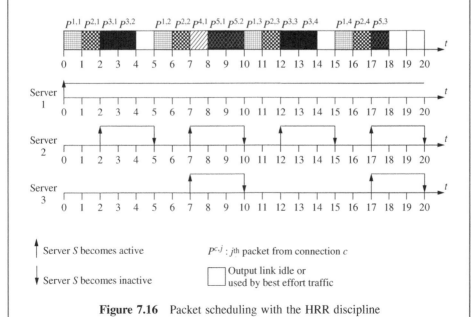

**Figure 7.16** Packet scheduling with the HRR discipline

___ *Continued on page 172* ___

---

*Continued from page 171*

> a connection are queued in the next list of the server that serves this connection just before a new round of this server begins. At time 0, server 1 becomes active (it stays always active); the two first packets of connections 1 and 2 ($P^{1,1}$ and $P^{2,1}$) are in the current list of server 1, thus it serves them, and activates server 2 at time 2. Once activated, server 2 serves connection 3 for 2 slots (packets $P^{3,1}$ and $P^{3,2}$ are transmitted) and as its current list is empty at time 4, it activates best effort server (or the output link remains idle during 1 slot). At time 5, server 2 becomes inactive, because $B_1$ is equal to zero. A new round of server 1 begins, and so on. The times when the different servers are active or inactive are given to aid understanding of easily the scheduling of packets.

---

**Exercise 7.5:   Determining end-to-end delay and jitter bounds for the stop-and-go discipline**

**Q1**   As the arriving frames on link $l$ and departing frames on link $l+1$ are synchronized by introducing a delay $\theta_{l,l+1}$, the time difference between $AF_l^p$ and $DF_{l+1}^p$ is $T + \theta_{l,l+1}$. Thus: $\overset{\mapsto}{DF_{l+1}^p} - \overset{\mapsto}{AF_l^p} = T + \theta_{l,l+1}$, ($l = 0, \ldots, N-1$), where $\overset{\mapsto}{F}$ denotes the start time of frame $F$.

**Q2**   The difference between $DF_l^p$ and $AF_l^p$ (i.e. the time difference of departing and arriving frames on the same link) is equal to $\tau_l$ (i.e. the sum of propagation delay plus the processing delay). Thus: $\overset{\mapsto}{AF_l^p} - \overset{\mapsto}{DF_l^p} = \tau_l$, ($l = 1, \ldots, N$).

**Q3**   $\overset{\mapsto}{AF_N^p} - \overset{\mapsto}{AF_0^p}$

$$= \overset{\mapsto}{AF_N^p} + (\overset{\mapsto}{AF_{N-1}^p} - \overset{\mapsto}{AF_{N-1}^p}) + (\overset{\mapsto}{AF_{N-2}^p} - \overset{\mapsto}{AF_{N-2}^p})$$

$$+ \ldots + (\overset{\mapsto}{AF_1^p} - \overset{\mapsto}{AF_1^p}) - \overset{\mapsto}{AF_0^p}$$

$$= (\overset{\mapsto}{AF_N^p} - \overset{\mapsto}{AF_{N-1}^p}) + (\overset{\mapsto}{AF_{N-1}^p} - \overset{\mapsto}{F_{N-2}^p}) + \ldots + (\overset{\mapsto}{AF_1^p} - \overset{\mapsto}{AF_0^p})$$

Using the results of the answers to Q1 and Q2, we have: $\overset{\mapsto}{AF_l^p} = \overset{\mapsto}{DF_{l+1}^p} - T - \theta_{l,l+1}$ and $\overset{\mapsto}{AF_{l+1}^p} = \overset{\mapsto}{AF_l^p} + \tau_{l+1}$, thus: $\overset{\mapsto}{AF_{l+1}^p} - \overset{\mapsto}{AF_l^p} = T + \tau_{l+1} + \theta_{l,l+1}$.

In consequence, we have:

$$\overset{\mapsto}{AF_N^p} - \overset{\mapsto}{AF_0^p} = \sum_{l=0}^{N-1} (T + \theta_{l,l+1} + \tau_{l+1}) = N \cdot T + \sum_{l=0}^{N-1} \theta_{l,l+1} + \sum_{l=1}^{N} \tau_l$$

*Continued on page 173*

_Continued from page 172_

**Q4** A packet $p$ occupies a certain position in the arriving frame $AF_0^p$ and a certain position in the arriving frame $AF_N^p$. The minimum stay of packet $p$ in the network is when packet $p$ arrives at the end of arriving frame $AF_0^p$ and it arrives at the destination at the beginning of frame $AF_N^p$. The maximum stay of packet $p$ in the network is when packet $p$ arrives at the beginning of arriving frame $AF_0^p$ and it arrives at the destination at the end of frame $AF_N^p$. We denote the minimum and maximum end-to-end delays of packet $p$ by $minE2E^p$ and $maxE2E^p$, respectively. Using the result of the answer to Q3, we have:

$$minE2E^p = \overrightarrow{AF}_N^p - \overrightarrow{AF}_0^p - T + \tau_0 = (N-1) \cdot T + \sum_{l=0}^{N-1} \theta_{l,l+1} + \sum_{l=0}^{N} \tau_l$$

$$maxE2E^p = \overrightarrow{AF}_N^p - \overrightarrow{AF}_0^p + T + \tau_0 = (N+1) \cdot T + \sum_{l=0}^{N-1} \theta_{l,l+1} + \sum_{l=0}^{N} \tau_l$$

**Q5** In Section 7.5.2, we mentioned that Golestani proved that the end-to-end delay and jitter are bounded by $(2N+1) \cdot T + \pi$ and $2 \cdot T$ respectively, where $\pi$ is the sum of end-to-end propagation and processing delays. As $\pi$ is equal to $\sum_{l=0}^{N} \tau_l$ and any additional delay $\theta_{l,l+1} (l = 0, \ldots, N-1)$ is less than $T$, $maxE2E^p$ is bounded by $(2N+1) \cdot T + \pi$. The difference between the minimum and maximum end-to-end delays ($minE2E^p$ and $maxE2E^p$) determined in the answers of the previous question is $2 \cdot T$. Thus we prove the bounds given by Golestani.

---

**Exercise 7.6:  *Scheduling with the jitter EDD discipline***

**Q1** Using equations (7.19), (7.21) and (7.22), the eligibility times and deadlines of the five packets at first switch are:

$$ET_1^{c,1} = 1, ET_1^{c,2} = 6, ET_1^{c,3} = 11, ET_1^{c,4} = 16, \text{ and } ET_1^{c,5} = 21$$

$$ExD_s^{c,1} = 5, ExD_s^{c,2} = 10, ExD_s^{c,3} = 15, ExD_s^{c,4} = 20 \text{ and } ExD_s^{c,5} = 25$$

The actual delay (i.e. waiting time plus transmission time) experienced by each packet at switch 1 depends on the load of this switch, but never exceeds the local deadline assigned to connection $c$ (i.e. $D_1^c = 4$). For example, the actual delays of packets 1 to 5 are 2, 4, 1, 4 and 1, respectively.

_Continued on page 174_

*Continued from page 173*

In consequence, the arrival times of packets, at switch 2, are 3, 10, 12, 20 and 22, respectively (Figure 7.17).

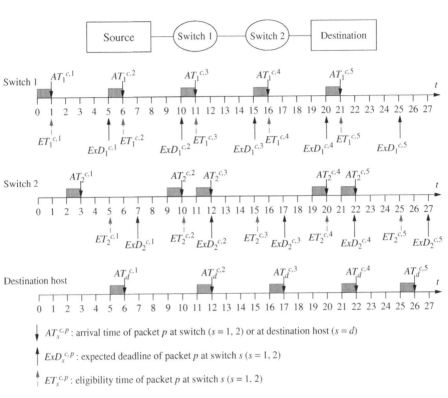

**Figure 7.17**   Example of delay EDD scheduling

Using equations (7.20)–(7.22), the eligibility times and deadlines of the five packets at switch 2 are:

$$ET_2^{c,1} = 5, ET_2^{c,2} = 10, ET_2^{c,3} = 15, ET_2^{c,4} = 20 \text{ and } ET_2^{c,5} = 25$$

$$ExD_2^{c,1} = 7, ExD_2^{c,2} = 12, ExD_2^{c,3} = 17, ExD_2^{c,4} = 22 \text{ and } ExD_2^{c,5} = 27$$

The actual delays of the five packets at switch 2 depend on the load of this switch, but never exceed the local deadline assigned to connection $c$ (i.e. $D_2^c = 2$). Recall that the time a packet is held before being eligible is not a component of the actual delay. For example, the actual delays of packets 1

*Continued on page 175*

*Continued from page 173*

to 5 are 1, 2, 2, 2 and 1, respectively. In consequence, the arrival times of packets at destination are 6, 12, 17, 22 and 26, respectively (Figure 7.17).

**Q2.** The end-to-end delays of packets 1 to 5 are 5, 6, 6, 6 and 5, respectively. The maximum end-to-end delay variation is 1. In consequence, end-to-end delay and jitter declared during connection establishment are guaranteed by the schedules given in Figure 7.17.

# 8

# Software Environment

This chapter presents some software components relevant to real-time applications. The first part of the chapter is concerned with operating systems. Real-time requirements for operating system behaviour forbid the use of standard Unix, although the Posix/Unix interface is very useful for software engineering. Three approaches are presented. In the first one, the real-time executive has been customized to provide a Posix interface. This is illustrated by VxWorks, the executive of the Mars Pathfinder rover, which is the second case study which will be presented in Chapter 9. The second approach is that of RT-Linux where a small companion kernel is attached to a Unix-like system. In the third approach, a system based on a Unix architecture has been engineered from scratch in order to fulfil real-time requirements. This is illustrated by LynxOs, the executive of the rolling mill acquisition system, which will be presented in Chapter 9 as the first case study. The second part of the chapter deals with programming languages designed with real-time potential. Some of them provide asynchronous programming. The Ada programming language is largely developed with the example of a mine pump control implementation. Real-time Java is outlined. Synchronous languages that make the assumption of instantaneously reacting to external events are also presented. The last part of the chapter is an overview of the real-time capabilities which are being added to distributed platforms that provide standardized middleware for non-real-time distributed applications. The challenge is to be able to use distributed objects and components and common-off-the-shelf hardware and software components that are developed extensively for non-real-time distributed applications. The chapter ends by summarizing the real-time capabilities of these software environments.

## 8.1 Real-Time Operating System and Real-Time Kernel

### 8.1.1 Overview

*Requirements*

A modern real-time operating system should provide facilities to fulfil the three major requirements of real-time applications. These are:

- guarantee of response from the computing system;
- promptness of a response, once it has been decided;
- reliability of the application code.

In interactive operating systems, the CPU activity is optimized to provide maximum throughput with the constraint of favouring some class of tasks. The primary concern is resource utilization instead of time constraints. All tasks are considered as aperiodic with unknown date of arrival and unknown execution times. They have no compulsory execution deadlines.

A real-time operating system must be able to take into account periodic tasks with fixed period and fixed deadlines, as well as sporadic tasks with unknown dates of occurrence but with fixed deadlines. The system must be controlled such that its timing behaviour is understandable, bounded and predictable. These properties can be aimed at by a layered approach based on a real-time task scheduler and on a real-time kernel.

The operating system kernel must enforce the real-time behaviour assumed by the real-time task scheduler, i.e. promptness and known latency. Timing predictions must include the insurance that the resources are available on time and therefore cope with access conflicts and fault tolerance.

The real-time kernel must provide efficient mechanisms for data acquisition from sensors, data processing and output to activators or display devices. Let us emphasize some of them.

1.  I/O management and control

    – a fast and flexible input and output processing power in order to rapidly capture the data associated with the priority events, or to promptly supply the actuators or the display devices;

    – the absence of I/O latency caused by file granularity and by I/O buffer management, and therefore the capability of predicting transfer delays of prioritized I/O.

2.  Task management and control

    – concurrency between kernel calls, limited only by the mutual exclusion to sensitive data, i.e. a fully preemptive and reentrant kernel;

    – fast and efficient synchronization primitives which will avoid unnecessary context switching;

    – a swift task context switch;

    – an accurate granularity of time servers;

    – a task scheduling which respects the user-defined priority, and which does not cause unexpected task switching or priority inversion.

3.  Resource management and control

    – contention reduction with predictable timings when concurrent tasks access shared resources such as memory busses, memory ports, interrupt dispatcher, kernel tables protected by mutual exclusion;

    – priority inversion avoidance;

    – deadlock prevention and watchdog services in the kernel.

## *Appraisal of real-time operating systems*

The appraisal of a real-time operating system relies mainly on real-time capabilities such as:

- promptness of response by the computer system;

- predictability of kernel call execution times;

- tuning of scheduling policies;

- assistance provided for program debugging in the real-time context when the application is running in the field;

- performance recorded in case studies.

Let us develop two aspects.

*1. Promptness of response*    The promptness of the response of a real-time kernel may be evaluated by two parameters, interrupt latency and clerical latency.

*Interrupt latency* is the delay between the advent of an event in the application and the instant this event is recorded in the computer memory. This interrupt latency is caused by:

- the propagation of the interrupt through the hardware components: external bus, interrupt dispatcher, interrupt board of the processor, interrupt selection;

- the latency in the kernel software resulting from non-preemptive resource utilization: masking interrupts, spin lock action;

- the delay for context switching to an immediate task.

This interrupt latency is usually reduced by a systematic use of the hardware priorities of the external bus, by kernel preemptivity and context switch to immediate tasks.

*Clerical latency* is the delay which occurs between the advent of an event in the application and the instant this event is processed by its target application task. This clerical latency is caused by:

- the interrupt latency;

- the transfer of data from the interrupt subroutine to the application programs context;

- the notification that the target application task is already eligible;

- the return to the current application task, which may be using some non-preemptive resource and, in that situation, must be protected against the election of another application task;

- the delay the target application task waits before being elected for running;

- the installation of the context of the target application task.

*2. Predictability of kernel call execution times*    A real-time kernel includes a complete set of methods for reducing time latency, which are reentrance, preemption, priority scheduling and priority inheritance. Therefore the execution time of each kernel call can be evaluated exactly when it is executed for the highest priority task. This time is that of the call itself plus the delay of the longest critical section in the kernel.

### Standard Unix unfitness for real-time

Facilities to easily equip a board level system with standard *de facto* interfaces such as network interfaces or graphical users interfaces like the X Window system, as well as program compatibility and therefore access to widely used packages and tools, are arguments for adopting a system like Unix. However, Unix presents a mix of corporate requirements and technical solutions which reflect the state of the art of the early 1970s when it was designed and which do not fit for real-time.

The shell program interprets the commands typed by the user and usually creates another task to provide the requested service. The shell then hangs up, waiting for the end of its child task before continuing with the shell script. The Unix kernel schedules tasks on a modified time-sliced round-robin basis; the priority is ruled by the scheduler and is not defined by the user.

The standard Unix kernel is not particularly interested in interrupts, which usually come from a terminal and from memory devices. Data coming into the system do not drive the system as they do in real-time systems. The kernel is, by design, not preemptive. Once an application program makes an operating system call, that call runs to completion. As an example of this, when a task is created by a *fork* the data segment of the created task is initialized by copying the data segment of the creator task; this is done within the system call and may last as long as some hundred milliseconds.

Thus, all standard Unix I/O requests are synchronous or blocked and a task cannot issue an I/O request and then continue with other processing. Instead, the requesting task waits until the I/O call is completed. A task does not communicate with I/O devices directly and turns the job over to the kernel, which may decide to simply store the data in a buffer. Early Unix designers optimized the standard file system for flexibility, not speed, or security, and consequently highly variable amounts of time may be spent finding a given block of data depending on its position in the file. Standard Unix allows designers to implement their own device drivers and to make them read or write data directly into the memory of a dedicated task. However, this is kernel code and the kernel then has to be relinked.

Standard Unix does not include much interprocess communication and control. The 'pipe' mechanism allows the output of a task to be coupled to the input of another task of the same family. The other standard interprocess communication facility is the 'signal'. The signal works like a software interrupt. Standard Unix permits programmers to set up shared memory areas and disk files. Later versions have a (slow) semaphore mechanism for protecting shared resources.

### Real-time standards

The challenge for real-time standards is between real-time kernels which are standardized by adopting the Unix standard interface and standard non-real-time Unixes modified for real-time enhancements.

A set of application programming interfaces (API) extending the Unix interface to real-time have been proposed as the Posix 1003.1b standards. These interfaces, which allow the portability of applications with real-time requirements, are:

- timer interface functions to set and read high resolution internal timers;

- scheduling functions which allow getting or setting scheduling parameters. Three policies are defined: SCHED_FIFO, a preemptive, priority-based scheduling, SCHED_RR, a preemptive, priority-based scheduling with quanta (round-robin), and SCHED_OTHER, an implementation-defined scheduler.

- file functions which allow creation and access of files with deterministic performance;

- efficient synchronization primitives such as semaphores and facilities for synchronous and asynchronous message passing;

- asynchronous event notification and real-time queued signals;

- process memory locking functions and shared memory mapping facilities;

- efficient functions to perform asynchronous or synchronous I/O operations.

## 8.1.2   VxWorks

Some real-time operating systems have been specifically built for real-time applications. They are called real-time executives. An example is VxWorks < VXWORKS >.[1] VxWorks has a modular design which allows mapping of several hardware architectures and enables scalability. It provides a symmetric system kernel to multiprocessor architectures of up to 20 processors.

It provides services for creating and managing tasks, priority scheduling, periodic tasks release by signalling routines, binary or counting semaphore synchronization, asynchronous signalization, mailbox-based, pipe or socket communication, time-outs and watchdogs management, attachment of routines to interrupts, exceptions or time-outs, interrupt to task communication allowing triggering of sporadic tasks, and several fieldbus input–output protocols and interfaces. Mutual exclusion semaphores can be refined (1) to include a priority inheritance protocol in order to prevent priority inversion, (2) to defer the suppression of a task which is in a critical section, and (3) to detect the cross-references of routines that use the same semaphore (this allows avoiding deadlock by embedded calls). All tasks share a linear address space which allows short context switches and fast communication by common data and code sharing. When a paging mechanism, usually called a memory management unit (MMU), is supported by the hardware architecture, it can be managed at the task level to implement local or global virtual memory, allowing better protection among tasks. However, since VxWorks is targeted to real-time applications, all tasks programs remain resident and there is no paging on demand or memory swapping.

A library of interfaces has been customized to provide a Posix interface. Among numerous available development tools are a GNU interface and an Ada compiler, native as well as cross-development environments, instrumentation and analysis tools.

---

[1] < xxx > means an Internet link which is given at the end of the chapter.

## 8.1.3   RT-Linux

The Linux operating system is actually a very popular system. Linux is a Unix-like general-purpose operating system and it provides a rich multitasking environment supporting processes, threads and a lot of inter-process communication and synchronization mechanisms such as mutexes, semaphores, signals, etc. The Linux scheduler provides the Posix scheduling interface including SCHED_FIFO, SCHED_RR classes and the SCHED_OTHER class which implements the Unix default time-sharing scheduler. However, the Linux operating system is limited when it is used for real-time development. A major problem is that the Linux kernel itself is non-preemptive and thus a process running a system call in the Linux kernel cannot be preempted by a higher priority process. Moreover, interrupt handlers are not schedulable.

To allow the use of the Linux system for real-time development, enhancements have been sought after in associating a companion real-time kernel improving the standard kernel: it is the dual kernel approach of the RT-Linux system where the RT-Linux real-time kernel is the higher priority task (Figure 8.1).

A companion real-time kernel is inserted, along with its associated real-time tasks. It may use a specific processor. It functions apart from the Linux kernel. It is in charge of the reactions to interrupts, and schedules as many real-time tasks as necessary for these reactions. To allow this, the Linux kernel is preempted by its companion kernel. However, when some real-time data have to be forwarded to the Linux programs, this communication between the companion kernel and Linux is always done in a loosely coupled mode and the transfer has to be finalized in the Linux program; the non-deterministic Linux scheduler wakes up the application program and therefore there is no longer real-time behaviour.

More precisely, the RT-Linux kernel< RTLINUX > modifies Linux to provide:

- A microsecond resolution time sense: in order to increase the resolution of the Linux software clock, which is around 10 milliseconds, the basic mechanism by which it is implemented has been altered. Rather than interrupting the processor at a fixed rate, the timer chip is programmed to interrupt the processor in time to process the earliest scheduled event. Thus the overhead induced by increasing the resolution timer is limited. The timer is now running in one-shot mode.

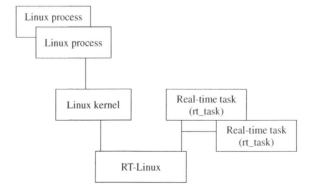

**Figure 8.1**   Real-time Linux architecture

- An interruption emulator for the Linux system: Linux is no longer allowed to disable hardware interrupts. Instead, the RT-Linux kernel handles all interrupts and emulates interrupt disabling/enabling for the Linux system. So, when Linux makes a request to disable interrupts, RT-Linux notes the request by simply resetting a software interrupt flag and then handles the interrupt for itself when it occurs. When Linux again enables interrupts, the real-time kernel processes all pending interrupts and then the corresponding Linux handlers can be executed.

- A real-time scheduler: the scheduler allows hard real-time, fully preemptive scheduling based on a fixed-priority scheme. The Linux system itself is scheduled as the lowest priority task and then runs when there are no real-time tasks ready to execute. When Linux is running, it schedules the Linux processes according to Posix scheduling classes. Linux is preempted whenever a real-time task has to execute.

Real-time tasks can be periodic tasks or interrupt-driven tasks (sporadic tasks) as defined by real-time primitives (Table 8.1, Figures 8.2 and 8.3). Tasks are programmed as loadable modules in the kernel and then run without memory protection. So a misbehaving task may bring the entire system down. However, running real-time tasks in the kernel reduces preemption overhead.

With the dual kernel approach, the programming model requires that the application be split into real-time and non-real-time components. Real-time tasks communicate with Linux processes using special queues called real-time (RT_FIFO). These queues have been designed so that a real-time task can never be blocked when it reads or writes data.

As an example consider a small application that polls a device for data in real-time and stores this data in a file (Figures 8.4 and 8.5). Polling the device is executed by a periodic real-time task, which then writes the data in a real-time FIFO (first-in first-out

**Table 8.1**   RT-Linux real-time task primitives

| Primitive | Action of the primitive |
|---|---|
| `int rt_task_init (RT_TASK *task, void fn(int data), int data, int stack_size, int priority)` | Creates a real-time task which will execute with the scheduling priority 'priority' |
| `int rt_task_delete (RT_TASK *task)` | Deletes a real-time task |
| `int rt_task_make_periodic (RT_TASK *task, RTIME start_time, RTIME period)` | The task is set up to run at periodically |
| `int rt_task_wait (void)` | Suspends a real-time periodic task until its next wake-up |
| `int rt_task_wakeup (RT_TASK *task)` | Wakes up an aperiodic real-time task, which becomes ready to execute |
| `int rt_task_suspend (RT_TASK *task)` | Suspends the execution of the real-time task |

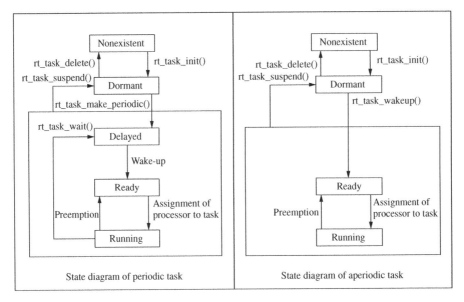

**Figure 8.2**   State diagram of task

```
#include <linux/errno.h>
#include <linux/rt_sched.h>
#include <linux/arch/i386/kernel/irq.h>

RT_TASK tasks[2];

void f_periodic (int t) {/* this function is executed by
                              a real-time periodic task */
while (1) {
      something to do ....
      rt_task_wait(); }}

void f_aperiodic (int t) {       /* this function is executed by
                              a real-time aperiodic task */
      something to do ....
      rt_task_suspend(&task([1]);  }

int ap_handler()  {              /* this handler wakes up the
                              aperiodic task */
      rt_task_wakeup(&task([1]);  }

int init_module(void) {
      rt_task_init(&tasks[0], f_periodic, 0, 3000, 4);
            /* the periodic task is created */
      rt_task_init(&tasks[1], f_aperiodic, 1, 3000, 5);
            /* the aperiodic task is created */
      rt_task_make_periodic((&task[0], 5, 10);
            /* the periodic task is initialized */
      request_RTirq(2, &ap_handler);
            /* a handler is associated with the IRQ 2 */
      return 0; }
void cleanup_module(void)
      {
      rt_task_delete(&tasks[0]); /* the periodic task is deleted */
      rt_task_delete(&tasks[1]);/* the aperiodic task is deleted */
      free _RTirq(2); /* IRQ 2 is free */
      }
```

**Figure 8.3**   An example of programming aperiodic and periodic real-time tasks

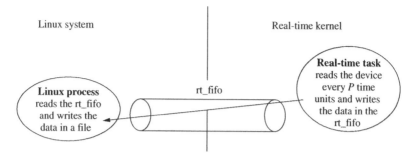

**Figure 8.4**   Real-time task communication with a Linux process

| The periodic real-time function is: | The Linux process is: |
|---|---|
| ```
void f_periodic () { int i;
  for (i=1; i<1000; i ++) {
    data = get_data();
    rt_fifo_put (fifodesc,
(char *) &data, sizeof(data));
    /* data are written in the
         fifo */
    rt_task_wait(); }}
``` | ```
int main () { int i,  f;  char
buf[10]
    rt_fifo_create(1,1000);
             /* fifo 1 is created
with size of 1000 bytes */
    f = open ("file", o_rdwr);
    for (i=1; i<1000; i ++)  {
     rt_fifo_read (1, buf,
     10 * sizeof(int));
     write(f, buf,
     10 * sizeof(int)); }
    rt_fifo_destroy(1);
             /* the fifo is destroyed */
    close(f);}
``` |

**Figure 8.5**   Device polling example

queue). A Linux process reads the data from the FIFO queue and stores them in a file (Barabonov and Yodaiken, 1996).

## 8.1.4   LynxOs

Some real-time operating systems have been obtained by engineering from scratch a Unix-based system. This is the case of LynxOs <LYNXOS>. A customized real-time kernel completely replaces the Unix kernel by another kernel which provides a real-time interface and a standard interface. The basic idea is that real-time applications do not need the Unix system or kernel but require Unix/Posix interfaces. These kernels have a native real-time nucleus, which presents the usual real-time capabilities. Their basic interface has been augmented with a full Posix interface providing source or binary compatibility for existing Unix, Posix or Linux programs. Thus, their interface is a superset of the Posix interface (i.e. Unix, Linux and Posix).

LynxOs provides Posix services:

- Posix 1003.1. Core services, such as process creation and control, signals, timers, files and directory operations, pipes, standard C library, I/O port interface and control.

- Posix 1003.1b. Real-time extensions, such as priority scheduling, real-time signals, clocks and timers, semaphores, message passing, shared memory, asynchronous and synchronous I/O, memory locking.

- Posix 1003.1c. Thread services, including thread creation, control and cleanup, thread scheduling, thread synchronization and mutual exclusion, signal handling.

Each process provides a paged virtual address space and supports the execution of threads, which share the address space of the process. Kernel threads share the kernel space. A memory management unit (MMU) performs the mapping from virtual to physical page address and enables each thread to run protected in its own space. Real-time tasks are implemented as threads. Applications or subsystems may be implemented as processes.

In order to provide deterministic behaviour, low kernel latency and short blocking times, a variety of architectural features have been provided, the basic ones being a fully preemptive and reentrant kernel, and a real-time global scheduler. Kernel threads and user threads share a common priority range of 256 levels and the highest priority thread runs regardless to which process it belongs or if it is a kernel thread. The priority inheritance protocol and the priority ceiling protocol are available. Additional aspects have been provided for lower kernel latency, such as locking pages in main memory, direct communication between I/O device and a thread, contiguous files and faster file indexing schemes.

Several features ease the development of applications, such as kernel plugins allowing dynamic loading of services and I/O drivers, Linux and Unix binary compatibility, native as well as cross-development environments, event tracing and performance analysis tools. LynxOs supports an Ada certified compiler and the Ada real-time annex.

# 8.2 Real-Time Languages

## 8.2.1 Ada

Ada is a modern algorithmic language with the usual control structures, and with the ability to define types and subprograms. It also serves the need for modularity, whereby data, types and subprograms can be packaged. It treats modularity in the physical sense as well, with a facility to support separate compilation.

In addition to these aspects, the language supports real-time programming, with facilities to define the invocation, synchronization and timing of parallel tasks. It also supports system programming, with facilities that allow access to system-dependent properties, and precise control over the representation of data (Ada, 1995a, b).

Besides real-time and embedded systems, Ada is particularly relevant for two kinds of applications: the very large and the very critical ones. The common requirement of these applications is reliable code. A strongly-typed language allows the compiler to detect programmer errors prior to execution. The debugging of run-time errors therefore concerns mainly the design errors.

The Ada programming language was published as ISO Standard 8652 in 1995. The GNAT compiler is distributed as free software < GNAT >. In the following, we summarize the major highlights of Ada 95 and give an example. Ada is a strongly typed language with conventional data and control structures, which are also found with specific idiosyncrasies in the Pascal, C and Java languages.

Ada facilitates object-oriented programming by providing a form of inheritance (via type extension using a tagged record type) and run-time polymorphism (via run-time dispatching operations). Type extension leads to the notion of class, which refers to a hierarchy of types.

The package is an important construct in Ada. It serves as the logical building block of large programs and is the most natural unit of separate compilation. In addition, it provides facilities for data hiding and for definition of abstract types.

Genericity and type extensibility make possible the production of reusable software components. Type extension using a tagged record type has been mentioned above. A generic is a template (with parameters) from which instances of subprograms and packages can be constructed. Generic instantiation, which involves the association of formal and calling parameters at compile time, is more powerful than mere macro expansion.

During the execution of a program, events or conditions may occur which might be considered exceptional. Ada provides an exception mechanism which allows exceptions to be raised explicitly within a block, and catching and handling of these exceptions in exception handlers at the block end. When no handler is found in the local block, then the exception is propagated to containing blocks until it is handled.

### *Concurrency and real-time programming*

Concurrent tasks can be declared statically or dynamically. A task type has a specification and a body. Direct communication between tasks is possible by a rendezvous protocol implying remote invocation of declared entry points that may be called from other tasks and acceptance of the call by the callee.

Asynchronous communication between tasks uses shared protected objects. A protected object type defines data that can be accessed by tasks in mutual exclusion only. In addition to mutual exclusion, a protected object can also be used for conditional synchronization. A task calling a protected object can be suspended until released by the action of some other task accessing the same protected object. A conditional routine is defined as an entry of the protected object and the condition is usually called a barrier expression. If the service performed by a protected object needs to be provided in two parts and the calling task has to be suspended after the first part until conditions are such that the second part can be done, the calling task can be suspended and requeued on another entry.

Tasks calling a protected object may be queued due to mutual exclusion or to the barrier expression. The queuing semantic and the choice of the queued task to elect for accessing the protected object are defined unambiguously. This allows validating concurrent programming implementations and proving their reliability (Kaiser and Pradat-Peyre, 1997).

All tasks and protected objects can be assigned priorities using the priority pragma. The task priorities are used by the scheduler for queuing ready tasks. The protected object priority is the ceiling priority that can be used to prevent priority inversion.

Task and protected object syntax is presented in more detail in the mine pump example below.

A task may be held up by executing a delay statement whose parameter specifies a duration of inactivity ('delay some_duration'; some_duration is of type duration, which is predefined) or indicates a date of awakening ('delay until some_date'; some_date is of type time).

The real-time systems annex of the Ada reference manual provides a set of real-time facilities which extends the core language. A dispatching policy can be selected to replace the basic FIFO scheduler. The task dispatching policy FIFO_Within_Priority allows fixed priority preemptive scheduling. The Ceiling_Locking policy specifies the use of the priority ceiling protocol. Other features, such as dynamic priorities and prioritized entry queues, can also be chosen by programming options.

Facilities are provided for interfacing and interacting with hardware devices, for giving access to machine code, for data representation and location, and for interrupt handling. Interfaces to assembly code, to other high-level languages and to the Posix API are assured by various compile directives defined as pragmas.

For interrupt handling, an interrupt handler is provided by a protected procedure (i.e. a procedure of a protected object) which is called by some mythical external task. The protected procedure can be attached to the interrupt, which has previously been defined as a system constant.

A restricted tasking profile, named Ravenscar profile, has been defined for use in high-integrity efficient real-time systems (Burns, 2001), <RAVEN>.

### Mine pump example

As an example to illustrate the use of the Ada language, we describe an implementation of a part of the mine pump problem extensively developed in Joseph (1996) and Burns (2001). A mine has several sensors to control a pump pumping out the water percolating in a sump and to monitor the methane level (Figure 8.6).

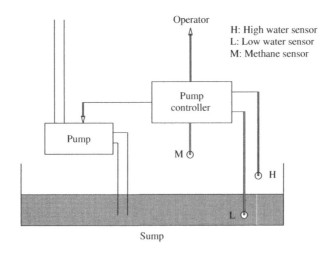

**Figure 8.6**   Control system of the mine pump

*Water level sensors interrupt handling*    Two water level sensors, H and L, detect when the percolating water is above the high or low levels respectively. These sensors raise interrupts. Cyclic tasks are designed to respond to these interrupts and switch the pump on or off, respectively (by turning the controller on or off). The cyclic tasks are released aperiodically. A protected object provides one protected procedure for each interrupt and one entry for each task. The aperiodic tasks and the protected object are grouped into one package.

```ada
package WaterSensors is                  -- package specification

  task HighSensor is                      -- task specification
    pragma Priority(4);                   -- task priority
  end HighSensor;
  task LowSensor is                       -- task specification
    pragma Priority(3);                   -- task priority
  end LowSensor;


end WaterSensors;

package body WaterSensors is              -- package body
  protected InterruptHandlers is
                              -- protected object specification
    procedure High; pragma Interrupt_Handler(High);
                              -- attached interrupt handler
    procedure Low; pragma Interrupt_Handler(Low);
                              --  attached interrupt handler
    entry ReleaseHigh; entry ReleaseLow;       -- called by tasks
    pragma Priority(10);          -- ceiling priority of the resource
  private
    HighInterrupt, LowInterrupt : Boolean := False;
                              -- data of the protected object
  end InterruptHandlers;

  protected body InterruptHandlers is  -- protected object body
    procedure High is
    begin HighInterrupt := True; end High;
    procedure Low is
    begin LowInterrupt := True; end Low;
    entry ReleaseHigh when HighInterrupt is
        -- the calling task is suspended as long as the barrier
        -- HighInterrupt is not True
    begin HighInterrupt := False; end ReleaseHigh;
    entry ReleaseLow when LowInterrupt is
        -- the calling task is suspended as long as the barrier
        -- LowInterrupt is not True
    begin LowInterrupt := False; end ReleaseLow;
  end InterruptHandlers;
```

```
task body HighSensor is        -- task body
begin
   loop                        -- infinite loop
      InterruptHandlers.ReleaseHigh; Controller.TurnOn;
                                -- aperiodically released
   end loop;
 end HighSensor;

 task body LowSensor is        -- task body
 begin
   loop                        -- infinite loop
      InterruptHandlers.ReleaseLow; Controller.TurnOff;
                                -- aperiodically released
   end loop;
 end LowSensor;

end WaterSensors;
```

*Methane sensor management*    The mine also has a methane sensor M. When the methane level reaches a critical level, an alarm must be sent to an operator. To avoid the risk of explosion, the pump must be operated only when the methane level is below the critical level.

A protected object stores the current methane reading. A periodic task refreshes the methane reading periodically by polling the methane sensor. If the methane value reaches the critical level, this task warns the operator and stops the pump. Another periodic task supervises the pump for safety purposes, stopping and starting the pump according to the current value of the methane reading and to the reliability of its value (a current methane reading which is too old is considered unreliable). Starting and stopping the pump are different actions than turning it on or off. The alarm is posted to a protected object which is read by an aperiodic operator task (not described here).

```
protected MethaneStatus is      -- protected object specification
  procedure Read(Ms : out MethaneValue; T : out Time);
                                -- out parameter for a result
  protected Write(V : MethaneValue; T : Time);
  pragma Priority(9);           -- ceiling priority
private
  CurrentValue := MethaneValue := MethaneValue'Last;
                                -- initially highest possible value
  TimeOfRead : Time := Clock;
                        -- Clock is a standard run-time function
end MethaneStatus;

protected body MethaneStatus is    -- protected object body
  procedure Read(Ms : out MethaneValue; T : out Time) is
  begin
     Ms := CurrentValue;
```

```
        T := TimeOfRead;
end Read;
  protected Write(V : MethaneValue; T : Time) is
  begin
      CurrentValue := V;
      TimeOfRead := T;
  end Write;
end MethaneStatus;


task MethanePolling is            -- task specification
  pragma Priority(8);             -- task priority
 end MethanePolling;


task body MethanePolling is       -- task body
    SensorReading : MethaneValue;
    Period : Duration := MethanePeriod;
                                  -- task period; this is a delay
    NextStart : Time;             -- this is a date
begin
  NextStart := Clock;             -- read the system clock
   loop
                    -- read hardware register in SensorReading
      if SensorReading >= MethaneThreshold then
         Controller.Stop;
                    -- request the controller to stop the pump
         OperatorAlarm.Set;          -- post a warning
      end if;
      MethaneStatus.Write(SensorReading, NextStart);
                      -- refresh the current value
      NextStart := NextStart + Period;
      delay until NextStart; -- new release date of periodic task
    end loop;
 end MethanePolling;


 task SafetyChecker is             -- task specification
    pragma Priority(5);            -- task priority
 end SafetyChecker;

task body SafetyChecker is         -- task body
  Reading : MethaneValue;
  Period : Duration := SafetyPeriod;  -- task period
  NextStart, LastTime, NewTime : Time;-- all dates
begin
  NextStart := Clock;                 -- read the system clock
  LastTime := NextStart;
```

```
  loop
     MethaneStatus.Read(Reading, NewTime);
                      -- current methane reading
     if Reading >= MethaneThreshold or
         NewTime - LastTime > Freshness then -- too old value
        Controller.Stop;
                      -- request the controller to stop the pump
     else
        Controller.Start;
                      -- request the controller to start the pump
     end if;
     NextStart := NextStart + Period;
     delay until NextStart; -- new release date of periodic task
  end loop;
end SafetyChecker;
```

```
protected OperatorAlarm is
  procedure Set;                      -- post a warning
  entry Release;                      -- wait for a warning
  pragma Priority(9);
private Alarm : Boolean := False;     -- shared data
end OperatorAlarm;
```

*Pump controller*    The pump controller is also a protected object. The aperiodic tasks that respond to the high and low water interrupts call TurnOn and TurnOff procedures. The periodic safety controller calls Stop and Start procedures.

```
protected Controller is
  procedure TurnOn;
  procedure TurnOff;
  procedure Stop;
  procedure Start;
  pragma Priority(9); -- ceiling priority of the resource
private
  Pump : Status := Off;            -- type Status is (On, Off)
  Condition : SafetyStatus := Stopped;
                   -- type SafetyStatus is (Stopped, Operational)
end Controller;
```

```
protected body Controller is
  procedure TurnOn is
  begin
    Pump := On;
    if Condition = Operational then TurnOnThePump; end if;
  end TurnOn;
  procedure TurnOff is
  begin
    Pump := Off;
    TurnOffThePump;
```

```
  end TurnOff;
  procedure Stop is
  begin
    TurnOffThePump;
    Condition := Stopped;
  end Stop;
  procedure Start is
  begin
    Condition := Operational;
    if Pump = On then TurnOnThePump; end if;
  end Start;
end Controller;
```

*Multitasking program*    The Main program declares all tasks and protected objects before starting them all concurrently. It imports some packages from the Ada real-time library. Some basic types and application constants are defined in a global package that appears first.

```
with Ada.Real_Time; use Ada.Real_Time;
procedure Main is                  -- this is the application boot
  package GlobalDefinitions is
      type Status is (On, Off);
      type SafetyStatus is (Stopped, Operational);
      type MethaneValue is range 0 .. 256;
      MethaneThreshold : constant MethaneValue := 32;
      Freshness : constant Duration := Milliseconds(30);
      MethanePeriod : constant Duration := Milliseconds(20);
      SafetyPeriod : constant Duration := Milliseconds(35);
  end GlobalDefinitions;
  -- Declaration of package WaterSensor with a protected object and
  -- two aperiodic tasks
  -- Declaration of protected objects MethaneStatus, OperatorAlarm
  -- and Controller
  -- Declaration of periodic tasks MethanePolling and SafetyChecker
begin -- at this point starts the multitasking of 5 concurrent tasks
  null;
end Main;
```

## 8.2.2   Ada distributed systems annex

*Partitions as units of distribution*

The Ada model for programming distributed systems is presented in the distributed systems annex (DSA) (Ada, 1995a, b). It specifies a partition as the unit of distribution. A partition, which may be active or passive, contains an aggregation of library units that execute in a distributed target execution environment. Typically, each active partition corresponds to a single execution site, and all its constituent units occupy the same address space. A passive partition resides at a storage node that is accessible to the processing nodes of the different active partitions that reference them. The principal interface between partitions is one or more package specifications. Support for the configuration of partitions to the target environment and its associated communication is not explicitly specified by the model. An example of such a support, named GLADE, is presented below.

The general idea is that the partitions execute independently other than when communicating. Programming the cooperation among partitions is achieved by library units defined to allow access to data and subprograms in different partitions. In this way, strong typing and unit consistency is maintained across a distributed system.

Library units are categorized into a hierarchy by pragmas, which are:

```
pragma Pure(...);
pragma Shared_Passive(...);
pragma Remote_Types(...);
pragma Remote_Call_Interface(...);
```

A pure unit does not contain any state. Thus a distinct copy can be placed in each partition. However, a type declared in a pure unit is considered to be a single declaration, irrespective of how many times the unit is replicated and the copying of it does not create derived types. Hence pure packages enable types to be declared to be used and checked in the communication between partitions.

A shared passive unit corresponds to a logical address space that is common to all partitions that reference its constituent library units. It allows the creation of a non-duplicated although shared segment.

Remote type units define types usable by communicating partitions. They are useful when one needs to pass access values, which correspond to access types that have a user-defined meaning, such as a handle to a system-wide resource. These access types are called remote access types.

A remote call interface (RCI) unit defines the interface of subprograms to be called remotely from other active partitions. Communication between active partitions is via remote procedure calls on RCI units. Such remote calls are processed by stubs at each end of the communication; parameters and results are passed as streams. This is all done automatically by the partition communication subsystem (PCS). A remote call interface body exists only in the partition which implements the remote object and is thus not duplicated. All other occurrences will have a stub allocated for remotely calling the object.

### Paradigms for distribution

An implementation of Ada for distributed systems needs a tool which provides mechanisms for configuring the program, i.e. associating the partitions with particular processing or memory elements in the target architecture.

GLADE is such a general-purpose tool, which is the companion of the GNAT compiler <GNAT> distributed as free software by Ada Core Technologies <ACT>. GLADE consists of a configuration tool called GNATDIST and a communication subsystem called GARLIC. These tools allow the building of a distributed application on a set of homogeneous or heterogeneous machines and use of the full standardized language.

However more simple paradigms of distribution can be implemented, such as the client/server paradigm as it is modelled in CORBA (Omg, 2001). ADABROKER is a CORBA platform which has been implemented in Ada and which is also available as free software < ADABROKER >. CIAO is a gateway from CORBA to Ada, which allows a client in CORBA to call services available in ADA DSA. It provides the CORBA client with a CORBA description (IDL description) of the DSA services (Pautet et al., 1999).

Other tools that use Ada in distributed system environments are presented in (Humpris, 2001).

### *Additional requirements for distributed real-time*

Recent real-time Ada workshops have focused on extensions to the DSA to include support for distributed real-time applications.

In real-time applications, in order to be able to predict and bound the response times of RPC requests it is necessary to be able to specify the priorities at which the RPC handlers are executed, and the priorities at which the messages are transmitted in the network. Thus several extensions of the ARM, which are close to the RT-CORBA specifications, are proposed (Pinho, 2001):

- A new global priority type, for representing a value with a global meaning in the distributed system. Appropriate mapping functions translate this global priority type to a value adequate for each CPU and network.

- Mechanisms for specifying the priority at which the RPC handlers start their execution, both initially and after servicing an RPC request.

- Mechanisms for specifying (at the client side) the priorities at which RPC requests are served in the server, as well as the message priorities in the network.

- Mechanisms for configuring the pool of RPC handlers, as well as more detailed semantics on the handling of pending RPC requests.

Recall that mechanisms to avoid or bound priority inversion are already present in the Ada real-time annex and have been implemented. Much of the real-time Ada workshop requirements are implemented in GLADE (Pautet and Tardieu, 2000; Pautet et al., 2001).

## 8.2.3   Real-time Java

The strengths of the Java language promote its use for real-time applications, especially in the context of client–server relationships and of Web usage. Its main strengths (Brosgol and Dobbing, 2001) are:

- elegant object-oriented programming features;

- a nice solution for multiple inheritance;

- portability due to the language semantics and the choice of a virtual machine implementation (JVM);

- large sets of libraries of very comprehensive APIs (Application programming interfaces) including Web-ready classes;

- strong industrial support.

However, Java also presents some weaknesses for real-time:

- the object centricity makes it clumsy to write programs that are essentially processing or using multitasking;

- the thread and mutual exclusion models lack a completely rigorous semantic;

- the dynamic memory allocation and garbage collection introduce a heavy time cost;

- the priority semantics and scheduling issues are completely implementation dependent;

- priority inversion is possible;

- there is no way to deal with low-level processing, interrupts and other asynchronous event handling.

Several consortia < RTJAVA > are considering real-time extensions to use Java in real-time applications. Several proposals of real-time classes and of variants of the JVM are being considered by the real-time engineering community. Some are detailed in Burns and Wellings (2001) and Brosgol and Dobbing (2001). However, the reader should note that Real-Time Java is an evolving specification and, at the time of writing, has not been completely tested by an implementation.

## 8.2.4  Synchronous languages

Synchronous languages (Halbwachs, 1993) allow the creation of programs that are considered to be reacting instantaneously to external events or, in other words, the duration of reaction is always shorter than the time between external events. Each internal or output event of the program is precisely and only dated by the flow of input events. The behaviour of a program is fully deterministic from the time point of view.

The notion of chronometric time is replaced by the notion of event ordering: the only relevant notions are the simultaneity and the precedence between events. Physical time does not play a special role, as it does in Ada for instance; it is just one of the events coming from the program environment. For example, the two statements: 'the train must stop within 10 seconds' and 'the train must stop within 100 metres', which express constraints of the same nature, will be expressed by similar precedence constraints in a synchronous language: 'The event Stop must precede the 10th (respectively the 100th) next occurrence of the event Second (respectively Metre)'. This is not the case in Ada where physical time is handled by special statements.

Any instant is a logical instant: the history of the system is a totally ordered sequence of logical instants; at each of these instants, and at these only, a set of events may occur (zero, one or several events). Events that occur at the same logical instant are considered simultaneous; those that happen at different instants are ordered according to their instants of occurrence. Apart from these logical instants, nothing happens either in the system or in its environment. Finally, all the tasks have the same knowledge of the events occurring at a given instant.

In practice, the synchrony hypothesis assumes that the program reacts rapidly enough to record all the external events in suitable order. If this assumption can be checked, the synchrony hypothesis is a realistic abstraction which allows a particularly efficient and measurable implementation. The object code is structured as a finite automaton, a transition of which corresponds to a reaction of the program. The corresponding code is loop-free and a bound of its execution time can be computed for a given machine. Thus the validity of the synchrony hypothesis can be checked.

Synchronous languages cannot pretend to solve all the problems raised by the design of real-time applications. A complex real-time application is usually made up of three parts:

- An interactive interface which acquires the inputs and posts the outputs. This part includes interrupt management, input reading from sensors and mapping physical input/output to logical data. It manages the human interface (keyboard, mouse, scrollbar) to call interactive services and the communication between loosely coupled components.

- One or more reactive kernels which compute the outputs from the logical inputs by selecting the suitable reaction.

- A level of data management which performs transformational tasks, stores data for logging and retrieval, and displays the application states on dashboards, under the control of the reactive kernel.

The synchronous language is useful for safely programming the reactive kernels when the synchrony hypothesis is valid. Let us summarize the presentation of the synchrony hypothesis by two figures. In Figure 8.7, the synchronous and asynchronous hypotheses are compared. Figure 8.8 shows an example where the computation times may be important and where the rate of input events may cause the synchrony hypothesis to fail. Thus, this hypothesis has to be checked with the application time constraints.

The oldest synchronous formalism is Statecharts (Harel, 1987). Another graphic formalism is ARGOS, which is based on parallel and hierarchical automata. Several synchronous languages have been developed: the oldest is ESTEREL, which is an imperative, textual language. LUSTRE is a functional, textual data-flow language, and SIGNAL is a relational language. A good presentation is given in Halbwachs (1993).

We now give a short example written in ESTEREL. It controls two trains which run on a circular network of five electrified rails (numbered from 1 to 5) and which must be separated by an empty rail. This track is illustrated in Figure 8.9. The program consists of a declaration part, an initialization part and five identical parts which describe the

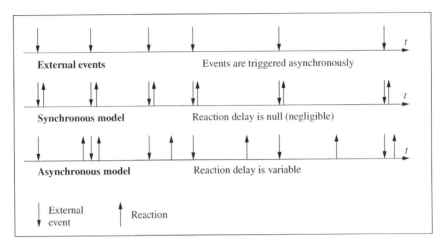

**Figure 8.7**   Synchronous and asynchronous hypotheses

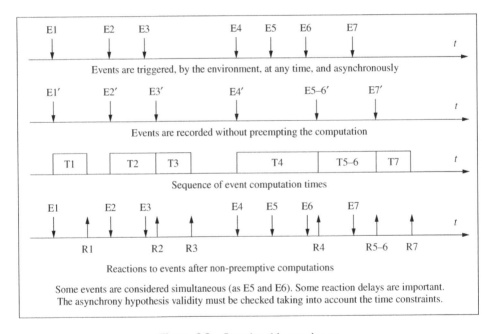

**Figure 8.8**   Questionable synchrony

rail management. Statements allow waiting for a signal ('await'), broadcasting a signal ('emit'), and writing parallel statements ('‖').

```
module TwoTrains:

    % external events triggered by sensors
    Input Sensor1, Sensor2, Sensor3, Sensor4, Sensor5, GO;
```

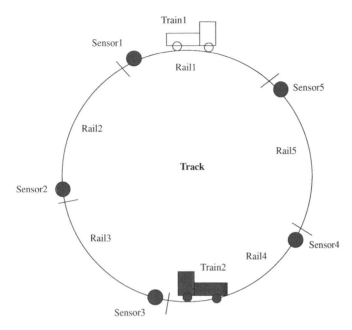

**Figure 8.9** Railway track

```
% internal events posted to the parallel modules
signal Rail1On, Rail1Off, Rail1Free, Rail2On,
       Rail2Off, Rail2Free, Rail3On, Rail3Off,
       Rail3Free, Rail4On, Rail4Off, Rail4Free,
       Rail5On, Rail5Off, Rail5Free;

% initialization module
await GO;
emit Rail1On;     % the train 1 starts on rail 1 on which
                  % power is switched on
emit Rail4On;     % the train 2 starts on rail 4 on which
                  % power is switched on
emit Rail3Free;   % this is the sole rail where the train may
                  % proceed
||    % parallel statement
% rail 1 management module

   loop
      [
      await Rail1On;     % wait the arrival of a train
      await Sensor1;     % wait the train passing by the sensor
      emit Rail1Off;     % switch off the power of rail 1
      ||
      await Rail3Free;   % rail 3 must be free before entering
                         % rail 2
      ];
```

```
    emit Rail2On;      % switch on power of rail 2
    emit Rail1Free;    % broadcasts the availability of rail 1
  end loop
||
% rail 2 management module, similar to rail 1 management module
||
% rail 3 management module, similar to rail 1 management module
||
% rail 4 management module, similar to rail 1 management module
||
% rail 5 management module, similar to rail 1 management module
end signal


end TwoTrains.      % end of module TwoTrains
```

## 8.3   Real-Time Middleware

In the past few years, object-oriented (OO) technology has become very popular. This technology contributes to reducing the development complexity and maintenance costs of complex applications and facilitating reuse of components. Having to deal with the complexity of design, analysis, maintenance and validation of real-time applications, the real-time systems engineering community is increasingly interested in using OO technology at different levels, mainly the design, programming and middleware levels. Thus, timing aspects should be integrated and handled at all these levels.

This engineering approach also motivates the use of distributed object computing middleware, such as CORBA. Distributed computing middleware resides between applications and the underlying infrastructure (operating system and network). Middleware provides an abstraction of the underlying system and network infrastructure to applications that use it. In non-real-time applications, this abstraction allows the development of applications without reference to the underlying system, network and interfaces. Nevertheless, to meet real-time constraints, real-time applications must be aware of, and have control over, the behaviour of the underlying infrastructure which is abstracted by the middleware. In consequence, middleware used by real-time applications must include functions allowing access to this underlying infrastructure and control of its behaviour. The current generation of distributed object-oriented middleware does not support real-time applications.

To take into account these needs, various works are being undertaken within the OMG (Object Management Group). These works aim to extend UML, Java and CORBA to make them suitable for real-time applications and to guarantee end-to-end quality of service. The main extensions focus on scheduling, memory management, concurrency and communication management. The middleware which has raised the most extensions to take into account real-time requirements is incontestably CORBA.

This work is sufficiently advanced and some components are now available on the market. This section focuses on Real-Time CORBA middleware.

Before presenting the concepts and mechanisms introduced in Real-Time CORBA, we briefly summarize the CORBA standard in the next section.

## 8.3.1 Overview of CORBA

The CORBA (Common Object Request Broker Architecture) standard specifies interfaces that allow interoperability between client and servers under the object-oriented paradigm. CORBA version 1.1 was released in 1992; the last version, at the time of writing, i.e. version 2.6, was released in December 2001 (OMG, 2001b).

CORBA provides a very abstract view of objects. The object exists only as an abstraction. An object is a combination of state and a set of methods that explicitly embodies an abstraction. An operation is a service that can be requested. It has an associated signature, which may restrict which actual parameters are valid. A method is an implementation of an operation. Each object is assigned an object reference, which is an identifier used in requests to identify the object. The interface determines the operations that a client may perform using the object reference. The access to distributed objects relies on an Object Request Broker (ORB) whose aim is to hide the heterogeneity of languages, platforms, computers and networks that implement the object services and to provide the interoperability among the different object implementations. The basic invocation of objects is based on the remote procedure call (RPC) mechanism.

CORBA supports both static and dynamic interfaces. The static invocation interfaces are determined at compile time, and are present in client codes using stubs (a client stub is a local procedure, part of the RPC mechanism, which is used for method invocation). The dynamic invocation interface allows clients to construct and issue a request whose signature (i.e. parameter number, parameters types and parameter passing modes) is possibly not known until run-time. That is, the request is fully constructed at run-time using information from the interface repository.

The main components of the CORBA architecture are shown in Figure 8.10 and are briefly summarized in the following:

*Interface definition language (IDL)*    IDL is a language that is used to statically define the object interfaces, to allow invocation to object operations with differing underlying implementations. From IDL definitions, it is possible to map CORBA objects into particular programming language. IDL syntax is derived from C++, removing the constructs of a simple implementation language and adding a number of keywords required to specify distributed systems.

*Interface architecture*    CORBA defines an architecture consisting of three specific interfaces: client-side interface, object implementation-side interface and ORB core interface.

- The client-side interface provides:
    - IDL stubs that are generated from IDL definitions and linked into the client program in order to implement the client part of the RPC; these are the static invocation interfaces;
    - dynamic invocation interfaces used to build requests at run-time.

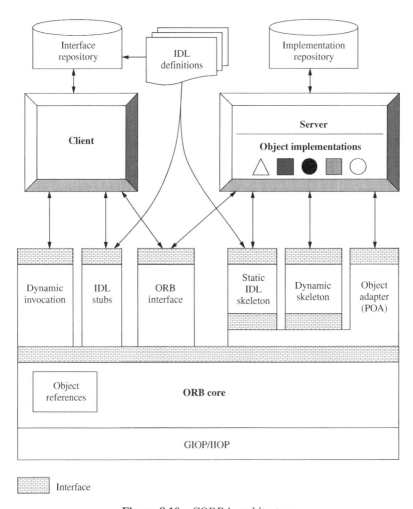

**Figure 8.10**    CORBA architecture

- Implementation-side interfaces allow calls from the ORB up to the object implementations. They include:

  - IDL skeletons which represent the server-side counterpart of the IDL stub interface; a skeleton is a component which assists an object adapter in implementing the server part of the RPC and in passing requests to particular methods;

  - dynamic skeleton interfaces provide at run-time binding mechanism for servers. Such an interface is analogous to the client side's dynamic invocation interface;

  - object adapter which processes requests on behalf of the object servers. It is the means by which object implementations access most ORB services, such as generation and interpretation of object references, method invocation and object activation.

- ORB interface, which allows the ORB to be accessed directly by clients and server programs.

*ORB core*    The ORB core is a set of communication mechanisms, which includes all functions required to support distributed computing, such as location of objects, object referencing, establishment of connections to the server, marshalling of request parameters and results, and activating and deactivating objects and their implementations.

*Object adapter*    The object adapter is the ORB component which provides object reference, activation and state-related services to an object implementation. There may be different adapters provided for different kinds of implementations. The CORBA standard defines a Portable Object Adapter (POA) that can be used for most ORB objects with conventional implementations.

*Interface repository*    The interface repository is used by clients to locate objects unknown at compile time, and then to build requests associated with these objects. Interfaces can be added to the repository to define operations for run-time retrieval of information from the repository.

*Implementation repository*    The implementation repository is a storage place for object implementation information. The object implementation information is provided at installation time and is stored in the implementation repository for use by the ORB to locate and activate implementations of objects.

*ORB interoperability*    This specifies a flexible approach for supporting networks of objects that are distributed across heterogeneous CORBA-compliant ORBs. The architecture identifies the roles of different domains of ORB-specific information. A domain is a distinct scope, within which common characteristics are exhibited, common rules observed, and over which distribution transparency is preserved. Domains are joined by bridges, which map concepts in one domain to the equivalent in another. A very basic inter-ORB protocol, called General Inter-ORB Protocol (GIOP), has been defined to serve as a common backbone protocol. The Internet Inter-ORB protocol (IIOP) is an implementation of GIOP on TCP/IP suitable for Internet applications.

## 8.3.2 Overview of real-time CORBA

Conventional CORBA does not define scheduling. The ability to enforce end-to-end timing constraints, through techniques such as global priority-based scheduling, must be addressed across the CORBA standard. The real-time requirements on the underlying systems include the use of real-time operating systems on the nodes in the distributed system and the use of adequate protocols for real-time communication between nodes in this distributed system. An important step towards distributed real-time systems supported by CORBA is the introduction of concepts related to time constraints in CORBA, without fundamental modification of the original CORBA.

In 1995, a Special Interest Group (SIG) was formed, at OMG, to initiate Real-Time CORBA (called RT-CORBA) and to assess the requirements and interest in providing real-time extensions to the CORBA model. The CORBA extension is done according to several phases. Two phases are already completed and led to two specifications, RT-CORBA 1.0 and 2.0, which we briefly present below. The RT-CORBA 1.0 standard is designed for fixed priority real-time operation. It was adopted in 1998, and integrated with CORBA in specification 2.4. RT-CORBA 2.0 targets dynamic scheduling, and was adopted in 2001.

An experimental RT-CORBA implementation, TAO (Schmidt et al., 1998), developed at Washington University in St Louis, has been extensively documented. TAO runs on a variety of operating system such as VxWorks, Chorus and Solaris. At present, only a few vendors have ported their ORBs to real-time operating systems.

## *RT-CORBA architecture*

RT-CORBA should include the following four major components, each of which must be designed and implemented taking into account the need for end-to-end predictability:

- scheduling mechanisms in the operating system (OS);
- real-time ORB;
- communication transport handling timing constraints;
- applications specifying time constraints.

RT-CORBA is positioned as a separate extension to CORBA (Figure 8.11). An ORB implementation compliant to RT-CORBA 1.0 must implement all of RT-CORBA except the scheduling service, which is optional.

*Thread pools*   RT-CORBA uses threads as a schedulability entity, and specifies interfaces through which the characteristics of a thread can be manipulated. To avoid unbounded priority inversion, real-time applications often require some form of pre-emptive multithreading. RT-CORBA addresses these concurrency issues by defining a standard *thread pool* model. This model enables preallocating pools and setting some thread attributes (default priority, and so on). Developers can configure thread pools to buffer or not buffer requests, thus providing further control over memory usage.

*Priority mechanisms*   RT-CORBA defines platform-independent mechanisms to control the priority of operation invocations. Two types of priorities are defined: CORBA priorities (handled at CORBA level) and native priorities (priorities of the target OS). Priority values must be mapped into the native priority scheme of a given scheduler before running the underlying schedulable entities. In addition, RT-CORBA supports two models for the priority at which a server handles requests from clients: the *server declared priority* model (the server dictates the priority at which object invocations are executed) and the *client propagated model* (the server honours the priority of the invocation set by the client). When using the server declared model an object must publish its CORBA priority in its object reference, so that the client knows at which priority level its requests are treated. The priority model is selected and configured by use of the `PriorityModelPolicy` interface. Priority selection may be applied to all the objects, or it can be overridden on a per-object reference basis. According to each implementation's needs, the RT-CORBA ORB implements a simple priority inheritance protocol, a priority ceiling protocol or some other inheritance protocol.

*Scheduling service*   The RT-CORBA scheduling service defines a high-level scheduling service so that applications can specify their scheduling requirements (worst case execution time, period, and so on) in a clear way independent of the target operating system.

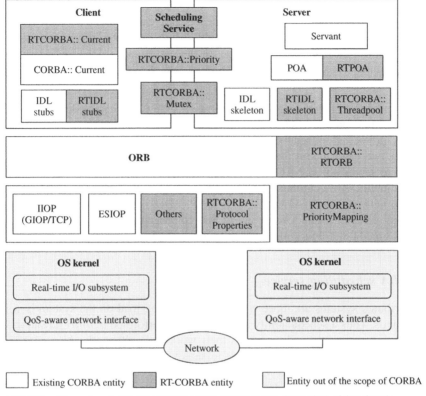

| Existing CORBA entity | RT-CORBA entity | Entity out of the scope of CORBA |

RTCORBA::Threadpool interface enables management (creation, destruction) of thread pools.

RTCORBA::Priority type defines RT-CORBA priorities as integer in [0 .. 32767].

RTCORBA::Current interface provides access to CORBA and native priorities of the current thread.

RTCORBA::PriorityMapping interface used for mapping RT-CORBA priorities into native priorities and vice versa.

RTPOA (Real-Time Portable Object Adapter) provides operations to support object-level priority settings at the time of object reference creation or servant activation.

RTCORBA::RTORB handles operations concerned with the configuration of the Real-Time ORB and manages the creation and destruction of instances of RT-CORBAIDL interfaces.

RTCORBA::Mutex interface provides mechanisms for coordinating contention for system resources. A conforming Real-Time CORBA implementation must provide an implementation of Mutex that implements some form of priority inheritance protocol.

RTCORBA::ProtocolProperties interface allows the configuration of transport protocol specific configurable parameters (send buffer size, delay, etc.).

**Figure 8.11**   Real-time CORBA architecture

*Real-time ORB services*   RT-CORBA ORBs, also called RTORB, handle operations concerned with the configuration of the real-time ORB and manage the creation and destruction of instances of other real-time CORBA IDL interfaces. Given that an ORB has to perform more than one activity at time, the allocation of the resources (processor, memory, network bandwidth, etc.) needed for those activities also has to be controlled in order to build predictable applications.

*Operating system*   One important component for RT-CORBA is the real-time operating system (RTOS). The RTOS performance and capabilities (priority set, context switch overhead, dispatching, resource locking mechanisms, thread management, admission control, etc.) considerably influence the performance. RT-CORBA does not provide portability for the real-time operating system. However, it is compatible with the Posix real-time extensions.

*Managing inter-ORB communication*   Contrary to the CORBA standard, which supports location transparency, RT-CORBA lets applications control the underlying communication protocols and end-systems. The guarantee of a predictable QoS can be achieved by two mechanisms: selecting and configuring protocol properties, and explicit binding to server objects. An RT-CORBA end-system must integrate protocols that guarantee timeliness of communications (i.e. bounded transfer delays and jitter). According to the network used (ATM, CAN, TCP/IP, FDDI, and so on), the mechanisms may be very different. RT-CORBA inter-ORB communication should use techniques and packet scheduling algorithms such as those studied in Chapters 6 and 7.

### RT-CORBA scheduling service

Static distributed systems are those where the processing load on the system is within known bounds. Thus a schedulability analysis can be performed *a priori*. Dynamic distributed systems cannot afford to predict their workload sufficiently. In consequence, the underlying infrastructure must be able to satisfy real-time constraints in a dynamically changing environment. RT-CORBA takes into account these two situations: the RT-CORBA 1.0 specification is designed for fixed-priority real-time operation, and RT-CORBA 2.0 targets dynamic scheduling, where priorities can vary during execution. In both RT-CORBA specifications (1.0 and 2.0), the scheduling service uses primitives of the Real-Time ORB. In RT-CORBA 1.0, the scheduling service implements fixed-priority scheduling algorithms such as rate monotonic or deadline monotonic. RT-CORBA 2.0 implements dynamic-priority scheduling algorithms such as earliest deadline first or least laxity first.

An application is able to use a uniform real-time scheduling policy enforced in the entire system. A scheduling service implementation will choose CORBA priorities, POA policies, and priority mappings in such a way as to realize a uniform real-time scheduling policy. Different implementations of the scheduling service can provide different real-time scheduling policies.

Note that RT-CORBA does not specify any scheduling policy (or algorithm), but it specifies interfaces to use according to application requirements. The primitives added in RT-CORBA to create a Real-Time ORB are sufficient to achieve real-time scheduling, but effective real-time scheduling is complicated. It requires that the RT-ORB primitives be used properly and that their parameters be set properly in all parts of the RT-CORBA system.

*1. Fixed-priority scheduling (RT-CORBA 1.0)*   In RT-CORBA 1.0, the concept of *activity* is used as an analysis/design entity. An activity may encompass several, possibly nested, operation invocations. RT-CORBA does not define further the concept of activity. The scheduling parameters (such as CORBA priorities) are referenced through the use of 'names' (strings). The application code uses names to uniquely identify

CORBA activities and CORBA objects. The scheduling service internally associates those names with scheduling parameters and policies. The scheduling service operates in a 'closed' CORBA system where fixed priorities are allowed to a static set of clients and servers. Therefore, it is assumed that the system designer is able to identify such a static set of CORBA activities and CORBA objects.

Whenever the client begins executing a region of code with a new deadline or priority, it invokes the `schedule_activity` operation with the name of the new activity. The scheduling service maps a CORBA priority to this name, and it invokes appropriate RT-ORB and RTOS primitives to schedule this activity.

The `create_POA` method accepts parameters for POA creation. All real-time policies of the returned POA will be set internally by this scheduling service method. This ensures a selection of real-time policies that is consistent.

The `schedule_object` operation is provided to allow the server to achieve object-level scheduling. A `schedule_object` call will install object-level scheduling parameters, for example, the priority ceiling of the object. These scheduling parameters are derived internally by the scheduling service.

*2. Dynamic scheduling (RT-CORBA 2.0)*   RT-CORBA A 2.0 replaces the term activity, used in RT-CORBA 1.0, by the definition of an end-to-end schedulable entity called *distributable thread* that may reside on multiple physical nodes. A distributable thread can execute operations on objects without regard for physical node boundaries.

Each distributable thread may have one or more scheduling parameter elements (e.g. priority, deadline or importance) that specify the acceptable end-to-end timeliness. The execution of a distributable thread is governed by the scheduling parameters on each node it visits. A scheduling discipline may have no scheduling parameter elements, only one, or several; the number and meaning of the scheduling parameter elements are scheduling-discipline specific. For example, simple deadline scheduling (such as EDF scheduling) may need only the thread deadline and maximum thread execution time.

Applications may announce their scheduling requirements. Distributable threads interact with the scheduler at specific scheduling points, including application calls, locks and releases of resources. Several scheduling discipline may exist. The RT-CORBA specification defines only the interface between the ORB/application and the scheduler. It is worth noting that schedulers will likely be dependent on the underlying operating system, and the RT-CORBA specification does not address these operating system interfaces, since they are outside the scope of CORBA.

Typically, distributed applications will be constructed as several distributable threads that execute logically concurrently. Each distributable thread will execute through one or a series of (distributed) scheduling segments, including some that may have nested segments. The `begin_scheduling_segment` operation enables association of scheduling parameter elements with a thread, the `update_scheduling_segment` operation enables modification of them, and the `end_scheduling_segment` operation causes the distributable thread to return to the previous scheduling parameter (if any). Also, RT-CORBA enables the application to create locally a scheduler-aware resource via `create_resource_manager`; these resources can have scheduling information associated with them via the `set_scheduling_parameter` operation. For example, a servant thread could have a priority ceiling protocol. The scheduling information associated with resources is discipline-specific.

# 8.4   Summary of Scheduling Capabilities of Standardized Components

Let us now summarize the efforts for providing components to be used as standardized real-time applications components. We consider two approaches, the first consisting in augmenting the promptness and predictability of actions, the second in controlling the timing of these actions.

## 8.4.1   Tracking efficiency

The basic idea of this approach is that real-time applications must be engineered with standard interfaces in order to be able to use components which are extensively used for non-real-time applications and are thus cheaper and safer (since they have been extensively tested). This approach supposes that the corresponding application programming interfaces (API) are widely accepted. This is the case for real-time operating systems that support all the Posix 1003.1 standards. A programming language such as Ada, standardized by ISO, proposes features ranging from task types to a specific real-time annex and imports external standards through library interfaces. Efforts for enabling Java to be used for real-time applications are done through the Real-Time Java extensions. For distributed platforms, several groups are attempting to standardize real-time aspects, leading to proposals for CORBA, distributed Ada or distributed Java.

However, the implementation of the interface specifications must be more efficient than non-real-time components. Real-time operating system kernels have been more or less engineered anew from scratch to implement a reentrant and preemptive kernel. Ada efficiency is obtained by static choices and decisions, allowing the detection of errors at compile time. Real-Time Java leads to the definition of a new virtual machine and specific packages for real-time classes. Real-Time CORBA requires customizing platforms and protocols.

## 8.4.2   Tracking punctuality

Efficient implementation is necessary for extending the usability of existing tools. However, efficiency is not sufficient. 'Real-time' does not mean 'real fast'. The true goal of real-time components is to be able to satisfy timing constraints. This is the goal of schedulers implementing some of the scheduling algorithms that have been extensively presented in this book.

All tools provide predefined fixed-priority preemptive schedulers: Posix 1003.1 compliant operating systems, Ada and Real-Time Java, real-time extensions of CORBA (fixed priorities for tasks and messages as well). Most of them take care of priorities inversion and implement priority ceiling or priority inheritance.

Variable priority schedulers are found more seldom and need to be specified by the user. This is defined by the SCHED_OTHER policy in Posix 1003.1 or by the queuing policy pragma in Ada. Real-Time Java and Real-Time CORBA are experimenting with variable priority issues. The difficulty of testing and validating applications in the context of variable priorities inhibits their use for industrial applications and therefore the development of environments supporting this kind of scheduler.

Dealing with timing faults, at run-time, and controlling the set of schedulable tasks with an online guarantee routine is still a research topic. However, the notion of importance is present in the Real-Time Java interface, but its use is not yet defined. More generally, coping with the time consumed by fault-tolerant techniques such as active or passive redundancy, or consensus (which are all out of the scope of this book) is still the subject of experiments with specific architectures and tools (Kopetz, 1997).

### 8.4.3 Conclusion

If we focus now on the ability to respect hard or soft real-time constraints, the state of the art shows a difference between centralized and distributed applications. Time constraints are more easily controlled in centralized, tightly coupled or homogeneous local network architectures. Thus, these architectures are required for hard real-time constrained applications. On the other hand, loosely coupled, open systems or heterogeneous architectures assume the ability of managing network resources in order to provide stringent control of message traffic and message deadlines. Today, this requires both theoretical and engineering developments. This explains why, for open and heterogeneous distributed architectures, only soft real-time applications are considered possible (realizable) in the near future.

# 8.5 Exercise

## 8.5.1 Question

---

*Exercise 8.1:* **Schedulability analysis of an extension of the mine pump example**

Consider an extended mine pump example where the tasks also perform data management, data logging and data display. This leads to some longer execution times. Additional tasks also control the carbon monoxide and airflow levels. The extended task configuration is given in Table 8.2.

**Table 8.2**  Task set parameters

| Task | Class | Period (T) | Relative deadline (D) | Worst-case computation time (C) |
|------|-------|------------|------------------------|----------------------------------|
| MethanePolling | Periodic | 200 | 100 | 58 |
| AirPolling | Periodic | 300 | 200 | 37 |
| CoPolling | Periodic | 300 | 200 | 37 |
| SafetyChecker | Periodic | 350 | 300 | 39 |
| LowSensor | Sporadic | 100 000 | 750 | 33 |
| HighSensor | Sporadic | 100 000 | 1000 | 33 |

*Continued on page 210*

---

*Continued from page 209*

**Q1**   Consider the task schedulability of the extended mine pump application under the rate monotonic and earliest deadline first techniques.

## 8.5.2   Answer

*Exercise 8.1:   Schedulability analysis of an extension of the mine pump example*

**Q1**   $U = 0.29 + 0.1233 + 0.1233 + 0.1114 = 0.6480$

$CH = 0.58 + 0.185 + 0.185 + 0.13 = 1.08$

Major cycle = [0, LCM(200, 300, 350)] = [0, 4200]

As tasks have deadlines shorter than the period, the sufficient condition for RM is not usable. For EDF, the sufficient condition $CH \leq 1$ does not hold. However, task schedules can be built without deadline missing. The schedule under RM is given by Table 8.3.

**Table 8.3**   Schedule under the rate monotonic algorithm

| Time interval | Elected task (fixed priority) | Comments |
|---|---|---|
| [0 .. 58[ | MethanePolling(1) | Deadline 100 is met |
| [58 .. 95[ | AirPolling(2) | Deadline 200 is met |
| [95 .. 122[ | CoPolling(3) | Deadline 200 is met |
| [122 .. 161[ | SafetyChecker (4) | Deadline 300 is met |
| [161 .. 200[ | Idle time of 39 time units | |
| [200 .. 258[ | MethanePolling(1) | Deadline 300 is met |
| [258 .. 300[ | Idle time of 42 time units | |
| [300 .. 337[ | AirPolling(2) | Deadline 500 is met |
| [337 .. 374[ | CoPolling(3) | Deadline 500 is met |
| [374 .. 400[ | SafetyChecker (4) | Preempted at 400 |
| [400 .. 458[ | MethanePolling(1) | Deadline 500 is met |
| [458 .. 471[ | SafetyChecker (4) | Deadline 650 is met |
| [471 .. 600[ | Idle time of 129 time units | |
| [600 .. 658[ | MethanePolling(1) | Deadline 700 is met |
| [658 .. 695[ | AirPolling(2) | Deadline 800 is met |
| [695 .. 722[ | CoPolling(3) | Deadline 800 is met |
| [722 .. 761[ | SafetyChecker (4) | Deadline 1000 is met |
| [761 .. 800[ | Idle time of 39 time units | |

The schedule under EDF is very similar. At time 400, *SafetyChecker* is not preempted and it finishes before *MethanePolling* is allowed to start.

*Continued on page 211*

*Continued from page 210*

> The idle time periods are sufficient to serve the sporadic tasks before their deadlines, whatever time they are triggered, and even if they are triggered simultaneously.

## 8.6   Web Links (April 2002)

< ACT > Ada Core Technologies: http://www.act-europe.fr/
< ADABROKER > Adabroker: http://adabroker.eu.org/
< GNAT > GNAT compiler: http://www.gnat.com
< LYNXOS > LynxOs operating system: http://lynuxworks.com
< RAVEN > Ravenscar Profile: http://www.cs.york.ac.uk/~burns/ravenscar.ps~
< RTJAVA > Real-Time Java: http://www.j-consortium.org, http://www.rtj.org,
< RTLINUX > RTLinux home page: http://www.rtlinux.org
< VXWORKS > VxWorks operating system: http://windriver.com)

# 9

# Case Studies

## 9.1 Real-Time Acquisition and Analysis of Rolling Mill Signals

### 9.1.1 Aluminium rolling mill

*Manufacturing process of an aluminium reel*

The Péchiney Rhénalu plant processes aluminium intended for the packaging market. The manufacturing process of an aluminium reel is made up of five main stages:

1. The founding eliminates scraps and impurities through heat and chemical processes, and prepares aluminium beds of $4\,m \times 6\,m \times 0.6\,m$ weighing 8–10 tons.

2. Hot rolling reduces the metal thickness by deformation and annealing and transforms a bed into a metal belt 2.5–8 mm thick and wound on a reel.

3. Cold rolling reduces the metal down to 250 micrometres ($\mu$m).

4. The thermal and mechanical completion process allows modification of the mechanical properties of the belt and cutting it to the customer's order requirements.

5. Varnishing consists of putting a coat of varnish on the belts sold for tins, food packaging or decoration.

The packaging market (tinned beverages and food) requires sheets with a strict thickness margin and demands flexibility from the manufacturing process. Each rolling mill therefore has a signal acquisition and analysis system that allows real-time supervision of the manufacturing process.

*Cold rolling*

Mill L12 is a cold rolling mill, single cage with four rollers, non-reversible, and kerosene lubricated. Its function is to reduce the thickness of the incoming belt, which may be between 0.7 and 8 mm, and to produce an output belt between 0.25 and 4.5 mm thick, and with a maximum width of 2100 mm. The minimum required thickness margins are 5 $\mu$m around the nominal output value. The scheme of the rolling mill is given in Figure 9.1.

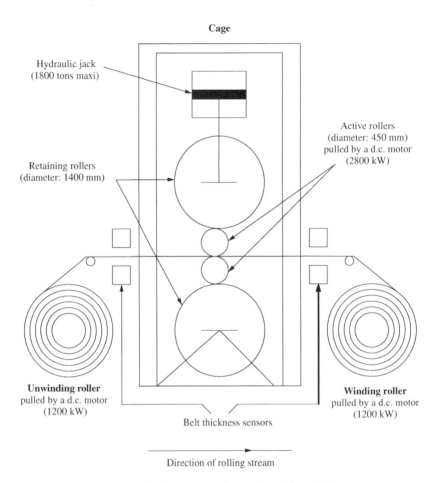

Cage

Hydraulic jack
(1800 tons maxi)

Active rollers
(diameter: 450 mm)
pulled by a d.c. motor
(2800 kW)

Retaining rollers
(diameter: 1400 mm)

**Unwinding roller**
pulled by a d.c. motor
(1200 kW)

**Winding roller**
pulled by a d.c. motor
(1200 kW)

Belt thickness sensors

Direction of rolling stream

**Figure 9.1**   Scheme of the cold rolling mill

The thickness reduction is realized by the joint action of metal crushing between the rollers and belt traction. The belt output speed may reach 30 m/s (i.e. 108 km/h). The rolling mill is driven by several computer-control systems which control the tightening hydraulic jack and the motors driving the active rollers, the winding and unwinding rollers, the input thickness variation compensation, the output thickness control and the belt tension regulation. Three of the controlling computers share a common memory.

Other functions are also present:

- production management, which prepares the list of products and displays it to the operator;

- coordination of arriving products, initial setting of the rolling mill and preparation of a production report;

- rolling mill regulation, which includes the cage setting, the insertion of the input belt, the speed increase, and the automatic stopping of the rolling mill;

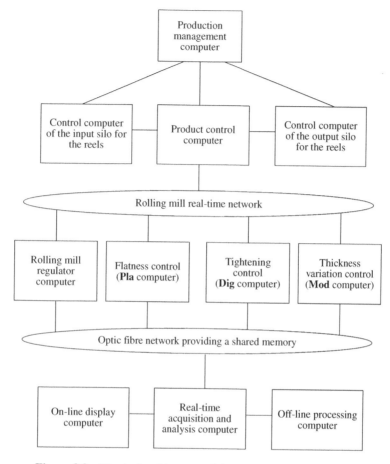

**Figure 9.2**   Physical architecture of the rolling mill environment

- management of two silos, automatic stores where the input reels and the output manufactured reels are stored.

Two human operators supervise the rolling mill input and output. The physical architecture of the whole application is given in Figure 9.2 where the production management computer, the control computers and their common memory, and the signal acquisition and analysis computer are displayed.

## 9.1.2   Real-time acquisition and analysis: user requirements

*Objectives of the signal acquisition and analysis system*

The objectives of the rolling mill signal acquisition and analysis are:

- to improve knowledge of the mill's behaviour and validate the proposed modifications;

- to help find fault sources rapidly;
- to provide operators with a manufacture product tracing system.

The signal source is the common memory of the three mill computers. The acquisition and analysis system realizes two operations:

- acquisition of signals which are generated by the rolling mill and their storage in a real-time database (RTDB);
- recording of some user configured signals on-demand.

## Special constraints

The manufacturing process imposes availability and security constraints:

- Availability: the mill is operational day and night, with a solely preventive maintenance break of 8 or 16 hours once a week.
- Security: no perturbation should propagate up to the mill controlling systems since this may break the belt or cause fire in the mill (remember that the mill is lubricated with kerosene, which is highly flammable).

## Signal acquisition frequency

The signal acquisition rate has to be equal to the signal production rate (which is itself fixed by the rolling evolution speed–the dynamics–and the Shannon theorem), and for the signal records to be usable, they have to hold all the successive acquired values during the requested recording period. The signals stored in the shared memory come from:

- the *Mod* computer, which writes 984 bytes every 4 ms (246 Kbytes/s) and additionally 160 bytes at a new product arrival (about once every 3 minutes);
- the *Dig* computer, which writes 544 bytes every 20 ms (27 Kbytes/s);
- the *Pla* computer, which writes 2052 bytes every 100 ms (20 Kbytes/s).

## Rolling mill signal recording

It is required to record the real-time signal samples during a given period and after some conditioning. The recorded signals must then be stored in files for off-line processing. The operator defines the starting and finishing times of each record and the nature of the recorded samples. Records may be of three kinds:

- on operator request: for example when he wants to follow the manufacturing of a particular product;
- perpetual: to provide a continuous manufacturing trace;

- disrupt analysis: to retrieve the signal samples some period before and after a triggering condition. This condition may be belt tearing, fire or urgency stop.

The recording task has been configured to record 180 bytes every 4 ms over a 700 s period and thus it uses files of 32 Mbytes. These records are then processed off-line, without real-time constraints.

### *Immediate signal conditioning*

The immediate signal conditioning includes raw signal analysis, real-time evolution display and dashboard presentation.

1. The raw signal analysis provides:
   - statistical information about a product and its quality trends;
   - computation of the belt length;
   - filtering treatment of the signal to delete noise and keep only the useful part of the signal, i.e. the thickness variations around zero.

2. Some values are displayed in real-time:
   - thickness variations of the input and output belt, with horizontal lines to point out the acceptable minimum and maximum;
   - flatness variations of the input and output belt. This flatness evolves during the production since heat dilates the rollers. Flatness is depicted on a coloured display called the flatness cartography. To get this cartography, the belt thickness is measured by 27 sensors spread across the belt width and is coded by a colour function of the measured value. The belt is plane when all the measures have the same colour. This allows easy visualization of the flatness variations as shown in Figure 9.3;
   - output belt speed. This allows estimation of the thickness variations caused by transient phases of the rolling mill;
   - planner of the regulations, in order to check them and to appraise their contribution to product quality;
   - belt periodic thickness perturbations which are mainly due to circumference defects of the rollers, caused by imperfect machining or by an anisotropic thermal dilatation. When the perturbations grow over the accepted margins, the faulty roller must be changed. These perturbations, at a 40 Hz frequency, are detected by frequency analysis using fast Fourier transform (FFT). Pulse generators located on the roller's axes pick up their rotation frequency. The first three harmonics are displayed. The FFT is computed with 1024 consecutive samples (the time window is thus $1024 \times 0.004 = 4\,\text{s}$).

3. The dashboard displays these evolutions, some numerical values, information and error messages, belt flatness instructions, and manufacturing characteristics (alloy, width, input and output nominal thickness, etc.). The screen resolution and its

This figure shows how the pressures are measured along a roller and
how they are displayed as a flatness cartography.

The belt applies different pressures on the roller

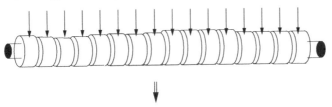

The roller generates different pressures on the sensors according to the applied force.
Each sensor measurement is coded by a colour function and the set of sensors provides
a flatness cartography.

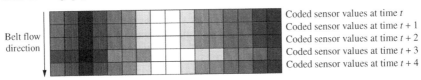

Belt flow
direction

Coded sensor values at time $t$
Coded sensor values at time $t + 1$
Coded sensor values at time $t + 2$
Coded sensor values at time $t + 3$
Coded sensor values at time $t + 4$

**Figure 9.3**   Roller geometry and flatness cartography

renewal rate (200 ms) are adapted to the resolution and dynamics of the displayed
signals as well as to the eye's perception ability.

### *Automatic report generation*

Every product passing in transit in the rolling mill automatically generates a report,
which allows appraising of its manufacturing conditions and quality. The reported
information is extracted from former computation and displays. The report is prepared
in Postscript format and saved in a file. The last 100 reports are stored in a circular
buffer before being printed. The reports are printed on-line, on operator request or
automatically after a programmed condition occurrence. The requirement is to be able
to print a report for every manufactured product whose manufacturing requires at least
5 minutes. The report printing queue is scanned every 2 seconds.

## 9.1.3   Assignment of operational functions to devices

### *Hardware architecture*

The geographic distribution shows three sets:

- the control cabin for the operator, where the signal display and report printing
  facilities must be available;

- the power station, where all signals should be available and where the
  acquisition and analysing functions are implemented (computation, recording,
  report generation);

- the terminal room, where the environment is quiet enough for off-line processing of the stored records and for configuring the system.

## Hardware and physical architecture choices

The Péchiney Rhénalu standards, the estimated numbers of interrupt levels and input–output cards, and the evaluation of the required processing power led to the following choices:

1.  For the real-time acquisition and analysis computing system: real-time executive LynxOs version 3.0, VME bus, Motorola 2600 card with Power PC 200 MHz, 96 Mbytes RAM memory, 100 Mbits/s Ethernet port and a SCSI 2 interface, 4 SCSI 2 hard disks, each with a 1 Mbyte cache memory, and 8 ms access time. With this configuration, LynxOs reports the following performance:

    - context switch in 4 microseconds;

    - interrupt handling in less than 11 microseconds;

    - access time to a driver in 2 microseconds;

    - semaphore operation in 2 microseconds;

    - time provided by `getimeofday()` system call with an accuracy of 3 microseconds.

2.  For off-line processing and on-line display: two Pentium PCs.

3.  For connecting the real-time acquisition and analysis computer and the two other functionally dependent PC computers: a fast 100 Mbytes CSMA/CD Ethernet with TCP/IP protocol.

4.  For acquiring the rolling mill data: the ultra fast optic fibre network Scramnet that is already used by the mill control computers. Scramnet uses a specific protocol simulating a shared memory and allowing processors to write directly and read at a given address in this simulated shared memory. Each write operation may raise an interrupt in the real-time acquisition and analysis computer and this interrupt can be used to synchronize it. The data are written by the emitting processor in its Scramnet card. The emission cost corresponds to writing at an address in the VME bus or in a Multibus, and the application can tolerate it. The writing and reading times have been instrumented and are presented Table 9.1.

**Table 9.1**   Scramnet access times

| Action | Number of useful bytes | Mean time (μs) | Useful throughput (Kb/s) |
|---|---|---|---|
| Writing by *Mod* | 984 | 689 | 1395 |
| Writing by *Dig* | 544 | 1744 | 305 |
| Writing by *Pla* | 2052 | 2579 | 777 |
| Reading by LynxOs | 984 | 444 | 2164 |

## 9.1.4  Logical architecture and real-time tasks

*Real-time database*

The application shares a common data table that is used as a blackboard by all programs, as shown in Figure 9.4. This table is resident in main memory and mapped into the shared virtual memory of the Posix tasks. Data are stored as arrays in the table.

To allow users to reference the signals by alphanumeric names, as well as allowing tasks to access them rapidly by addresses in main memory, dynamic binding is used and the binding values are initialized anew at each database restructuring. This use of precompiled alphanumeric requests causes this table to be called a real-time database (RTDB).

*Real-time tasks*

The set of periodic tasks and the recording of the rolling steps (rolling start, acceleration, rolling at constant speed, deceleration, rolling end) are synchronized by the emission of the *Mod* computer signals every 4 ms. This fastest sampling rate fixes the basic cycle. In the following we present the tasks, the precedence relations between some of them, the empirically chosen priorities, and the task synchronization implementation. The schemas of some tasks are given in Figures 9.5 and 9.8.

*The three acquisition tasks: modcomp, digigage and planicim*   The acquisition of rolling mill signals must be done at the rate of the emitting computer. This hard

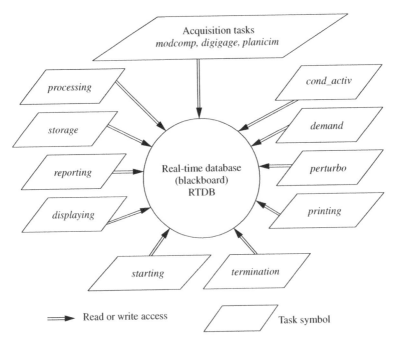

**Figure 9.4**   Real-time database utilization

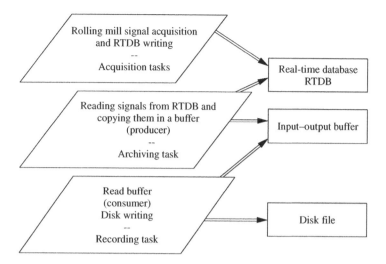

**Figure 9.5** The recorded data flow

timing constraint (due to signal acquisition frequency) is necessary for recording the rolling mill dynamics correctly. Flatness regulation signals come from the *Pla* computer with a period of 100 ms. Thickness low regulation signals come from the *Dig* computer with a period of 20 ms. Thickness rapid regulation signals are issued from the *Mod* computer with a period of 4 ms. One acquisition task is devoted to each of these signal sources. An interrupt signalling the end of writes in Scramnet is set by the writer. We note the three acquisition tasks as *modcomp, digigage* and *planicim*. The acquisition task deposits the acquired signals in the RTDB memory-resident database. The interrupt signal allows checking whether the current computation time of a task remains lower than its period. A trespassing task, i.e. one causing a timing fault, is set faulty and stopped. This also causes the whole acquisition and analysis system to stop, without any perturbation of the rolling mill control or the product manufacturing.

*Activation conditions task: cond_activ* The activation condition task (called *cond_activ*) is the dynamic interpreter of the logic equations set specifying the list of samples to record or causing automatic recording to start when the signals detect that a product has gone out of tolerance. These logic equations are captured at system configuration, parsed and compiled into an evaluation binary tree. This task is triggered every 4 ms by the *modcomp* task with a relative deadline value equal to its period.

*Immediate signal processing task: processing* The signal processing task (called *processing*) reads the new signal samples in the database, computes the data to be displayed or stored and writes them in the database. It computes the statistical data, the FFT, the belt length, and the filtering of some signals. This processing must be done at the acquisition rate of the fastest signals to recording the rolling mill dynamics correctly. This task is triggered every 4 ms by the *modcomp* task with a relative deadline value equal to its period.

*Record archiving tasks: storage, perturbo and demand* The three record archiving tasks, called *storage, perturbo* and *demand*, must operate at the acquisition rate of the fastest signals. This means that some timing constraints have to be taken into account to record the rolling mill dynamics correctly. Thus the tasks are released every 4 ms by the *modcomp* task with a relative deadline value equal to its period. Each task reads the recorded signals in the database and transfers them to files on disks, using producer–consumer schemes with a two-slot buffer for each file. The archiving tasks (i.e. *storage, perturbo* and *demand* tasks) write to the buffers while additional tasks, called *recording* consume from the buffers the data to be transferred to disks. Those *recording* tasks, one per archiving task, consume very little processor time and this can be neglected. They have a priority lower than the least priority task of period 4 ms (their priority is set to 5 units below their corresponding archiving task).

*Signal displaying task: displaying*   Signal displaying (task called *displaying*) requires a renewal rate of 200 ms. This is a deadline with a soft timing constraint, since any data which is not displayed at a given period may be stored and displayed at the next period. There is no information loss for the user, who is concerned with manufacturing a product according to fixed specifications. For this he or she needs to observe the minimum, maximum and mean values of the signal since the last screen refresh. The display programs use an X11 graphical library and the real-time task uses the PC as an X server.

*Report generating task: reporting*   The reports must be produced (by the task called *reporting*) with a period of 200 ms. This task also has a soft deadline.

*Report printing task: printing*   Report printing (the task is named *printing*) is required either automatically or by the operator. The task is triggered periodically every two seconds and it checks the Postscript circular buffer for new reports to print.

*Initializing task: starting*   The application initialization is an aperiodic task (called *starting*) which prepares all the resources required by the other tasks. It is the first to run and executes alone before it releases the other tasks. A configuration file specifies the number, type and size of files to create. There may be up to 525 files, totalling 2.5 Gbytes. All files are created in advance, and are allocated to tasks on demand. At the first system installation, this file creation may take up to one hour.

*Closing task: termination*   The application closure is performed by an aperiodic task (called *termination*) which releases all used resources. It is triggered at the application end.

### Precedence relationships

The successive signal conditionings involve precedence relationships between the tasks: acquisition must be done before signal processing and the evaluation of activation conditions. These tasks must in turn precede record archiving, display and report generation. *Starting* precedes every task and *termination* stops them all before releasing their resources. Figure 9.6 shows the precedence graph.

When the task *modcomp* has set the signal samples in the database, it activates the other periodic tasks which use these samples; *digigage* and *planicim,* which have larger periods, also deposit some samples. The 4 ms period tasks check a version number to know when the larger period samples have been refreshed.

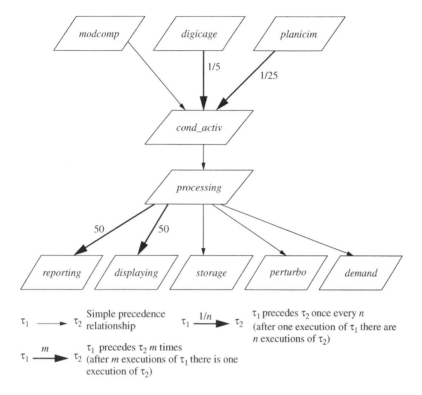

**Figure 9.6**  Tasks precedence graph

## Empirical priorities of tasks

The LynxOs system has a fixed priority scheduler, with 255 priority levels, the higher level being 255. The priorities have been chosen on a supposed urgency basis and the higher priorities have been given to the tasks with the harder timing constraints. It has been checked that the result was a feasible schedule.

Table 9.2 presents the empirical constant priorities given to each task, the period $T$, the measured computation time $C$ (the minimum, maximum and mean values have been recorded by measuring the start and finish time of the requests with the getimeofday() system call), the relative deadline $D$ and the reaction category in case of timing fault.

## Synchronization by semaphores

In the studied system, the periodic tasks are not released by a real-time scheduler using the system clock. The basic rate is given directly by the rolling mill and by the end-of-write interrupt which is generated every 4 ms by the *Mod* computer.

The task requests triggering and the task precedence relationships are programmed with semaphores which are used as synchronization events. Recall that a semaphore $S$ is used by means of two primitives, $P(S)$ and $V(S)$ (Silberschatz and Galvin, 1998; Tanenbaum and Woodhull 1997).

**Table 9.2** The tasks of the acquisition and analysis system

| Task | Priority | T ms | Cmin (μs) | Cmax (μs) | Cmean (μs) | D (ms) | Reaction to faults |
|------|----------|------|-----------|-----------|------------|--------|--------------------|
| *starting* | 50 | | | | | 30 000 | 5 |
| *modcomp* | 50 | 4 | 600 | 992 | 613 | 1 | 1 |
| *cond_activ* | 38 | 4 | 136 | 221 | 141 | 4 | 2 |
| *processing* | 36 | 4 | 92 | 496 | 106 | 4 | 2 |
| *storage* | 34 | 4 | 128 | 249 | 136 | 4 | 3 |
| *perturbo* | 33 | 4 | 112 | 218 | 120 | 4 | 3 |
| *demand* | 32 | 4 | 155 | 348 | 167 | 4 | 3 |
| *digigage* | 30 | 20 | 860 | 1430 | 1130 | 10 | 1 |
| *planicim* | 29 | 100 | 1800 | 2220 | 1920 | 50 | 1 |
| *displaying* | 27 | 200 | 512 | 1950 | 1510 | 200 | 4 |
| *reporting* | 26 | 200 | 475 | 2060 | 1620 | 200 | 4 |
| *printing* | 18 | 2000 | | | | 300 000 | 4 |
| *termination* | 50 | | | | | | 5 |

The periodic tasks are programmed as cyclic tasks which block themselves on their private semaphore (a semaphore initialized with state 0) at the end of each cycle. An activation cycle corresponds to a request execution. Thus *modcomp* blocks itself when executing *P(S_modcomp)*, *cond_activ* when executing *P(S_cond_activ)*, *processing* when executing *P(S_processing)*, *demand* when executing *P(S_demand)*, and so on. At each 4 ms period end, all the tasks are blocked when there is no timing fault.

The *Mod* computer end-of-write interrupt causes the execution of a *V(S_modcomp)* operation, which awakes the *modcomp* task. When this task finishes and just before blocking again by executing *P(S_modcomp)*, it wakes up all the other periodic tasks by executing *V(S_cond_activ)*, *V(S_processing)*, ..., *V(S_demand)*. Every 5 cycles it wakes task *digigage*; every 25 cycles it wakes task *planicim*; ...; every 500 cycles it wakes task *printing*. The execution order is fixed by the task priority (there is only one processor and the cyclic tasks are not preempted for file output since the *recording* tasks have lower priorities). This implements the task precedence relationships. The synchronization of the 11 cyclic tasks is depicted in Figure 9.7.

Task *modcomp* also monitors each task $\tau_x$ it awakes. In nominal behaviour, $\tau_x$ is blocked at the time of its release. This is checked by *modcomp* reading $S\_\tau_x$'s state ($S\_\tau_x$ is the private semaphore of $\tau_x$). $S\_\tau_x$'s state represents the history of operations on $S\_\tau_x$ and it memorizes therefore whether, before being preempted by *modcomp*, the cyclic task $\tau_x$ was able or not to execute the $P(S\_\tau_x)$ operation which ends the cycle, blocking $\tau_x$ anew. This solution is correct only in a uniprocessor computer and if *modcomp* is the highest priority task and able to preempt the other tasks.

To sum up, the task *modcomp* starts each 4 ms cycle when receiving the Scramnet interrupt mapped to a *V* semaphore operation. It executes its cyclic program, checks the time limit of the tasks and then awakes all the tasks concerned with the current cycle. Figure 9.8 presents the task schema of *modcomp* and of the archiving tasks.

Finally, when a task needs signals acquired by a task other than *modcomp*, it reads the database and checks for them. Each of the data structures resulting from acquisition or processing is given a version number that is incremented at each update. The client programs have their own counter and compare its value to the current version number to check for a new value. The version numbers are monotonously increasing. If their

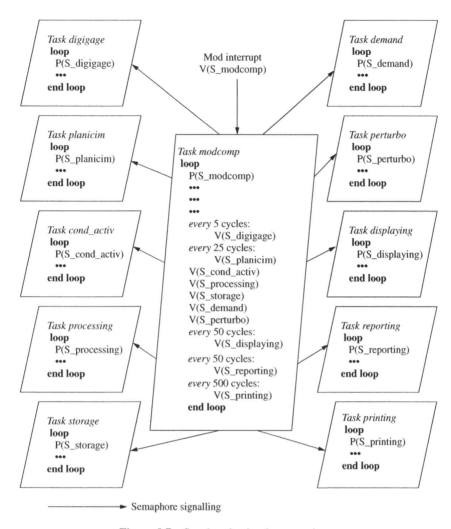

**Figure 9.7**   Synchronization by semaphores

incrementation can be made by an atomic operation (between tasks), there is no need to use a mutual exclusion semaphore.

### Reactions to timing faults

Timing faults are detected by task *modcomp* as explained above. The reaction depends on the criticality of the faulty task (Table 9.2) and is related to one of the following categories:

- Category 1: the computing system is stopped since the sampled signals do not represent the rolling mill dynamics. The values have not been read at the same sampling instant (this category concerns the three acquisition tasks, *modcomp*, *digigage* and *planicim*).

```
Archiving task/** tasks storage, perturbo and demand
  begin
    open database
    open synchronization table
    open allocation table
    start the buffer consumer task
    while (no required stop) loop
      wait for a required archive
      read configuration and open archiving file
      create the two slots buffer for the recorded signals
        /** each buffer size is set to the recorded signal size and rate
      wait for the start recording authorization /** blocked by P(S_producer)
      while (not(end recording condition) or not(max recording time)) loop
        write each signal in its current buffer
        if the current buffer is full then
          activate the consumer recording task   /** with V(S_consumer)
          point to the other buffer        /** with P(S_producer)
        end if
      end loop
      wait until the last buffer is saved
      close the archiving file
    end loop      /** loop controlled by (no required stop)
    close database
    close synchronization table
    close allocation table
  end/** archiving task

Recording task
  begin
    while (no required stop) loop
      wait until a buffer is ready /** with P(S_Consumer)
      transfer the buffer to the file, indicate free buffer /** with V(S_producer)
    end loop /** loop controlled by (no required stop)
  end/** Recording task

Acquisition task         /** task modcomp
  begin
    Scramnet initialization
    open database
    open synchronization table
    while(no required stop)loop
      wait the Scramnet interrupt /** with P(S_modcomp)
      read Scramnet and write the samples in the database
      monitor other tasks
      awake the other tasks,   τ_x  /** with V(S_τ_x)
    end loop                 /** loop controlled by (no required stop)
    close database
    close synchronization table
  end/** acquisition task
```

**Figure 9.8** *Modcomp* and archiving task schemes

- Category 2: the computing system is stopped since the computed values are incorrect and useless (this category concerns the conditions elaboration task, *cond_activ*, and the signal processing task: *processing*).

- Category 3: the function currently performed by the task is stopped since its results are not usable (this category concerns the three record archiving tasks, *storage, perturbo* and *demand*).

- Category 4: the current function is not stopped but the fault is recorded in the logbook (journal). The recurrent appearance of this fault may motivate the operator to alleviate the processor load by augmenting the task period or reducing the number of required computations (this category concerns the signal displaying task, *displaying*, the report generating task, *reporting*, and the report printing task, *printing*).

- Category 5: nothing is done since the fault consequences are directly noticed by the operator (this category concerns the initializing and the closing task).

It should be noted that these reactions have some correlation with the task precedence relationships.

## 9.1.5   Complementary studies

Complementary studies of this rolling mill are suggested below.

### *Scheduling algorithms*

Let us suppose that the task requests are released by a scheduler that uses the LynxOs real-time clock whose accuracy is 3 microseconds. The precedence relationships are no longer programmed but the scheduler takes care of them.

- Study the schedulability of the 11 periodic tasks with an on-line empirical fixed priority scheduler as in the case study.

- Study the schedulability of the 11 periodic tasks with the RM algorithm.

- Study the schedulability of the 11 periodic tasks with the EDF algorithm

### *Scheduling with shared exclusive resources*

Let us suppose that the shared data in the database are protected by locks implemented with mutual exclusion semaphores (*P* or *V* operation time is equal to 2 microseconds). Analyse the influence of access conflicts, context switches (the thread context switch time is equal to 4 microseconds) and the additional delays caused by the database locking with different lock granularity.

### *Robustness of the application*

Compute the laxity of each task and the system laxity for:

- evaluating the global robustness. For example, consider slowing down the processor speed as much as acceptable for the timing constraints.

- evaluating the margin for the task behaviour when its execution time increases.

- estimating the influence of random perturbations caused by shared resource locking.

To introduce some timing jitter, it is necessary to increase the processor utilization factor of some tasks. Reducing the period of some tasks can do this, for example. Then, once a jitter has appeared:

- introduce a start time jitter control for the signal displaying task,

- introduce a finish time jitter control for the *processing* and *reporting* tasks. This allows simulating a sampled data control loop monitoring the actuators.

### *Multiprocessor architecture*

Let us suppose a multiprocessor is used to increase the computing power. Study the task scheduling with two implementation choices. In the first one, the basic rate is still given by the rolling mill, and cyclic task synchronization and wake up are done by program. In the second case, the LynxOs real-time clock (accuracy of 3 microseconds) and a real-time scheduler are used.

Task precedence must be respected and the mixing of priorities and event-like semaphores cannot be used, since the uniprocessor solution is no longer valid. The fault detection that the redundancy allowed is not valid either.

### *Network*

The use of Scramnet is costly. Examine the possibilities and limits of other real-time networks and other real-time protocols. Consider several message communication schemes between the application tasks. Finally, as in the example presented in Section 6.4.3, consider message scheduling when the network used is CAN, FIP or a token bus.

## 9.2 Embedded Real-Time Application: Mars Pathfinder Mission

### 9.2.1  Mars Pathfinder mission

After the success of early Mars discovery missions (Viking in 1976), a long series of mission failures have limited Mars exploration. The Mars Pathfinder mission was an important step in NASA discovery missions. The spacecraft was designed, built and operated by the Jet Propulsion Laboratory (JPL) for NASA. Launched on 4 December 1996, Pathfinder reached Mars on 4 July 1997, directly entering the planet's atmosphere and bouncing on inflated airbags as a technology demonstration of a new way to deliver a lander of 264 kg on Mars. After a while, the Pathfinder stationary lander released a micro-rover, named Sojourner. The rover Sojourner, weighing 10.5 kg, is a six-wheeled vehicle controlled by an earth-based operator, who used images obtained by both the rover and lander systems. This control is possible thanks to two communication devices: one between the lander and Earth and the other between the lander and the rover, done by means of high frequency radio waves. The Mars Pathfinder's rover rolled onto the surface of Mars on 6 July at a maximum speed of 24 m/h. Sojourner's mobility provided the capability of discovering a landing area over hundreds of square metres on Mars.

The scientific objectives included long-range and close-up surface imaging, and, more generally, characterization of the Martian environment for further exploration. The Pathfinder mission investigated the surface of Mars with several instruments: cameras, spectrometers, atmospheric structure instruments and meteorology, known as ASI/MET, etc. These instruments allowed investigations of the geology and surface morphology at sub-metre to one hundred metres scale. During the total mission, the spacecraft relayed 2.3 gigabits of data to Earth. This huge volume of information included 16 500 images from the lander camera and 550 images from the rover camera, 16 chemical analyses and 8.5 million measurements of atmospheric conditions, temperature and wind.

After a few days, not long after Pathfinder started gathering meteorological data, the spacecraft began experiencing total resets, each resulting in losses of data. By using an on-line debug, the software engineers were able to reproduce the failure, which turned out to be a case of priority inversion in a concurrent execution context. Once they had understood the problem and fixed it, the onboard software was modified and the mission resumed its activity with complete success. The lander and the rover operated longer than their design lifetimes. We now examine what really happened on Mars to the rover Sojourner.

## 9.2.2 Hardware architecture

The simplified view of the Mars Pathfinder hardware architecture looks like the one-processor architecture, based on the RS 6000 microprocessor, presented in Figure 9.9. The hardware on the rover includes an Intel 8085 microprocessor which is dedicated to particular automatic controls. But we do not take into account this processor because it has a separate activity that does not interfere with the general control of the spacecraft.

The main processor on the lander part is plugged on a VME bus which also contains interface cards for the radio to Earth, the lander camera and an interface to a specific 1553 bus. The 1553 bus connects the two parts of the spacecraft (stationary lander and rover) by means of a high frequency communication link. This communication link was inherited from the Cassini spacecraft. Through the 1553 bus, the hardware on the lander part provides an interface to accelerometers, a radar altimeter, and an instrument for meteorological measurements, called ASI/MET.

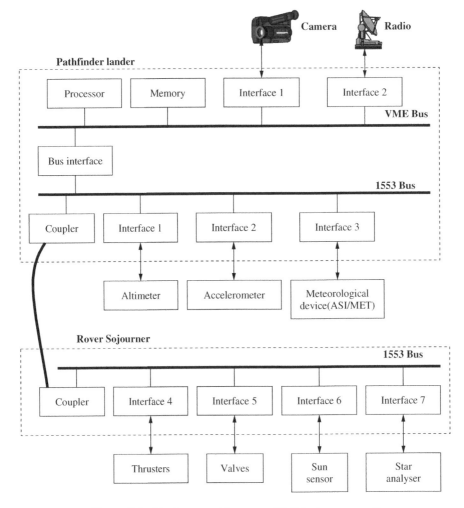

**Figure 9.9** Hardware architecture of Pathfinder spacecraft

The hardware on the rover part includes two kinds of devices:

- Control devices: thrusters, valves, etc.
- Measurement devices: a camera, a sun sensor and a star scanner.

## 9.2.3 Functional specification

Given the hardware architecture presented above, the main processor of the Pathfinder spacecraft communicates with three interfaces only:

- radio card for communications between lander and Earth;
- lander camera;
- 1553 bus interface linked to control or measurement devices.

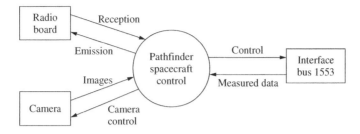

**Figure 9.10**  Context diagram of Pathfinder mission according to SA-RT method

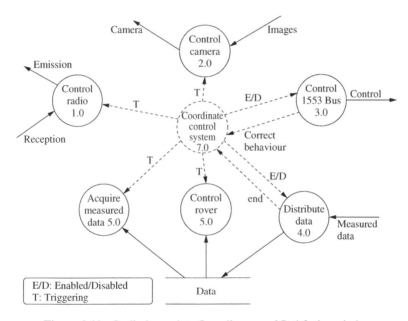

**Figure 9.11**  Preliminary data flow diagram of Pathfinder mission

The context diagram of this application is presented in Figure 9.10 according to the Structured Analysis for Real-Time systems (SA-RT) (Goldsmith, 1993; Hatley and Pirbhai, 1988). As explained above, there are only three terminators, external entities connected to the monitoring system. The first step of decomposition is shown as a preliminary data flow diagram in Figure 9.11. In order to simplify the analysis of this complex application, only the processes active during the Mars exploration phase have been represented. Other processes, active during the landing phase or the flight, have been omitted. The control process, numbered 7.0, corresponds to the scheduling of the other functional processes and could be specified by a state transition diagram.

## 9.2.4  Software architecture

The software architecture is a multitasking architecture, based on the real-time embedded system kernel VxWorks (Wind River Systems). The whole application includes over 25 tasks. These tasks are either periodic (bus management, etc.) or aperiodic (error analysis, etc.). The synchronization and communications are based on reader/writer paradigm or message queues. Some of these tasks are:

- mode control task (landing, exploration, flight, etc.);

- surface pointing control task (entering Mars's atmosphere);

- fault analysis task (centralized analysis of the error occurring in the tasks);

- meteorological data task (ASI/MET);

- data storage task (in EEPROM);

- 1553 bus control task (see further detailed explanations);

- star acquisition task;

- serial communication task;

- data compression task;

- entry/descent task.

It is important to outline that the mission had quite different modes (flight, landing, exploration), so a specific task is responsible for managing the tasks that have to be active in each mode. In this study we are only interested in the exploration mode. Moreover, in order to simplify the understanding of the problem, the application presented and analysed here is derived from the original real Pathfinder mission.

The simplified software task architecture is presented in Table 9.3 and in Figure 9.12 according to a diagram of the Design Approach for Real-Time Systems (DARTS) method (Gomaa, 1993). This task diagram consists of the different tasks of the application and their communications. All the tasks of the analysed application are considered to be periodic and activated by an internal real-time clock (RTC). It is important to notice that four tasks (*Data_Distribution*, *Control_Task*, *Measure_Task*, *Meteo_Task*) share a critical resource, called *Data*, that is used in mutual exclusion. Two operations are provided by the data abstraction module: read and write. The different tasks are

**Table 9.3**  Task set of Pathfinder application in the exploration mode

| Priority | Task | Comments |
|---|---|---|
| The highest | *Bus_Scheduling* | 1553 bus control task |
| ↑ | *Data_Distribution* | 1553 bus data distribution task |
| ↑ | *Control_Task* | Rover control task |
| ↑ | *Radio_Task* | Radio communication management task |
| ↑ | *Camera_Task* | Camera control task |
| ↑ | *Measure_Task* | Measurement task |
| The lowest | *Meteo_Task* | Meteorological data task |

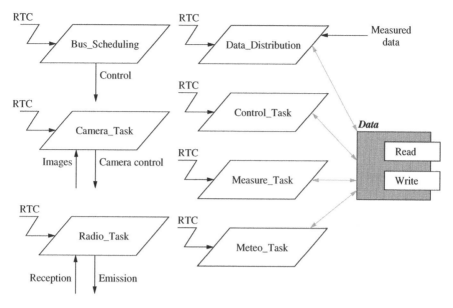

**Figure 9.12**   Task architecture of Pathfinder mission (RTC: real-time clock)

reader and writer tasks that can access these data in a critical section. The theory presented in Chapter 3 has been applied to this case study.

## 9.2.5  Detailed analysis

The key point of this application is the management of the 1553 bus that is the main communication medium between tasks. The software schedules this bus activity at a rate of 8 Hz (period of 125 ms). This feature dictates the architecture software which controls both the 1553 bus itself and the devices attached to it.

The software that controls the 1553 bus and the attached instruments is implemented as two tasks:

- The first task, called *Bus_Scheduling*, controls the setup of the transactions on the 1553. Each cycle, it verifies that the transaction has been correctly realized, particularly without exceeding the bus cycle. This task has the highest priority.

- The second task handles the collection of the transaction results, i.e. the data. The second task is referred to as *Data_Distribution*. This task has the third highest priority in the task set; the second priority is assigned to the entry and landing task, which has not been activated in the studied exploration mode. So the main objective of this task is to collect data from the different instruments and to put them in the shared data module *Data*.

A typical temporal diagram for the 1553 bus activity is shown in Figure 9.13. First the task *Data_Distribution* is awakened. This task is completed when all the data distributions are finished. After a while the task *Bus_Scheduling* is awakened to set

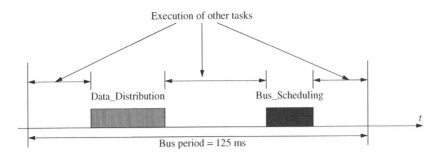

**Figure 9.13**  Typical temporal diagram for the 1553 bus activity

up transactions for the next cycle. The times between these executions are devoted to other tasks. This cycle is repeated indefinitely.

Except for the periods of the first two tasks *Bus_Scheduling* and *Data_Distribution*, which are specified with exact values corresponding to the real application, the timing characteristics of tasks (execution time and period) were estimated in order to get a better demonstrative example. These task parameters are presented in Table 9.4 in decreasing priority order. The timing parameters ($C_i$ and $T_i$) have been reduced by assuming a processor time unit of 25 ms. In order to simplify the problem, we assume that the critical sections of all tasks using the shared critical resource have a duration equal to their execution times. Except for the task called *Meteo_Task*, the parameters are considered as fixed. The *Meteo_Task* has an execution time equal to either 2 or 3, corresponding to more or less important data communication size.

The processor utilization factor of this seven-task set is equal to 0.72 (respectively 0.725) for an execution time of *Meteo_Task* equal to 2 (respectively 3). We can note that both values are lower than the limit ($U \leq 0.729$) given by the sufficient condition for RM scheduling (see condition (2.12) in Chapter 2). So this application would be schedulable if the tasks were independent. But the relationships between tasks, due to the shared critical resource *Data*, lead to simulation of the execution of the task set with the two different values of the *Meteo_Task* execution time. This simulation has to be done over the LCM of the task periods, that is to say 5000 ms (or 200 in reduced time).

In Figure 9.14, the execution sequence of this task set for the *Meteo_Task* execution time equal to 2 is shown. As we can see, the analysis duration is limited to the reduced

**Table 9.4**  Pathfinder mission task set parameters

| Task | Priority | Parameters (ms) | | Reduced parameters | | Critical section duration |
|---|---|---|---|---|---|---|
| | | $C_i$ | $T_i$ | $C_i$ | $T_i$ | |
| Bus_Scheduling | 7 | 25 | 125 | 1 | 5 | — |
| Data_Distribution | 6 | 25 | 125 | 1 | 5 | 1 |
| Control_Task | 5 | 25 | 250 | 1 | 10 | 1 |
| Radio_Task | 4 | 25 | 250 | 1 | 10 | — |
| Camera_Task | 3 | 25 | 250 | 1 | 10 | — |
| Measure_Task | 2 | 50 | 5000 | 2 | 200 | 2 |
| Meteo_Task | 1 | {50, 75} | 5000 | {2, 3} | 200 | {2, 3} |

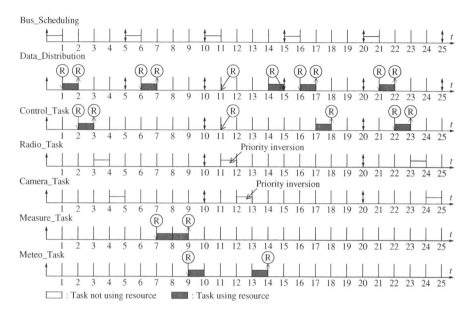

**Figure 9.14** Valid execution sequence of Pathfinder mission for a *Meteo_Task* task with execution time equal to 2

time 25 because, when the execution of the *Measure_Task* and *Meteo_Task* tasks have completed, the study can be limited to the next period of the other tasks. The obtained execution sequence is valid in the sense that all tasks are within their deadlines. The *Measure_Task* and *Meteo_Task* tasks end their executions at time 14 and the others produce a valid execution sequence in the time range [20, 30] that is indefinitely repeated until the end of the major cycle, equal to 200.

It is worth noticing that all the waiting queues are managed according to the task priority. Moreover, the tasks which use the critical resource *Data* are assumed to acquire it at the beginning of their activation and to release it at the end of their execution. When this resource request cannot be satisfied because another task is using the critical resource, the kernel primitive implementing this request is supposed to have a null duration.

It is not difficult to see that a priority inversion phenomenon occurs in this execution sequence. At time 11, the *Data_Distribution* task which is awakened at time 10, should get the processor, but the *Meteo_Task* task, using the critical resource, blocks this higher priority task. The *Camera_Task* and *Radio_Task* tasks, which do not need the shared exclusive resource and are awakened at time 11, have a priority higher than task *Meteo_Task*, and as a consequence they get the processor one after the other at times 11 and 12. Then *Meteo_Task* task can resume its execution and release the critical resource at time 14. Finally the higher priority task, *Data_Distribution* task, resumes its execution and ends just in time before its deadline 15 (Figure 9.14).

The priority inversion phenomenon leads to an abnormal blocking time of a high priority task, here *Data_Distribution* task, because it uses a critical resource shared by a lower priority task, *Meteo_Task*, and two intermediate priority tasks, *Camera_Task* and *Radio_Task* tasks, can execute.

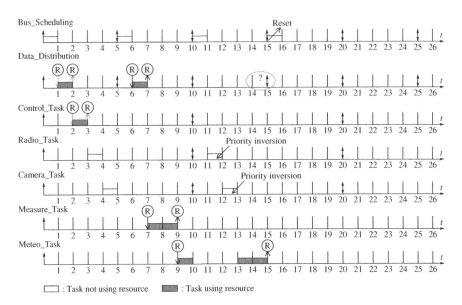

**Figure 9.15**   Non-valid execution sequence of Pathfinder mission for a *Meteo_Task* task with execution time equal to 3

Let us suppose now that *Meteo_Task* has an execution time equal to 3. The new execution temporal diagram, presented in Figure 9.15, shows that the *Data_Distribution* task does not respect its deadline. This temporal fault is immediately detected by the *Bus_Scheduling* task and leads to a general reset of the computer: this caused the failure of Pathfinder mission. This reset initialized all hardware and software. There is no loss of collected data. However, the remainder of the activities were postponed until the next day.

In order to prevent this priority inversion phenomenon, it is necessary to use one specific resource management protocol as seen in Chapter 3. Figure 9.16 illustrates the efficiency of the priority inheritance protocol. The execution sequence is now valid even though *Meteo_Task* task has an execution duration equal to 3. In fact the intermediate priority tasks, *Camera_Task* and *Radio_Task* tasks, are executed after *Meteo_Task* task because this task inherits the higher priority of *Data_Distribution* task. In this case, it is interesting to notice that the *Meteo_Task* task execution time can be as long as 3 units without jeopardizing the valid execution sequence.

In order to avoid the priority inversion phenomenon, one can also use another protocol based on the assignment of the highest priority to the task which is in a critical section. Actually, this resource management protocol leads to forbidding the execution of other tasks during critical sections (Figure 9.17). But a drawback of this protocol is that a lower priority task using a resource can block a very high priority task, such as the *Bus_Scheduling* task in the considered application.

## 9.2.6   Conclusion

Being focused on the entry and landing phases of the Pathfinder mission, engineers did not take enough care over testing the execution of the exploration mode. The actual

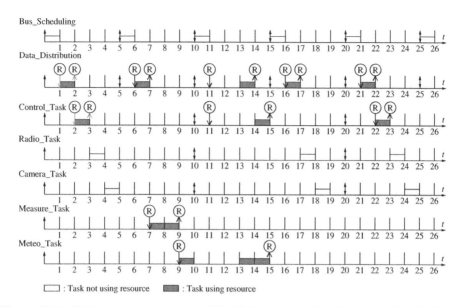

**Figure 9.16**   Valid execution sequence of Pathfinder mission by using a priority inheritance protocol and for a *Meteo_Task* task with execution time equal to 3

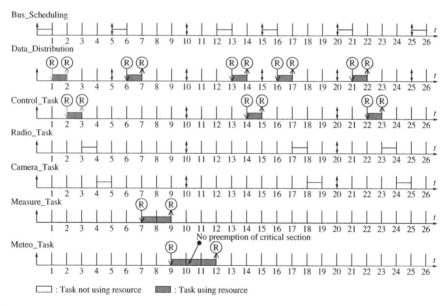

**Figure 9.17**   Valid execution sequence of Pathfinder mission by using a highest priority protocol and for a *Meteo_Task* with execution duration equal to 3

data rates were higher than estimated during the pre-flight testing and the amount of science activities, particularly meteorological instrumentation, proportionally greater. This higher load aggravated the problem of using the critical resource (communication on 1553 bus). It is important to outline that two system resets had occurred in the pre-flight testing. As they had never been reproducible, engineers decided that they were probably caused by a hardware glitch. As this part of the mission was less critical, the software was not protected against the priority inversion phenomenon by using a mutex semaphore implementing priority inheritance. A VxWorks mutex object includes a Boolean parameter that indicates whether priority inheritance should be performed by the semaphore management. In this case the mutex parameter was off. Once the problem was understood the modification appeared obvious: change the creation flags of the semaphore and enable the priority inheritance. The onboard software was modified accordingly on the spacecraft. This application, which we have simplified for a better understanding, has been studied by assuming a scheduling based on fixed priority (RM algorithm) and a priority inheritance protocol for managing the exclusive resource. This study can be prolonged by analysing the execution sequence produced by the following scheduling contexts:

- scheduling with variable priorities (for example, earliest deadline first);

- other resource management protocol (for example, priority ceiling protocol).

# 9.3   Distributed Automotive Application

## 9.3.1   Real-time systems and the automotive industry

Nowadays, car manufacturers integrate more and more microcontrollers that manage the brakes, the injection, the performance, and the passenger comfort (Cavalieri et al., 1996). For instance, the engine control system aims to manage the engine performance in terms of power, to reduce fuel consumption and to control the emission of exhaust fumes. This control is obtained by sending computed values to the actuators: electronic injectors, electromagnetic air valve for managing the idling state of the engine (i.e. the driver does not accelerate) and fuel pump. The ABS system prevents the wheels from locking when the driver brakes. The system must also take into account sudden variations in the road surface. This regulation is obtained by reading periodically the rotation sensors on each wheel. If a wheel is locked, then the ABS system acts directly on the brake pressure actuator. Complementary information on the process control functionalities can be found, for instance, in Cavalieri et al. (1996). The different processors, named ECUs (Electronic Component Units), are interconnected with different fieldbuses such as CAN (Control Area Network) and VAN (Vehicle Area Network) (ISO, 1994a,b,c).

One of the recent efforts from car manufacturers and ECU suppliers is the definition of a common operating system called OSEK/VDX (OSEK, 1997). The use of this operating system by all ECUs in the future will enhance the interoperability and the reusability of the application code. Such an approach drastically reduces the software development costs.

## 9.3.2   Hardware and software architecture

The specific application that we are going to study is a modified version derived from an actual one embedded in the cars of PSA (Peugeot-Citroën Automobile Corp.)

(Richard et al., 2001). The application is composed of different nodes interconnected by one CAN network and one VAN network. Prominent European fieldbus examples targeted for automotive applications are CAN and VAN. These fieldbuses have to strive to respect deterministic response times. Both correspond to the medium access control (MAC) protocol, based on the CSMA/CA (Carrier Sense Multiple Access / Collision Avoidance) protocol.

CAN is a well-known network; it was presented in Section 6.4.3. We just recall that the maximum message length calculation should include the worst-case bit stuffing number and the 3 bits of IFS (Inter Frame Space). For a message of $n$ bytes, this length is given by $47 + 8n + \lfloor (34 + 8n)/4 \rfloor$, where $\lfloor x \rfloor$ ($x \geq 0$) denotes the largest integer less than or equal to $x$.

### Hardware architecture

The complete application is composed of nine ECUs (or nodes) interconnected by one CAN network and one VAN network as shown by Figure 9.18. They are: Engine controller, Automatic Gear Box, Anti-lock Brake System/Vehicle Dynamic Control, Suspension controller, Wheel Angle Sensor/Dynamic Headlamp Corrector, Bodywork, and three other specialized units dedicated to passenger comfort functions (Table 9.5). To make understanding of the rest of this chapter easier, Table 9.5 links a number to each main ECU of the application.

CAN is used for real-time control systems such as engine control and anti-lock brakes whereas VAN is used in bodywork for interconnecting ECUs without tight time-critical constraints. The bodywork computer (node 6) ensures the gateway function between CAN and VAN. The need for exchanges between these two networks is obvious. For example, for displaying the vehicle speed, a dashboard in the bodywork needs information from the ECU connected to CAN; when requiring more power, the engine controller can send a signal to the air condition controller to inhibit air conditioning. And this latter is also under real-time constraints.

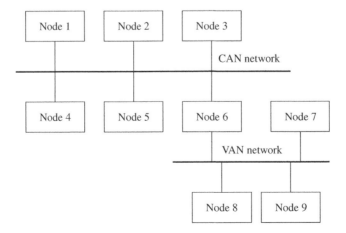

**Figure 9.18** Hardware architecture of the automotive application

**Table 9.5** Functions of the main nodes of the distributed automotive application

| Node | Function |
|---|---|
| Node 1 | Engine controller |
| Node 2 | Automatic gear box |
| Node 3 | Anti-locking brake system/Vehicle dynamic control |
| Node 4 | Wheel angle sensor/Dynamic headlamp corrector |
| Node 5 | Suspension controller |
| Node 6 | Bodywork (between CAN and VAN networks) |
| Nodes 7, 8, 9 | Passenger comfort functions |

## 9.3.3 Software architecture

The entire application has 44 tasks distributed among the different processors and 19 messages conveyed by the two networks. More precisely, the critical part of the application uses the CAN network, and has 31 tasks and 12 messages, whereas the non-critical part uses the VAN network and has 13 tasks and 7 messages. In order to simplify the study of this complex example, we limit the temporal analysis to the nodes connected to the CAN network, that is to say to the critical real-time part of the application. So the corresponding software architecture of the automotive application is given in Figure 9.19.

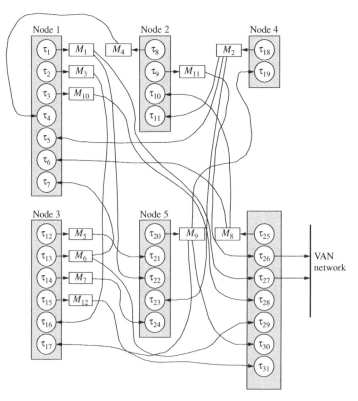

**Figure 9.19** Software architecture of the automotive application restricted to the critical real-time communications on the CAN network

We now present the model of the application used in the temporal analysis. We describe all the tasks on each processor, and all the messages on the CAN network. Each task is defined by $(r_i, C_i, D_i, T_i)$ parameters, defined in Chapter 1. In this application, the arrival time $r_i$ is null for any task. Moreover, the tasks are periodic and deadlines are equal to periods. The timing requirements are summarized in Table 9.6, for each processor.

For evaluating the implementation, we assume that all ECUs run under OSEK/VDX OS. Moreover, the actual complex task description has been split into many small basic tasks (in an OSEK/VDX sense). Table 9.7 presents the communication data between tasks for all the messages. The period of a message is trivially inherited from the sender of this message and its deadline is inherited from the task it is addressed to. In our case, deadlines are equal to periods, so deadlines can also be inherited from the sender of the message. For a message, the transmission delay is computed as a function of the number of bytes according to the formula recalled in Section 9.3.2. The messages are listed by priority order.

**Table 9.6** Task parameters of the distributed automotive application

| Node | Task | Computation time (ms) | Period (ms) |
|------|------|-----------------------|-------------|
| Node 1 | $\tau_1$ | 2 | 10 |
| | $\tau_2$ | 2 | 20 |
| | $\tau_3$ | 2 | 100 |
| | $\tau_4$ | 2 | 15 |
| | $\tau_5$ | 2 | 14 |
| | $\tau_6$ | 2 | 50 |
| | $\tau_7$ | 2 | 40 |
| Node 2 | $\tau_8$ | 2 | 15 |
| | $\tau_9$ | 2 | 50 |
| | $\tau_{10}$ | 2 | 50 |
| | $\tau_{11}$ | 2 | 14 |
| Node 3 | $\tau_{12}$ | 1 | 20 |
| | $\tau_{13}$ | 2 | 40 |
| | $\tau_{14}$ | 1 | 15 |
| | $\tau_{15}$ | 2 | 100 |
| | $\tau_{16}$ | 1 | 20 |
| | $\tau_{17}$ | 2 | 20 |
| Node 4 | $\tau_{18}$ | 4 | 14 |
| | $\tau_{19}$ | 4 | 20 |
| Node 5 | $\tau_{20}$ | 1 | 20 |
| | $\tau_{21}$ | 1 | 20 |
| | $\tau_{22}$ | 1 | 10 |
| | $\tau_{23}$ | 2 | 14 |
| | $\tau_{24}$ | 2 | 15 |
| Node 6 | $\tau_{25}$ | 2 | 50 |
| | $\tau_{26}$ | 2 | 50 |
| | $\tau_{27}$ | 2 | 10 |
| | $\tau_{28}$ | 2 | 100 |
| | $\tau_{29}$ | 2 | 40 |
| | $\tau_{30}$ | 2 | 20 |
| | $\tau_{31}$ | 2 | 100 |

**Table 9.7** Message characteristics of the distributed automotive application. The transmission delay computation is based on CAN with a bit rate of 250 Kbit/s

| Message | Sender task | Receiver task | Number of bytes | Size (bits) | Propagation delay (ms) | Period (ms) | Priority |
|---------|-------------|---------------|-----------------|-------------|------------------------|-------------|----------|
| $M_1$ | $\tau_1$ | $\tau_{27}$, $\tau_{22}$ | 8 | 130 | 0.5078 | 10 | 12 |
| $M_2$ | $\tau_{18}$ | $\tau_{11}$, $\tau_5$, $\tau_{23}$ | 3 | 82 | 0.3203 | 14 | 11 |
| $M_3$ | $\tau_2$ | $\tau_{16}$ | 3 | 82 | 0.3203 | 20 | 10 |
| $M_4$ | $\tau_8$ | $\tau_4$ | 2 | 73 | 0.2852 | 15 | 9 |
| $M_5$ | $\tau_{12}$ | $\tau_{21}$ | 5 | 101 | 0.3945 | 20 | 8 |
| $M_6$ | $\tau_{13}$ | $\tau_7$, $\tau_{29}$ | 5 | 101 | 0.3945 | 40 | 7 |
| $M_7$ | $\tau_{14}$ | $\tau_{24}$ | 4 | 92 | 0.3594 | 15 | 6 |
| $M_8$ | $\tau_{25}$ | $\tau_{10}$, $\tau_6$ | 5 | 101 | 0.3945 | 50 | 5 |
| $M_9$ | $\tau_{20}$ | $\tau_{19}$, $\tau_{17}$, $\tau_{30}$ | 4 | 92 | 0.3594 | 20 | 4 |
| $M_{10}$ | $\tau_3$ | $\tau_{28}$ | 7 | 121 | 0.4727 | 100 | 3 |
| $M_{11}$ | $\tau_9$ | $\tau_{26}$ | 5 | 101 | 0.3945 | 50 | 2 |
| $M_{12}$ | $\tau_{15}$ | $\tau_{31}$ | 1 | 63 | 0.2461 | 100 | 1 |

## 9.3.4 Detailed temporal analysis

*Temporal analysis of nodes considered as independent*

As a first step of the temporal analysis, we ignore the communications between nodes. The scheduling analysis of the different ECUs is quite easy because the defined tasks are considered independent. So we can calculate the processor utilization factor $U$ and the scheduling period $H$ for each processor, as defined in Chapter 1 (Table 9.8).

Moreover, on each node, we have a real-time system composed of independent, preemptive periodic tasks that are in phase and have deadlines equal to their respective periods. If we assign the fixed priorities according to the rate monotonic algorithm (tasks with shorter periods have higher priorities), we can check the schedulability of the node only by comparing its utilization factor $U$ to the upper bound of the processor utilization factor determined by Liu and Layland (1973) (see condition (2.12) in Chapter 2). Notice that this schedulability condition is sufficient to guarantee the feasibility of the real-time system, but it is not necessary. This means that, if a task set has a processor utilization factor greater than the limit, we have to carry on and use other conditions for the schedulability or simulate the task execution over the scheduling period.

**Table 9.8** Basic temporal parameters of each node

| Node | $U$ | Upper bound (Liu and Layland, 1973) | $H$ (ms) |
|------|-----|-------------------------------------|----------|
| Node 1 | 0.686 | 0.729 | 4200 |
| Node 2 | 0.356 | 0.757 | 1050 |
| Node 3 | 0.337 | 0.735 | 600 |
| Node 4 | 0.486 | 0.828 | 140 |
| Node 5 | 0.476 | 0.743 | 420 |
| Node 6 | 0.470 | 0.729 | 200 |

From the results presented in Table 9.8, we conclude that each node is weakly loaded, less than 69% for the highest processor utilization factor. Therefore all the task sets, if considered independent, satisfy the sufficient condition of Liu and Layland (1973) and the fixed-priority assignment, according to the rate monotonic algorithm, can schedule these task sets. Neither further analysis nor simulation over a scheduling period is necessary to prove the schedulability of the application.

Anyway, in order to illustrate the scheduling analysis with priority fixed according to the RM algorithm, we present the execution sequences of tasks of two nodes and display the emission and reception of messages by the different tasks. It is assumed hereafter that the messages are sent at the end of the tasks and received at their beginning. Recall that we do not consider message communications. The simulations have been plotted only over a tiny part of the scheduling period: 20 ms. Figure 9.20 deals with the execution of node 3, and Figure 9.21 corresponds to the execution sequence of node 5.

To summarize this section, each node of this automotive application, considered alone, can easily schedule tasks by using a fixed-priority assignment, according to the rate monotonic algorithm. We can widen this result to the case of message communications, if we consider a slack synchronization between tasks. This case occurs when a kind of 'blackboard' is used as a communication technique in a real-time system: the sender writes or over-writes the message at each emission and the writer always reads the last message (sometimes a message may be lost).

The cost of reading and writing a message is included in the task computation times. The access to the 'blackboard' is supposed to be atomic (or at least mutually exclusive, or best, according to a reader–writer synchronization pattern). The slack synchronization means that if the $k$th value of a message is not available, the receiving task can perform its computation with the previous $(k-1)$th value of the message.

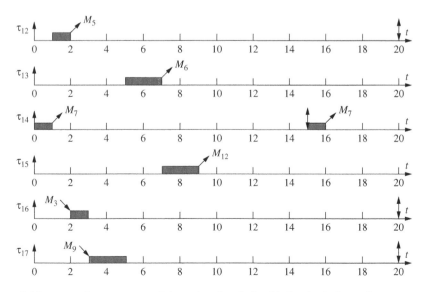

**Figure 9.20** Execution sequence of the tasks of node 3 with fixed-priority assignment according to the rate monotonic algorithm

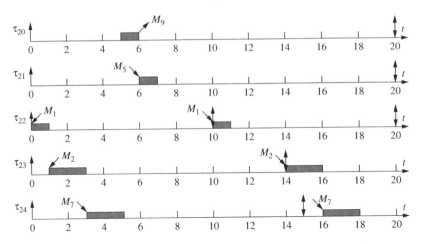

**Figure 9.21** Execution sequence of the tasks of node 5 with fixed-priority assignment according to the rate monotonic algorithm

### Temporal analysis of the distributed application

When distributed systems are considered with tight synchronizations, the tasks are mutually dependent because they exchange messages. The analysis must take into account the synchronization protocol of the communicating tasks, and also the scheduling policies of the messages through the network. The network is a shared resource for each communicating task. For example, between the previously analysed nodes (3 and 5), we have three communication relationships:

- $\tau_{12}$ (node 3) sends message $M_5$ to $\tau_{21}$ (node 5);

- $\tau_{14}$ (node 3) sends message $M_7$ to $\tau_{24}$ (node 5);

- $\tau_{20}$ (node 5) sends message $M_9$ to $\tau_{17}$ (node 3).

In distributed systems, a dysfunction can occur if a message is sent after the receiver task execution. This fact is illustrated in Figures 9.20 and 9.21: task $\tau_{20}$ sends the message $M_9$ to task $\tau_{17}$ after this task has completed its execution. A simple solution to this problem lies in the use of two-place memory buffers related to each communication message. The message emitted at the $k$th period is used at period $k + 1$. The first request of $\tau_{17}$ must be able to use a dummy message. This is possible if the calculation of task $\tau_{17}$ remains valid within this message time lag. But this solution needs hardware and/or software changes in order to manage this specific buffer. So we want to stay in a classical real-time system environment.
A solution can be found following two methods:

- Method 1 assumes the use of synchronization primitives (e.g. lock and unlock semaphores) in the task code in order to produce the right sequence with a fixed-priority assignment (this solution is used in the rolling mill signal acquisition presented as the first case study).

- Method 2 modifies the task parameter $r_i$, keeping the initial priority in accordance with the method presented in Section 3.1.

In the first method, the schedulability analysis is based on the response time analysis method for distributed systems called holistic analysis (Tindell and Clark, 1994). This is an *a priori* analysis for distributed systems where the delays for messages being sent between processors must be accurately bounded. In this modelling, the network is considered as a non-preemptive processor. When a message arrives at a destination processor, the receiver task is released, and can then read the message. We can say that the receiver task inherits a release jitter $J_r$ in the same way that a message inherits release jitter from the sender task corresponding to its worst-case response time $TR_s : J_r = TR_s + d_{CAN}$ where $d_{CAN}$ is the transmission delay of the message (Section 6.4.3 gives an example of computation of $d_{CAN}$ delay). A solution to the global problem can be found by establishing all the scheduling equations (worst-case response time for each task on every node and the release jitters induced by the message communication). Then it is possible to solve the problem and find the maximum execution time bounds, which must be lower than deadlines. We can summarize by saying that this method validates the application by evaluating the worst-case response times of all the tasks of the distributed application. With synchronization primitives, the dysfunction, explained above in Figures 9.20 and 9.21, cannot occur because when task $\tau_{17}$ starts running, it is blocked waiting for the message $M_9$. So this method permits us to validate this application with the RM priority assignment (Richard et al., 2001).

In the second method, the release time of each task receiving a message is modified in order to take into account the execution time of the sender task and the message communication delay. These two delays correspond to the waiting times of the sender task (respectively message) due to higher priority tasks of the same node (respectively higher priority messages in the network). It is of an utmost importance to integrate in calculations the occurrence number of higher priority tasks (respectively higher priority messages) arriving during the period of the sender task (respectively message). An example of these results is shown in Table 9.9 only for the nodes 3 and 5 corresponding to the previously analysed sequences. In Figures 9.22 and 9.23, it is quite clear that task $\tau_{20}$ sends the message $M_9$ to task $\tau_{17}$ before its execution. It is also obvious that the

**Table 9.9**  Modifications of task parameters of the distributed automotive application according to the second method

| Node | Task | Period | RM priority | Modified $r_i$ |
|------|------|--------|-------------|----------------|
| Node 3 | $\tau_{12}$ | 20 | 5 | 0 |
| | $\tau_{13}$ | 40 | 2 | 0 |
| | $\tau_{14}$ | 15 | 6 | 0 |
| | $\tau_{15}$ | 100 | 1 | 0 |
| | $\tau_{16}$ | 20 | 4 | 10 |
| | $\tau_{17}$ | 20 | 3 | 9 |
| Node 5 | $\tau_{20}$ | 20 | 2 | 0 |
| | $\tau_{21}$ | 20 | 1 | 5 |
| | $\tau_{22}$ | 10 | 5 | 3 |
| | $\tau_{23}$ | 14 | 4 | 5 |
| | $\tau_{24}$ | 15 | 3 | 3 |

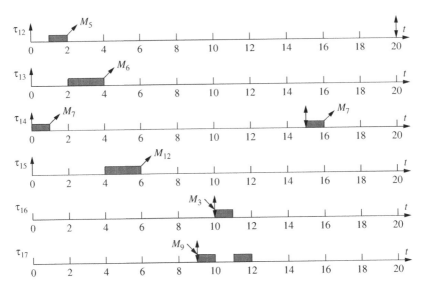

**Figure 9.22**   Execution sequence of the tasks of node 3 with the RM priority assignment and modified release times (see Table 9.9) in the case of the second method

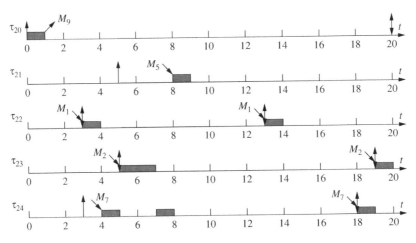

**Figure 9.23**   Execution sequence of the tasks of node 5 with the RM priority assignment and modified release times (see Table 9.9) in the case of the second method

whole application remains schedulable since only the release times have been changed; the processor utilization factor and the deadlines are the same. In this context, the system of independent, preemptive tasks with relative deadlines equal to their respective periods, on each node, is schedulable with an RM priority assignment because the schedulability condition does not depend on the release times.

# Glossary

**Absolute deadline ($d$)**  An absolute time before which a task should complete its execution: $d = r + D$.

**Acceptance test (or Guarantee routine)**  On-line scheduling creates and modifies the schedule as new task requests are triggered or when a deadline is missed. A new request may be accepted if there exists at least a schedule within which all previously accepted task requests as well as this new candidate meet their deadlines. This test is called an acceptance test and also a guarantee routine.

**Aperiodic (or asynchronous) message or packet**  A message (or a packet) whose send requests are initiated at irregular (random) times.

**Aperiodic task**  A task whose requests are initiated at irregular (random) times.

**Arrival (Release or Request) time of message or packet**  The time at which a message (packet) enters the queue of messages (packets) ready to send.

**Arrival (Release or Request) time of task**  The time at which a task enters the queue of ready tasks.

**Asynchronous message**  *See* Aperiodic message.

**Background processing**  The execution of a lower-priority task while higher-priority tasks are not using the processor.

**Best effort strategy (policy)**  A scheduling policy that tries to do its best to meet deadlines, but there is no guarantee of meeting the deadlines.

**Blocked task**  A task waiting for the occurrence of some event (e.g. resource release).

**Capacity of periodic server**  The maximum amount of time assigned to a periodic server to use, in each period, for the execution of aperiodic tasks.

**Centralized scheduling**  Scheduling within which all decisions are taken by a single node.

**Clairvoyant scheduling algorithm**  An ideal scheduling algorithm that knows the future of the arrival times of all the tasks to be scheduled.

**Completion (or finishing) time**  The time at which a task completes its execution.

**Computation (execution or processing) time of task**  The amount of time necessary to execute the task without interruption.

**Connection admission control**  A function of a QoS-aware network that tests if there are sufficiently resources to accept a new connection.

**Connection-oriented network**  A network in which an end-user must establish a connection before transmitting data.

**Context of task**  The set of data used to describe the state of a task. This set contains task priority, registers, etc.

**Context switch**  An operation undertaken by the operating system kernel to switch the processor from one task to another. The context of the task currently executing is saved and replaced by the context of another task.

**Critical** (or **exclusive**) **resource** A resource that cannot be used by more than one task at any time.

**Critical** (or **time-critical**) **task** A task that needs to meet a hard deadline.

**Critical section** A code fragment of a task during which mutually exclusive access to a critical resource is guaranteed.

**Deadline** *See* Absolute deadline and Relative deadline.

**Deadline monotonic** (or **Inverse deadline**) **algorithm** A scheduling algorithm which assigns static priorities to tasks according to their relative deadlines: the task with the shortest relative deadline is assigned the highest priority.

**Deadlock** A situation in which two or more tasks are blocked indefinitely because each task is waiting for a resource acquired by another blocked task.

**Deferrable server** Deferrable server policy is an extension of the polling server policy, which improves the response time of aperiodic requests. It looks like the polling server. However, the deferrable server preserves its capacity if no aperiodic requests are pending at the beginning of its period. Thus, an aperiodic request that enters the system just after the server suspends itself can be executed immediately.

**Delay jitter** *See* Jitter of packet.

**Dependence of tasks** Relationships between tasks, which may be precedence links or resource sharing.

**Dependent tasks** Tasks which have precedence or resource constraints.

**Deterministic strategy** (or **policy**) The requirements must be guaranteed so that the requested level will be met, barring 'rare' events such as equipment failure. Deterministic strategy is required for hard real-time tasks and messages.

**Discipline** *See* Service discipline.

**Dispatcher** The part of the operating system kernel that assigns the processor to the ready tasks.

**Distributed architecture** A hardware architecture composed of a set of processors connected by a communication network. The tasks on remote processors communicate by messages, not by a shared memory.

**Distributed scheduling** Scheduling in distributed real-time systems in which local scheduling decisions are taken after some communication (state exchanges) between cooperating nodes.

**Distributed system** A system that is concurrent in nature and that runs in an environment consisting of multiple nodes, which are in geographically different locations and are interconnected by means of a local area or wide area network.

**Dynamic scheduling** A scheduling in which the task characteristics (deadlines, periods, computation times, and so on) are not known in advance, but only when the task requires its execution for the first time.

**Earliest deadline first (EDF) algorithm** A scheduling algorithm which assigns dynamic priorities to tasks according to their absolute deadlines: the task with the shortest deadline is assigned the highest priority.

**End-to-end delay of packet** The time elapsing between emission of the first bit of a packet by the source and its reception by the destination.

**End-to-end transfer delay of packet** *See* End-to-end delay of packet.

**Exclusive resource** *See* Critical resource.

**Execution time of task** *See* Computation time of task.

**Feasible schedule** A schedule in which all the task deadlines are met.

**Feasible task set**   A task set for which there exists a feasible schedule.

**Finishing time**   *See* Completion time.

**Flow**   Messages issued by a periodic or sporadic source form a flow from source to destination.

**Frame-based discipline**   Discipline that uses fixed-size frames, each of which is divided into multiple packet slots. By reserving a certain number of packet slots per frame, connections are guaranteed with bandwidth and delay bounds.

**Global scheduling**   A scheduling that deals with distributed real-time systems and tries to allocate tasks to processors to minimize the number of late tasks, and eventually to optimize other criteria.

**Guarantee routine**   *See* Acceptance test.

**Guarantee strategy** (or **policy**)   *See* Deterministic strategy.

**Hard real-time system**   A system designed to meet the specified deadlines under any circumstances. Late results are useless and may have severe consequences.

**Hard time constraint**   A timing constraint that should be guaranteed in any circumstances.

**Hardware architecture**   Architecture composed of a set of components (processors, memory, input–output devices, communication medium, and so on).

**Hybrid task set**   A set composed of both types of tasks, periodic and aperiodic.

**Idle time of processor**   The set of time intervals where the processor laxity is strictly positive (i.e. set of time intervals where the processor may be idle without jeopardizing the guarantee of task deadlines).

**Importance** (or **criticality**) **of task**   A parameter specified at the design stage to define the level of importance (criticality) of a task. The scheduler should guarantee, in any circumstances, the deadlines of the most important tasks.

**Independent tasks**   Tasks with no precedence or resource constraints.

**Inverse deadline algorithm**   *See* Deadline Monotonic algorithm.

**Jitter of packet** (or **delay jitter**)   The variation of end-to-end transfer delay (i.e. the difference between the maximum and minimum values of transfer delay).

**Jitter of task**   Two main forms of jitter may be distinguished: (1) jitter which specifies the maximum difference between the start times (relative to the release times) of a set of instances of a periodic task, and (2) the jitter which specifies the maximum difference between the release times and the finishing times of a set of instances of a periodic task.

**Laxity of processor**   (*LP*) The maximum amount of time a processor may remain idle without jeopardizing the guarantee of deadlines of accepted tasks.

**Laxity of task**   (*L*) The maximum time that a task can be delayed and still complete within its deadline.

**Least laxity first (LLF) algorithm**   A scheduling algorithm which assigns dynamic priorities to tasks according to their laxity: the task with the shortest laxity is assigned the highest priority.

**Load factor of processor**   The processor load factor of a set of $n$ periodic tasks is equal to $\sum_{i=1}^{n} C_i/D_i$ ($C_i$ is the computation time of task $i$ and $D_i$ is its relative deadline).

**Local scheduling**   In distributed real-time systems, local scheduling is the part of scheduling that deals with the assignment of a local processor to the tasks allocated to this processor.

**Major cycle** (or **scheduling period** or **hyper period**)   The time interval after which the schedule is repeated indefinitely. It is used for system analysis.

**Middleware**   Software that resides between applications and the underlying infrastructure (operating system and network). Middleware provides an abstraction of the underlying system and network infrastructure to applications that use it.

**Monoprocessor scheduling**   Scheduling for a monoprocessor architecture.

**Multiprocessor scheduling**   Scheduling for a multiprocessor architecture.

**Mutual exclusion**   A mechanism allowing only one task to have access to shared data at any time, which can be enforced by means of a semaphore.

**Non-preemptive task**   A task that cannot be preempted by the dispatcher during its execution to assign the processor to another ready task.

**Non-preemptive scheduling**   A scheduling in which a task, once started, continuously executes without interruption unless it stops itself or requires access to a shared resource. The scheduler cannot withdraw the processor from a task to assign it to another one.

**Non-work-conserving discipline**   Discipline in which the output link may be idle even when a packet is waiting to be served (it is a idling discipline).

**Off-line scheduling algorithm**   A scheduling in which the order of task execution is determined off-line (i.e. before application start). Then the schedule is stored in a table which is used by the dispatcher, at application run-time, to assign the processor to tasks.

**On-line scheduling algorithm**   A scheduling in which the schedule (the order of task execution) is determined on-line using the parameters of active tasks.

**Optimal scheduling algorithm**   An algorithm that is able to produce a feasible schedule for any feasible task set.

**Overload**   A situation in which the amount of computation time required by tasks during a given time interval exceeds the available processor time during the same interval. Timing faults occur during overload situations.

**Packet-switching network**   Any communication network that accepts and delivers individual packets of information using packet switching techniques.

**Period** ($T$)   The period of a task (respectively message or packet) is the time interval between two successive instances of a periodic task (respectively message or packet).

**Periodic** (or **synchronous**) **message** or **packet**   A message (or packet) sent at regular time intervals (i.e. periodically).

**Periodic task**   A task that is activated periodically (i.e. at regular equally spaced intervals of time).

**Polling server**   A scheduling policy to serve aperiodic tasks. A polling server becomes active at regular intervals equal to its period and serves pending aperiodic requests within the limit of its capacity. If no aperiodic requests are pending, the polling server suspends itself until the beginning of its next period and the time originally preserved for aperiodic tasks is used by periodic tasks.

**Precedence constraint**   Two tasks have a precedence constraint when a task cannot start before the completion of the other one.

**Preemptive task**   A task that may be interrupted by the scheduler during its execution, and resumed later.

**Preemptive scheduling**    A scheduling in which a running task can be interrupted to assign the processor to another task. The preempted task will be resumed later.

**Priority of task**    A parameter statically or dynamically associated with tasks and used by the scheduler to assign the processor to the ready tasks.

**Priority of message** (or **packet**)    A parameter statically or dynamically associated with messages (respectively with packets) and used by the scheduler to assign the output link to the ready messages (respectively packets).

**Priority-based discipline**    In priority-based disciplines, packets have priorities assigned according to the reserved bandwidth or the required delay bound for the connection. The packet service is priority-driven.

**Priority ceiling protocol**    An algorithm that provides bounded priority inversion; that is, at most one lower priority task can block a higher priority task.

**Priority inheritance**    A mechanism used when tasks share resources. When a task waiting for a resource has a higher priority than the task using the resource, this latter task inherits the priority of the waiting task.

**Priority inversion**    A case where a medium priority task is executed prior to a high priority task; this occurs because the latter is blocked — for an unbounded amount of time — by a low priority task. It is a consequence of shared resource access.

**Probabilistic strategy** (or **policy**)    The constraints are guaranteed at a probability known in advance.

**Process**    *See* Task.

**Processing time of task**    *See* Computation time of task.

**Progressive triggering of tasks**    Periodic tasks are progressively triggered when they do not have the same value for their first release time.

**QoS**    *See* Quality of service.

**Quality of service (QoS)**    Term commonly used to mean a collection of parameters such as reliability, loss rate, security, timeliness and fault tolerance.

**Rate monotonic (RM) algorithm**    A scheduling algorithm that assigns higher (static) priorities to tasks with shorter periods.

**Rate monotonic analysis (RMA)**    A collection of quantitative methods and algorithms that allows understanding, analysis, and prediction of the timing behaviour of real-time applications with periodic tasks.

**Rate-allocating discipline**    Discipline that allows packets on each connection to be transmitted at higher rates than the minimum guaranteed rate, provided the switch can still meet guarantees for all connections.

**Rate-based discipline**    Discipline that provides a connection with a minimum service rate independent of the traffic characteristics of other connections.

**Rate-controlled discipline**    Discipline that guarantees a rate for each connection, and the packets from a connection are never allowed to be sent above the guaranteed rate.

**Real-time network**    A network with mechanisms that can guarantee transfer delay and jitter bounds.

**Real-time operating system kernel**    An operating system kernel with capabilities to handle timing constraints.

**Real-time scheduling**    Scheduling that handles timing constraints.

**Real-time system** A system composed of tasks that have timing constraints to be guaranteed. A real-time system is a system that must satisfy explicit timing constraints or it will fail.

**Relative deadline** (*D*) A period of time during which a task should complete its execution: $D = d - r$. The relative deadline is the maximum allowable response time of a task.

**Release time of packet** (*r*) *See* Arrival time.

**Request time of packet** (*r*) *See* Arrival time.

**Resource** Hardware or software component of the system used by tasks to carry out their computation.

**Resource constraint** Tasks that share common resources have resource constraints.

**Response time of task** The time elapsed between the arrival time and the finishing time of a task.

**Response time of message** The time elapsed between the arrival time of a message at the sender node and its reception at the receiver node.

**Schedulability test** A schedulability test allows checking whether a periodic task set that is submitted to a given scheduling algorithm might result in a feasible schedule.

**Schedulable task set** A set of tasks for which there exists a feasible schedule.

**Schedule of messages** (or **packets**) An allocation of the output link (medium) to messages (or packets), so that their deadlines are met.

**Schedule of task** An assignment of tasks to the processor, so that task deadlines are met.

**Scheduler of tasks** The part of an operating system kernel that schedules tasks.

**Scheduler of packets** The part of a switch (or of a router) that schedules packets.

**Scheduler-based discipline** Discipline that assigns dynamic priorities to packets based on their deadlines.

**Scheduling of messages** (or **packets**) Allocating network resources (mainly the bandwidth) to messages (respectively packets) in order to meet their timing constraints.

**Scheduling of tasks** The activity of deciding the order in which tasks are executed on processor.

**Scheduling period** (or **hyper period**) *See* Major cycle.

**Server of tasks** A periodic task used to serve aperiodic requests. *See also* Sporadic server, Deferrable server, Polling server.

**Service discipline** A combination of a connection admission control (CAC) and a packet scheduling algorithm.

**Simultaneous triggering of tasks** (or **in phase tasks**) A set of periodic tasks are simultaneously triggered when they have the same value for their first release time.

**Soft real-time system** A system in which the performance is degraded when timing failures occur, but no serious consequences are observed.

**Soft time constraint** A timing constraint that may be violated from time to time with no serious consequences.

**Sporadic message** (or **packet**) An aperiodic message (or packet) characterized by a known minimum inter-arrival time between consecutive instances.

**Sporadic server** A scheduling strategy to serve aperiodic requests. A sporadic server preserves its capacity of service when there are no aperiodic requests to serve. The sporadic server does not replenish its capacity to its full value at the beginning of each new period, but only after it has been consumed by aperiodic task executions.

**Sporadic task**   An aperiodic task characterized by a known minimum inter-arrival time between consecutive instances of this task.

**Start time** ($s$)   The time at which a task begins its execution.

**Static scheduling**   A scheduling in which all the task characteristics (deadlines, periods, computation times, and so on) are statically known (i.e. they are known before the start of the real-time application).

**Statistical strategy** (or **policy**)   A strategy that promises that no more than a specified fraction of tasks or packets will see performance below a certain specified value.

**Synchronous message**   *See* Periodic message.

**Task** (or **process**)   A unit of concurrency that can be handled by a scheduler. A real-time application is composed of a set of tasks.

**Time-critical task**   *See* Critical task.

**Timing fault**   A situation in which a timing constraint is missed.

**Transfer delay jitter**   *See* Jitter of packet.

**Utilization factor of processor** ($U$)   The fraction of the processor time used by a set of periodic tasks. $U = \sum_{i=1}^{n} C_i/T_i$ ($C_i$ is the computation time of task $i$ and $T_i$ its period).

**Work-conserving discipline**   Discipline that schedules a packet whenever a packet is present in the switch (it is a non-idling discipline).

**Worst-case computation** (or **execution**) **time** ($C$)   The worst case of execution time that may be experienced by a task.

# Bibliography

*Ada 95 Reference Manual: Language and Standard Libraries*. International standard ANSI/ISO/IEC-8652, 1995.

*Ada 95 Rationale: Language and Standard Libraries*, Intermetrics, 1995. Also available from Springer-Verlag, LNCS 1247.

AFNOR, *FIP Bus for Exchange of Information between Transmitters, Actuators and Programmable Controllers*, French standard NF C46-603, April 1990.

Agrawal G., Chen B. and Zhao W., Local synchronous capacity allocation schemes for guaranteeing messages deadlines with the timed token protocol, in *Proceedings of IEEE INFOCOM'93*, San Francisco, CA, pp. 186–193, 1993.

Andersson B., Baruah S. and Jonsson J., Static-priority scheduling on multiprocessors, in *Proceedings of IEEE Real-Time Systems Symposium*, London, pp. 193–202, December 2001.

Aras C., Kurose J.F., Reeves D.S. and Schulzrinne H., Real-time communication in packet switched networks, in *Proceedings of the IEEE*, **82**(1): 122–139, 1994.

Atlas A. and Bestavros A., Statistical rate monotonic scheduling, in *Proceedings of IEEE Real-Time Systems Symposium*, Madrid, December 1998.

Bacon J., *Concurrent systems*, Addison-Wesley, Harlow, 1997.

Baker T.P., Stack-based scheduling of real-time processes, in *Proceedings of IEEE Real-Time Systems Symposium*, pp. 191–200, 1990.

Banino J.S., Kaiser C., Delcoigne J. and Morisset G., The DUNE-IX real-time operating system, *Computing Systems*, **6**(4): 425–480, 1993.

Barabonov M. and Yodaiken V., Real-time Linux, *Linux Journal*, March, 1996.

Baruah S., Koren G., Mishra B., Raghunatham A., Rosier L. and Shasha D., On line scheduling in the presence of overload, in *Proceedings of IEEE Foundations of Computer Science Conference*, San Juan, Puerto Rico, pp. 101–110, 1991.

Bennett J.C.R. and Zhang H., WF2Q: worst-case fair weighted fair queueing, in *Proceedings of IEEE INFOCOM'96*, San Francisco, CA, pp. 120–128, March 1996.

Bennett J.C.R. and Zhang H., Hierarchical packet fair queueing algorithms, in *Proceedings of SIGCOMM'96*, Stanford, CA, pp. 143–156, August 1996. Also in *IEEE/Transactions on Networking*, **5**(5): pp. 675–689, October 1997.

Bertossi A. and Bonucelli M., Preemptive scheduling of periodic jobs in uniform multiprocessor systems, *Information Processing Letters*, **16**: 3–6, 1983.

Blazewicz J., Scheduling dependent tasks with different arrival times to meet deadlines, in Beilner H. and Gelenbe E. (eds) *Modeling and Performance Evaluation of Computer Systems*, North Holland, Amsterdam, pp. 57–65, 1977.

Brosgol B. and Dobbing B., Real-time convergence of Ada and Java, in *Proceedings of ACM SIGAda 2001 International Conference, AdaLetters* **22**(4), December 2001.

Burns A., Guide for the use of the Ada Ravenscar profile in high integrity systems, *Ada User Journal*, **22**(4), September 2001.

Burns A. and Wellings A., *Real-time Systems and Programming Languages*. Addison-Wesley, Harlow, 1997.

Burns A. and Wellings B., *Real-Time Systems and Programming Languages*. Addison Wesley, Harlow, 2001.

Buttazzo G.C., *Hard Real-Time Computing Systems, Predictable Scheduling, Algorithms and Applications*, Kluwer Academic, Dordrecht, 1997.

Buttazzo G.C. and Stankovic J.A., Red: a robust earliest deadline scheduling algorithm, in *Proceedings of 3rd International Workshop on Responsive Computing Systems*, 1993.

Buttazzo G.C., Lipari G. and Abeni L., Elastic task model for adaptive rate control, in *Proceedings of IEEE Real-Time Systems Symposium*, Madrid, December 1998.

Campbell R.H., Horton K.H. and Belford G.G, Simulations of a fault tolerant deadline mechanism, *Digest of Papers FTCS-9*, pp. 95–101, 1979.

Cardeira C. and Mammeri Z., Neural networks for satisfying real-time task constraints, in *Proceedings of SPRANN'94 IMACS Symposium on Signal Processing, Robotics and Neural Networks*, Lille, pp. 498–501, 1994.

Cavalieri S., Di-Stefano A. and Mirabella O., Mapping automotive process control on IEC/ISA fieldbus functionalities, *Computers in Industry*, **28**: 233–250, 1996.

CENELEC, WorldFIP, European standard EN 50170-3, April 1997.

Chen B., Agrawal G. and Zhao W., Optimal synchronous capacity allocation for hard real-time communications with the timed token protocol, in *Proceedings of the 13th IEEE Real-Time Systems Symposium*, pp. 198–207, 1992.

Chen M.I. and Lin K.J., Dynamic priority ceilings: a concurrency control protocol for real-time systems, *Real-Time Systems Journal*, **2**(4): 325–346, 1990.

Chetto H. and Chetto M., How to insure feasibility in distributed system for real-time control, in *Proceedings of International Symposium on High Performance Computer Systems*, Paris, 1987.

Chetto H. and Chetto M., An adaptive scheduling algorithm for fault-tolerant real-time systems, *Software Engineering Journal*, **6**(3): 93–100, 1991.

Chetto H. and Delacroix J., Minimisation des temps de réponse des tâches sporadiques en présence des tâches périodiques, in *RTS'93*, Paris, pp. 32–52, 1993 (in French).

Chetto H., Silly M. and Bouchentouf T., Dynamic scheduling of real-time tasks under precedence constraints, *Journal of Real-Time Systems*, **2**: 181–194, 1990.

Chu W.W. and Lan L.M.T., Task allocation and precedence relations for distributed real-time systems, *IEEE Transactions on Computers*, **C-36**(6): 667–679, 1987.

Chung J.Y., Liu J.W.S. and Lin K., Scheduling periodic jobs that allow imprecise results, *IEEE Transactions on Computers*, **39**(9): 1156–1174, 1990.

Clark R.K., Scheduling dependent real-time activities, PhD thesis, Carnegie Mellon University, May 1990.

Cruz R.L., A calculus for network delay, Part I: network elements in isolation, *IEEE Transactions on Information Theory*, **37**(1): 114–131, January 1991a.

Cruz R.L., A calculus for network delay, Part II: network analysis, *IEEE Transactions on Information Theory*, **37**(1): 132–141, January 1991b.

Damm A., Reisinger J., Schnakel W. and Kopetz H., The real-time operating system of Mars, *Operating Systems Review*, **23**(3): 141–157, 1989.

Delacroix J., Stabilité et Régisseur d'ordonnancement en temps réel, *Technique et Science Informatiques*, **13**(2): 223–250, 1994 (in French).

Delacroix J., Towards a stable earliest deadline scheduling algorithm, *Journal of Real-Time Systems*, **10**(3): 263–291, 1996.

Delacroix J. and Kaiser C., Un modèle de tâches temps réel pour la résorption contrôlée des surcharges, *RTS'98*, pp. 45–61, 1998 (in French).

Demers A., Keshav S. and Shenker S., Analysis and simulation of a fair queueing algorithm, in *Proceedings of ACM SIGCOMM'89*, Austin, TX, September 1989, pp. 1–12. Also in *Journal of Internetworking Research and Experience*, **1**(1): 3–26, October 1990.

Dertouzos M.L. and Mok A.K.L., Multiprocessor on-line scheduling of hard real-time tasks, *IEEE Transactions on Software Engineering*, **15**(12): 1497–1506, 1989.

Deutsche Institut für Normung, *PROFIBUS standard part 1 and 2* — DIN 19 245, 1991.

Dhall S.K., Scheduling periodic-time critical jobs on single processor and multiprocessor computing systems, PhD thesis, University of Illinois, April 1977.

Eager D.L., Lazowska E.D. and Zahorjan J., Load sharing in distributed systems, *IEEE Transactions on Software Engineering*, **SE-12**: 662–675, 1986.

Ferrari D. and Verma D.C., Scheme for real-time channel establishment in wide-area networks, *Journal of IEEE Selected Areas in Communications*, **8**(3): 368–79, 1990.

Figueira N.R. and Pasquale J., An upper bound on delay for virtual clock service discipline, *IEEE/ACM Transactions on Networking*, **3**(4): 399–408, August 1995.

Goldsmith S., *A Practical Guide to Real-Time Systems Development*, Prentice Hall, New York, 1993.

Golestani S.J., A stop-and-go queueing framework for congestion management, in *Proceedings of ACM SIGCOMM'90*, Philadelphia, PA, pp. 8–18, September 1990.

Golestani S.J., Congestion-free communication in high-speed packet networks, *IEEE Transactions on Communications*, **39**(12): 1802–12, December 1991.

Golestani S.J., A self-clocked queueing scheme for broadband applications, in *Proceedings of IEEE INFOCOM'94*, Toronto, Ontario, Canada, pp. 636–646, June 1994.

Gomaa H., *Software Design Methods for Concurrent and Real-Time Systems*, Addison Wesley, Reading, MA, 1993.

Goyal P., Vin H.M. and Cheng H., Start-time fair queueing: a scheduling algorithm for integrated services packet switching networks, in *Proceedings of ACM SIGCOMM'96*, Stanford, CA, pp. 157–168, August 1996. Also in *IEEE/ACM Transactions on Networking*, **5**(5): 690–707, October 1997.

Graham R., Bounds on the performance of scheduling algorithms, *Computer and Job Shop Scheduling Theory*, John Wiley & Sons, Chichester, pp. 165–227, 1976.

Greenberg A.G. and Madras N., How fair is fair queuing?, *Journal of ACM*, **39**(3): 568–598, July 1992.

Grolleau E. and Choquet-Geniet A., Scheduling real-time systems by means of Petri nets, in *Proceedings of the 25th IFAC Workshop on Real-Time Programming*, Palma, Spain, pp. 95–100, May 2000.

Haberman A.N., Prevention of system deadlocks, *Communications of ACM*, **12**(7): 373–377 and 385, 1969.

Halbwachs N., *Synchronous Programming of Reactive Systems*, Kluwer Academic, Dordrecht, 1993.

Harel D., Statecharts: a visual approach to complex systems, *Science of Computer Programming*, **8**(3): 1987.

Hatley D. and Pirbhai I., *Strategies for Real-Time System Specification*, Dorset Hous, 1988.

Havender J.W., Avoiding deadlocks in multitasking systems, *IBM System Journal*, **7**(2): 74–84, 1968.

Hou C.J. and Shin K.G., Allocation of periodic task modules with precedence and deadline constraints in distributed real-time systems, in *Proceedings of Real-Time Systems Symposium*, Phoenix, AZ, pp. 146–155, 1992.

Humpris D., Integrating Ada into a distributed systems environment, *Ada User Journal*, **22**:(1), March 2001.

Ishii H., Tada M. and Masuda T., Two scheduling problems with fuzzy due-dates, *Fuzzy Sets and Systems*, **46**: 339–347, 1992.

ISO, Token-passing bus access method and physical layer specifications — International Standard ISO 8802-4, 1990.

ISO, Road vehicles — Low-speed serial data communication, Part 2: low-speed controller area network (CAN) — International Standard ISO 11519-2, 1994a.

ISO, Road vehicles — Interchange of digital information: Controller Area Network for high speed communication, ISO 11898, 1994b.

ISO, Vehicle Area Network, Serial Data Communication — Road vehicles, Serial data communication for automotive application, ISO 11519-3, 1994c.

Jensen E.D, Locke C.D. and Tokuda H., A time-driven scheduling model for real-time operating systems, in *Proceedings of IEEE Real-Time Systems Symposium*, pp. 112–122, 1985.

Johnson M.J., Proof that timing requirements of the FDDI token ring protocol are satisfied, *IEEE Transactions on Communications*, **COM-35**(6): 620–625, 1987.

Joseph M. (ed.), *Real-Time Systems: Specification, Verification and Analysis*, Prentice Hall, Englewood Cliffs, NJ, 1996.

Kaiser C., De l'utilisation de la priorité en présence d'exclusion mutuelle, Research report RR 84, INRIA, 24 pages, 1981 (in French).

Kaiser C. and Pradat-Peyre J.F., Comparing the reliability provided by tasks or protected objects for implementing a resource allocating service: a case study, in *Proceedings of Tri-Ada'97 Conference*, Saint-Louis, MO, November 1997.

Kaiser C. and Pradat-Peyre J.F, Reliable, fair and efficient concurrent software with dynamic allocation of identical resources, in *Proceedings of 5th Maghrebian Conference on Software Engineering and Artificial Intelligence*, Tunis, pp. 109–125, 1998.

Kalmanek C., Kanakia H. and Keshav S., Rate controlled servers for very high-speed networks, in *Proceedings of IEEE Global Telecommunications Conference (GLOBECOM)*, San Diego, CA, pp. 300.3.1–300.3.9, December 1990.

Kandlur D.D., Shin K.G. and Ferrari D., Real-time communication in multi-hop networks, in *Proceedings of the 11th International Conference on Distributed Computing Systems (ICDCS'91)*, Arlington, TX, pp. 300–307, May 1991. Also in *IEEE Transactions on Parallel and Distributed Systems*, **5**(10): 1044–1056, October 1994.

Keshav S., On the efficient implementation of fair queueing, *Internetworking Research and Experience*, **2**: 157–173, 1991.

Klein M., Ralya T., Pollak B, Obenza R. and Harbour M.G., *A Practitioner's Handbook for Real-Time Analysis*, Kluwer Academic, Dordrecht, 1993.

Kopetz K., *Real-Time Systems. Design Principles for Distributed Embedded Applications*, Kluwer Academic, Dordrecht, 1997.

Koren G. and Shasha, D., D-OVER: an optimal on-line scheduling algorithm for overloaded real-time systems, Technical Report 138, INRIA, 45 pages, 1992.

Kweon S.K. and Shin K.G., Traffic-controlled rate monotonic priority scheduling of ATM cells, in *Proceedings of 15th IEEE INFOCOM*, 1996.

Lehoczky J., Sha L. and Ding Y., The rate monotonic scheduling algorithm: exact characterization and average case behavior, in *Proceedings of Real-Time Systems Symposium*, pp. 166–171, 1989.

Lehoczky J.P., Sacha L. and Ding Y., An optimal algorithm for scheduling soft-aperiodic tasks in fixed-priority preemptive systems, in *Proceedings of the IEEE Real-Time Systems Symposium*, pp. 110–123, 1992.

Lelann G., Critical issues for the development of distributed real-time systems, Research Report 1274, INRIA, 19 pages, 1990.

Leung J. and Merrill M., A note on preemptive scheduling of periodic real-time tasks, *Information Processing Letters*, **11**(3): 115–118, 1980.

Levi S.T., Tripathi S.K., Carson S.D. and Agrawala A.K., The MARUTI hard real-time operating system, *ACM Operating Systems Review*, **23**(3): 90–105, 1989.

Liu C. and Layland J.W., Scheduling algorithms for multiprogramming in a hard real-time environment, *Journal of ACM*, **20**(1): 46–61, 1973.

Liu J.W.S, *Real-Time Systems*, Prentice Hall, Englewood Cliffs, NJ, 2000.

Liu J.W.S., Lin K., Shih W., Yu A., Chung J. and Zhao W., Algorithms for scheduling imprecise computations, *IEEE Computer Special Issue on Real-Time Systems*, **24**(5): 58–68, May 1991.

Malcolm N. and Zhao W., Hard real-time communication in multiple-access networks, *Journal of Real-Time Systems* (8): 35–77, 1995.

Manufacturing Automation Protocol, MAP: 3.0 Implementation release — MAP Users Group, 1987.

McNaughtan R., Scheduling with deadlines and loss functions, *Management Science*, **6**: 1–12, 1959.

Mok A.K. and Chen D., A multiframe model for real-time tasks, *IEEE Transactions on Software Engineering*, **23**(10): 635–645, 1997.

Mok A.K.L. and Dertouzos M.L., Multiprocessor scheduling in real-time environment, in *Proceedings of the 7th Texas Conference on Computing Systems*, pp. 1–12, 1978.

Nagle B.J., On packet switches with infinite storage, *IEEE Transactions on Communications*, **35**(4): 435–438, 1987.

Nakajima T., Kitayama T., Arakawa H. and Tokuda, H., Integrated management of priority inversion in real-time Mach, in *Proceedings of IEEE Real-Time Systems Symposium*, pp. 120–130, 1993.

Nassor E. and Bres G., Hard real-time sporadic tasks scheduling for fixed priority schedulers, in *International Workshop on Response Computer Systems (Office of Naval Research / INRIA)*, Golfe Juan, France, 1991.

Natarajam S. (ed.), *Imprecise and Approximate Computation*, Kluwer Academic, Dordrecht, 1995.

Nissanke N., *Realtime Systems*, Prentice Hall, Englewood Cliffs, NJ, 1997.

OMG, Real-Time CORBA. A white paper — Issue 1.0., OMG, December 1996.

OMG, Real-time CORBA 2.0: Dynamic scheduling specification, OMG, September 2001a.

OMG, The Common Object Request Broker: Architecture and specification, Revision 2.6, OMG, December 2001b.

OSEK, OSEK/VDX operating system, version 2.0r1, http://www-iiit.etec.uni-karlsruhe.de/~osek/, 1997.

Parekh A.K. and Gallager R.G., A generalized processor sharing approach to flow control in integrated services networks: the single-node case, *IEEE/ACM Transactions on Networking*, **1**(3): 344–357, 1993.

Parekh A.K. and Gallager R.G., A generalized processor sharing approach to flow control in integrated services networks: the multiple node case, *IEEE/ACM Transactions on Networking*, **2**(2): 137–150, 1994.

Pautet L. and Tardieu S., GLADE: a framework for building large object-oriented real-time distributed computing, in *Proceedings of ISORC'00*, 2000.

Pautet L., Quinot T. and Tardieu S., Corba &DSA: divorce or marriage?, in *Proceedings of International Conference on Reliable Software Technologies, Ada-Europe'99, in LNCS 1622*, Springer-Verlag, pp. 211–225, June 1999.

Pautet L., Quinot T. and Tardieu S., Building modern distributed systems, in *Proceedings of the 6th International Conference on Reliable Software*, 2001.

Pedro P. and Burns A., Worst case response time analysis of hard real-time sporadic traffic in FIP networks, in *Proceedings of 9th Euromicro Workshop on Real-Time Systems*, Toledo, Spain, pp. 3–10, June 1997.

Pimentel J.R., *Communication Networks for Manufacturing*. Prentice Hall, Reading, MA, 1990.

Pinho L.M., Session summary: distribution and real-time, in *Proceedings of the 10th International Real-Time Ada Workshop, Ada Letters*, **21**(1): 2001.

Rajkumar R., *Synchronization in Real-Time Systems. A Priority Inheritance Protocol*, Kluwer Academic, Dordrecht, 1991.

Ramamritham K. and Stankovic J.A., Dynamic task scheduling in distributed hard real-time systems, *IEEE Software*, **1**: 65–75, 1984.

Ramamritham K., Stankovic J.A. and Shiah P., Scheduling algorithms for real-time multiprocessor systems, *IEEE Transactions on Parallel and Distributed Systems*, **1**(2): 184–194, 1990.

Richard M., Richard P. and Cottet F., Task and message priority assignment in automotive systems, in *Proceedings of the IFAC Conference on Fieldbus Systems and their Applications (FET), Nancy*, France, pp. 105–112, November 2001.

Sahni S.K., Preemptive scheduling with due dates, *Operational Research*, **27**: 925–934, 1979.

Sathaye S. and Strosnider J.K., Conventional and early token release scheduling models for the IEEE 802.5 token ring, *Journal of Real-Time Systems*, (7): 5–32, 1994.

Schmidt D.C., Levine D.L. and Mungee S., The design of the TAO real-time object request broker, *Computer Communications* **21**: 294–324, 1998.

Schwan K., Gopinath P. and Bo W., CHAOS — kernel support for objects in the real-time domain, *IEEE Transactions on Computers*, **C-36**(8): 904–916, 1987.

Scoy R., Bamberger J. and Firth R., An overview of DARK, in Agrawala A., Gordon K. and Hwang P. (eds) *Mission Critical Operating Systems*, IOS Press, Amsterdam, 1992.

Sevcik K.C. and Johnson M.J., Cycle time properties of the FDDI token ring protocol, *IEEE Transactions on Software Engineering*, **SE-13**(3): 376–385, 1987.

Sha L., Rajkumar R. and Lehoczky J.P., Priority inheritance protocols: an approach to real-time synchronisation, *IEEE Transactions on Computers*, **39**(9): 1175–1185, 1990.

Shih W., Liu W.S., Chung J. and Gillies D.W., Scheduling tasks with ready times and deadlines to minimize average error, *Operating Systems Review*, **23**(3): 1989.

Shin K. and Chang Y., Load sharing in distributed real-time systems with state change broadcasts, *IEEE Transactions on Computers*, **38**(8): 1124–1142, 1989.

Shreedhar M. and Varghese G., Efficient fair queueing using deficit round robin, in *Proceedings of ACM SIGCOMM'95*, August 1995, Cambridge, MA, pp. 231–242. Also in *IEEE/ACM Transactions on Networking*, **4**(3): 375–385, June 1996.

Silberschatz A. and Galvin P., *Operating System Concepts*, Addison-Wesley, Reading, MA, 1998.

Sorenson P.G., A methodology for real-time system development, PhD Thesis, University of Toronto, Canada, 1974.

Sprunt B., Sha L. and Lehoczky J.P., Aperiodic task scheduling for hard real-time systems, *Journal of Real-Time Systems*, **1**(1): 27–60, 1989.

Spuri M. and Buttazzo G.C., Efficient aperiodic service under earliest deadline scheduling, in *Proceedings of the IEEE Real-Time Systems Symposium*, pp. 2–11, 1994.

Spuri M. and Buttazzo G.C., Scheduling aperiodic tasks in dynamic priority systems, *Journal of Real-Time Systems*, **10**(2): 179–210, 1996.

Stallings W., *Handbook of Computer-Communications Standards: Local Area Network Standards*, Macmillan, London, 1987.

Stallings W., *Local and Metropolitan Area Networks*, Prentice Hall, Englewood Cliffs, NJ, 2000.

Stankovic J.A., Misconceptions about real-time computing, *Computer*, **21**: 10–19, 1988.

Stankovic J.A., Distributed real-time computing: the next generation, Technical Report TR92-01, University of Massachusetts, 1992.

Stankovic J.A. and Ramamritham K., The Spring Kernel: a new paradigm for real-time operating system, *ACM Operating Systems Review*, **23**(3): 54–71, 1989.

Stankovic J.A., Ramamrithmam K. and Cheng S., Evaluation of a flexible task scheduling algorithm for distributed hard real-time systems, *IEEE Transactions on Computers*, **34**(12): 1130–1143, 1985.

Stankovic J.A., Spuri, M., Di Natale M. and Buttazzo G.C., Implications of classical scheduling results for real-time systems, *IEEE Computer*, **28**(8): 16–25, 1995.

Stankovic J.A., Spuri, M., Ramamritham K. and Buttazzo G.C., *Deadline Scheduling for Real-Time Systems — EDF and Related Algorithms*. Kluwer Academic, Dordrecht, 1998.

Stankovic J.A., Ramamritham K., Niehaus D., Humphrey M. and Gary W. The Spring System: integrated support for complex real-time systems, *International Journal of Time-Critical Computing Systems*, **16**(2/3): 223–251, 1999.

Stephens D.C., Bennett J.C.R. and Zhang H., Implementing scheduling algorithms in high-speed networks, *IEEE Journal on Selected Areas in Communications*, **17**(6): 1145–1158, 1999.

Stiliadis D. and Varma A., Design and analysis of frame-based fair queueing: a new traffic scheduling algorithm for packet-switched networks, in *Proceedings of ACM SIGMETRICS'96*, Philadelphia, PA, pp. 104–115, May 1996.

Storch M.F. and Liu J.W.S., Heuristic algorithms for periodic job assignment, in *Proceedings of Workshop on Parallel and Distributed Real-Time Systems*, Newport Beach, CA, pp. 245–251, 1993.

Tanenbaum A.S., *Distributed Operating Systems*, Prentice Hall, Englewood Cliffs, NJ, 1994.

Tanenbaum A.S. and Woodhull A.S., *Operating Systems: Design and Implementation*, Prentice Hall, Englewood Cliffs, NJ, 1997.

Tia T.S. and Liu J.W.S., Assigning real-time tasks and resources to distributed systems, *International Journal of Mini and Microcomputers*, **17**(1): 18–25, 1995.

Tindell K.W. and Clark, J., Holistic schedulability analysis for distributed hard real-time systems, *Microprocessors and Microprogramming*, **40**: 117–134, 1994.

Tindell K., Burns A. and Wellings A., Allocating hard real-time tasks: an NP-hard problem made easy, *Journal of Real-Time Systems*, **4**(2): 145–65, 1992.

Tindell K., Burns A. and Wellings A.J., Calculating controller area network (CAN) message response times, *Control Engineering Practice*, **3**(8): 1163–1169, 1995.

Tokuda H. and Mercer C., ARTS: a distributed real-time kernel, *ACM Operating Systems Review*, **23**(3): 1989.

Tokuda H. and Nakajima T., Evaluation of real-time synchronisation in real-time Mach, in *Proceedings of USENIX 2nd Mach Symposium*, 1991.

Turner J.S., New directions in communications (or which way to information age?), *IEEE Communications Magazine*, **24**(10): 8–15, 1986.

Verissimo P., Barret P., Bond P., Hilborne A., Rodrigues L. and Seaton D., The extra Performance Architecture (XPA) in DELTA-4, in Powell D. (ed.) *A Generic Architecture for Dependable Distributed Computing*, Springer-Verlag, London, 1991.

Verma D., Zhang H. and Ferrari D., Delay jitter control for real-time communication in a packet switching networks, in *Proceedings of Tricomm'91*, Chapel Hill, NC, pp. 35–46, April 1991.

Wang K. and Lin T.H., Scheduling adaptive tasks in real-time systems, in *Proceedings of IEEE Real-Time Systems Symposium*, Puerto-Rico, pp. 206–215, December 1994.

Weiss M.A., *Data Structures and Algorithm Analysis in Ada*, Addison-Wesley, Reading, MA, 1994.

Yao L.J., Real-time communication in token ring networks, PhD Thesis, University of Adelaide, 1994.

Zhang H., Service disciplines for guaranteed performance service in packet-switching networks, *Proceedings of the IEEE*, **83**(10): 1374–1396, 1995.

Zhang H. and Ferrari D., Rate-controlled static-priority queueing, in *Proceedings of IEEE INFO-COM'93*, San Francisco, CA, pp. 227–236, March 1993.

Zhang H. and Ferrari D., Improving utilization for deterministic service in multimedia communication, in *Proceedings of International Conference on Multimedia Computing Systems*, 1994.

Zhang L., VirtualClock: a new traffic control algorithm for packet switching networks, in *Proceedings of ACM SIGCOMM'90, September, 1990*, Philadelphia, PA, pp. 19–29. Also in *ACM Transactions on Computer Systems*, **9**(2): 101–124, 1991.

Zhang S. and Burns A., Guaranteeing synchronous message sets in FDDI networks, in *Proceedings of 13th Workshop on Distributed Computer Control Systems*, Toulouse, pp. 107–112, 1995.

Zhao W. and Ramamritham K., Virtual time CSMA protocols for hard real-time communication, *IEEE Transactions on Software Engineering*, **13**(8): 938–952, 1987.

Zheng Q., Shin K. and Shen C., Real-time communication in ATM networks, in *Proceedings of 19th Annual Local Computer Network Conference*, Minneapolis, Minnesota, pp. 156–165, 1994.

# Index

absolute deadline, 9
acceptance techniques, 39
acceptance test, 16
Ada, 186
admission control, 129, 135
anomalies, 95
arrival pattern, 158
arriving frames, 154
asynchronous system, 2
automotive application, 238
auxiliary virtual clock, 139, 144

background scheduling, 33, 39
bandwidth, 129
bandwidth allocation granularity, 159
best effort, 129, 135
best-effort strategy, 110
bit-by-bit round-robin, 140, 143
BR, 140
burst, 134, 145
burstiness, 134, 145, 159
bursty traffic, 134
bus arbitrator, 115
bus arbitrator table, 115

CAC, 136
CAN, 109, 111, 113, 117, 238
cell, 130
clerical latency, 179
client, 201
client propagated model, 204
cold rolling mill, 213
communication delay, 106
computing systems, 5
connection, 130
connection admission control, 136
connection establishment, 136
connectionless, 130
connection-oriented, 129, 130
constant priority, 16
constant priority scheduling, 18
consumers, 115
consumption buffer, 115
Controller Area Network, 113
CORBA, 200
critical resource, 55, 59, 61
critical section, 12, 55, 59

criticality, 13, 86
CSMA/CA, 109, 113
CSMA/CD, 111

D_Order, 160
deadline mechanism model, 82
deadline missing tolerance, 79
deadline monotonic, 29, 53
deadline-based, 147
deadlock, 59, 60, 61, 62, 67
deferrable server, 35
deficit round-robin, 143
delay, 129, 145
delay bounds, 135
delay earliest-due-date, 139, 146
delay EDD, 146, 160
delay jitter, 105, 135, 159
delay variation, 135
delay-jitter controlling, 159, 161
departing frames, 154
dependency of tasks, 12
deterministic strategy, 110
differentiated services, 164
DiffServ, 164
discipline, 129, 136
distortion, 159
distributed real-time systems, 103, 110
dominant, 114
domino effect, 79
dynamic allocation, 105
dynamic scheduling, 207

earliest deadline first, 31, 53, 104, 122
EDF, 31, 37, 39, 79, 100, 146
elastic task model, 81
elected, 10
election table, 16
eligibility time, 158, 159, 161
end-to-end delay, 105, 133, 142, 146, 148,
        154, 156, 159, 162
end-to-end jitter, 149
end-to-end transfer delay, 105, 106, 135
ESTEREL, 197
execution modes, 87

Printed and bound by CPI Group (UK) Ltd, Croydon, CR0 4YY

27/10/2024

14580218-0004